Praise for *A Tide of Dreams*

"Carey Henry Keefe has done it—the remarkable, unknown, inside story of a rich red slice of Crimson Tide Americana!"

—Ellen Vaughn, *New York Times* bestselling author

"Carey Henry Keefe has written a love story, or better said, a story of many loves. I imagine she started out to write about her love for her grandfather, Carney Laslie. That story alone would have made a book worth reading. However, the devotion of a group of men who experienced the common bond of playing football for the University of Alabama Crimson Tide takes the reader on an adventure. These men may have never said the word, but they lived a lifetime of love for each other through the trials of World War II, family, winning and losing football games. On first impression many people will think this is a football book. After reading Keefe's excellently written text, all will know it is an account of devotion, sacrifice, and of love."

—Ken Gaddy, retired director of the Paul W. Bryant Museum

"Not just a repetition of game stats or Xs and Os for analysts of national priorities, Carey Keefe's *Tide of Dreams* gives a keen insight into the role of collegiate football in the American experience, particularly from the Depression years to the coming of the 1950s television revolution. Never overlooked is the influence of wives and young families on the headline coaches, a factor which gives depth and humanity to the sporting evaluation, well beyond the usual 'Rah! Rah! Cis boom bah!'"

—William Crisp, novelist, author of *375th Personnel Recovery Detachment*, nephew of legendary Alabama coach Henry Gorham Coach "Hank" Crisp

"Carey Henry Keefe's fascinating and poignant book reveals what goes on behind the scenes to create a winning college football team: the sacrifices assistant coaches' families make, the loneliness of being on the recruiting circuit for months at a time, the uncertainty of living contract year to contract year, and the challenge of working with a head coach with a big ego and a bad temper."

—Kathryn Smith, author of *The Gatekeeper: Missy LeHand, FDR, and the Untold Story of the Partnership that Defined a Presidency*

"Just when you think you know everything about Coach Bear Bryant, Carey Henry Keefe adds a new dimension to his life with this moving portrait about his lifelong friendship and coaching partnership with her grandfather, Carney Laslie, and her godfather, Frank Moseley. This narrative travels from their early days as players at the U of A to the little-explored wartime training camps where they prepped the first generation of top gun fliers and mastered the ingredients for producing championship football teams."

—Anne R. Keene, author *The Cloudbuster Nine: The Untold Story of Ted Williams and the Baseball Team that Helped Win WWII*, granddaughter of the commander of the US Navy Pre-Flight School in Chapel Hill, NC

"Carey Henry Keefe peels away the competitive and sometimes violent nature of football to shine a bright light on its humanity. Loyalty, integrity, and something akin to family shape her narrative, compelling themes that are as universal and as breathtaking as a perfect spiral or a last-minute touchdown. There are lessons in these pages, and Keefe offers them with elegance and heart."

—Greg Fields, author of *Through the Waters and the Wild*, 2022 winner of the Independent Press Award for Literary Fiction

"More than a book about football, *A Tide of Dreams* is a story of pride, perseverance, ambition, and, above all, loyalty. With meticulous research and a personal connection to one of the protagonists, Carey Henry Keefe has created a remarkable behind-the-scenes look at three men who led very public lives in the pressure-filled world of college sports. They were not supermen, and their careers were sometimes rocky, but Keefe shows us, flaws and all, their inspiring drive to succeed and their commitment to one another. This is a story not to be missed and is beautifully told by a fine writer."

—Clifford Garstang, author of *The Shaman of Turtle Valley* and *Oliver's Travels*

"The subtitle of Carey Henry Keefe's *A Tide of Dreams* says it all: UNTOLD. Not only does this spectacular piece of work reveal behind-the-curtain stories of the much-written-about Coach Paul 'Bear' Bryant, but it chronicles in a fascinating way the simultaneous journeys of Bryant and his two closest coaching confidantes and friends—Carney Laslie and Frank Moseley. Beginning in the early 1930s as rugged Crimson Tide football players, this trio of great football minds remained inseparable for most of their careers. Especially poignant are their World War II days when they utilized football techniques and workouts to train what would become the world's greatest fighter pilots. Following their service, the trio reunited as coaches and continued to lead young men on the gridiron for years to come. *A Tide of Dreams* is more than a story of three football buddies doing what they loved most; it's a magnificent display of friendship, love, and loyalty."

—Tommy Ford, thirty-three-year retiree of the University of Alabama Athletics Department, author or co-author of twelve books on Crimson Tide football

A Tide of Dreams

by Carey Henry Keefe

ISBN 978-1-64663-685-3

Cover Photo:
Foreground: Carney Laslie, Background: Paul "Bear" Bryant. Paul W. Bryant Museum/The University of Alabama. Used with permission. The Bryant Museum. © Catapult Sports.

Back Cover Photos: Top Left: Kentucky Alumni Magazine
Left: John C. Wyatt Lexington Herald-Leader photographs, University of Kentucky Libraries Special Collections Research Center
Bottom Right: © The Courier-Journal – USA TODAY NETWORK

Published by

 köehlerbooks™

3705 Shore Drive
Virginia Beach, VA 23455
800-435-4811
www.koehlerbooks.com

A TIDE
OF DREAMS

THE UNTOLD BACKSTORY OF COACHES PAUL "BEAR" BRYANT, CARNEY LASLIE AND FRANK MOSELEY

CAREY HENRY KEEFE

VIRGINIA BEACH
CAPE CHARLES

Lovingly dedicated to Poppa and Mama-Alice.
And to my parents, who gave me the confidence
to pursue my own dreams.

Why They Coached

THEY LOVED THE GAME.

"Football in reality is very much the American way of life. As in life, the players are faced with challenges, and they have an opportunity to match skills, strength, poise, and determination against each other. The participants learn to cooperate, associate, depend upon, and work with other people. They have a great opportunity to learn that if they are willing to work, strive harder when tired, look people in the eye, and rise to the occasion when opportunity presents itself, they can leave the game with strong self-assurance, which is vitally important in all phases of life. At the same time they are developing these priceless characteristics, they get to play and enjoy fellowship with the finest grade and quality of present-day American youth."

—Paul W. "Bear" Bryant[1]

The other reason:
they loved to win.

Contents

PART VI

Introduction

IT WASN'T LONG AFTER I returned from pitching my first novel at a writer's conference in the fall of 2010 in New York City, armed with a fresh appreciation of the process of publication and a copy of *The Portable MFA Handbook*, that the story within these pages re-presented itself. I always knew it was a story worth telling. I had planned one day to pen a quick biography and distribute it to family members in time for Christmas. But it didn't take long for me to realize that my assessment was quite naïve. For the account not to be perceived as a tale "my momma's momma told her and then my momma told me" required skills congruent with those of an investigative journalist who was comfortable searching library and newspaper archives, willing to contact strangers, ask questions, and discreetly solicit information. In short, it would be a monumental undertaking. Adding to my self-doubt was knowing that I knew only enough about college football to enjoy the game and was far from knowledgeable enough to write a book that would encompass the sport in all its glory as well as the controversy.

During the course of research and writing, I regularly questioned my abilities along with the wisdom of biting off clearly more than I could chew, knowing it might—to carry on with the analogy—actually swallow me whole in the process. But it was in the earliest days of the project, which I liken to an incubation period, that while visiting a charming bookstore in Charlottesville, Virginia, perusing a row of miscellaneous titles not even dedicated to the topic of sports, I happened upon John Watterson's comprehensive book, *The History of College Football*. Thumbing through the 400-plus-page book, I knew then I held what would be my bible of football history; a guide to follow as I pieced together the history of these three men whose lives mirrored the history of the sport. The realization felt electric, and from that moment on, the project took on a life of its own.

A year or so into the writing, I was so grateful for Mr. Watterson's work that I was compelled to send him an email, only to discover that he lived a mere forty-five-minute drive from my house. He graciously agreed to meet, and I had the distinct pleasure of telling him personally how much his book had helped me thus far. When I timidly asked if he might like to read the manuscript once I got to the point of completion, he did not hesitate: "If I never read anything about football again it will be too soon," he declared. It had taken him eleven years to write *The History* and he had had his fill. (Postscript: eight years later, I contacted him again to gauge his interest, and he was delighted to do me the honor of reading the completed project.)

At the end of the day, *A Tide of Dreams* is not so much about the game of college football as it is about friendship and loyalty, aspirations and dreams, lived out within the realm of a sport that has helped shape our nation's own trajectory of survival. The intensity of this period of history always fascinated me and, along with the intriguing blend of the three men's personalities, kept me energized and focused to recount their story as accurately and true to the historical narrative as possible. The result was an endeavor that not only took over my study where piles of books, three-ring binders, and various articles and newspapers clippings covered every surface, but also spilled over onto our dining room table and buffet, where eight-by-ten black-and-white photos lay spread out, a visual testimony of places and faces supporting the narrative at hand.

A reader of the manuscript near its completion commented to me upon finishing, "Well, it's not really a story about football." Yes and no. It is, but it isn't. I have tried to correct terminology where it has been pointed out to me and have had eyes reviewing the manuscript who were sensitive to identifying errors where the game itself, people, and/or dates were concerned. The challenge with respect to the game, of course, is that it underwent many changes from the 1920s to the '60s. I have tried to stick with relating pertinent information with the construct of the game in the time period it was played, but I also kept details simplified for the purpose of not confusing readers who might not be as savvy or interested as others in their understanding of why, how, or when the changes occurred. Although I could have saved myself from making a mistake (or twenty) by investing in David Nelson's *Anatomy of a Game* (see epilogue), I chose not to, as it is not only out of print but for my purposes too detailed. For those much more well versed in the technicalities of the game, I apologize in advance for any inadvertent errors in relating the details of any of the games, for I know it is like nails on a chalkboard to those with more than a novice's understanding of the game.

The sport continues to undergo changes, and as of this writing, college football players have the ability to accept compensation in exchange for their playing on a team. The current shift in the NCAA's strict oversight that allowed athletes to receive scholarships only, to allowing athletes to accept lucrative endorsement contracts, as well as allowing universities to recruit by offering hefty financial incentives (otherwise known as "pay-for-play"), could end the era of college football as we know it today.

—Carey Henry Keefe, Author

The Winningest Coach

"Men are brothers by life lived ... It is this that we know together ... all of us, all ages. We have played this magnificent, wild, extravagant, difficult and often dangerous game—not merely watched it played ... We know the feel of it, the desperate excitement, the triumph, the despair ... It is this which gives the game its power over our memories and minds—a power which those who have never played find inexplicable—even incredible."

—Archibald MacLeish, Pulitzer Prize-winning poet,
addressing the National Football Foundation Hall of Fame
December 1969

BLACKSBURG, VIRGINIA
AUGUST 1979

THE HELICOPTER CARRYING PAUL "Bear" Bryant landed unceremoniously on the small patch of backyard at the Moseley home in Blacksburg, Virginia. He had come that day to pay homage to his old friend and past assistant coach, my godfather, Frank Moseley, who had passed away at age sixty-eight of lung cancer. Other than the deafening *thump, thump, thump* of the whirlybird, Bryant arrived and departed with little fanfare and no entourage. He paid his condolences to Edy, Frank's devoted wife of thirty-five years and then, after finishing off the peanut butter sandwich Edy had made, lumbered slowly back across the green lawn, hunched low to avoid the swirling blades, and climbed aboard. I had last seen him eight years before at the funeral of my grandfather, Coach Carney Laslie. I was thirteen at the time. The passing years had taken a noticeable toll: a tiredness to his measured walk that matched his face, well known for its deeply etched lines and weather-beaten complexion. I watched as the University of Alabama's black, nondescript helicopter slowly lifted off the ground, carrying the man I knew as "Uncle Paul" back to Tuscaloosa.

I joined Edy back in the kitchen, and we continued to reminisce about the early years when the three men—Frank Moseley, "Bear" Bryant, and Carney Laslie—coached together. It wasn't long before Alene, the Moseleys' daughter, joined us.

"Mama, I can't believe it. Did you really just make Bear Bryant a sandwich when we have all that wonderful food sitting on the buffet in the dining room?" she scolded good-naturedly.

"Oh, honey, that's all he wanted. I knew him when all of us—your daddy and Carney included—felt lucky enough to have a peanut butter and jelly sandwich for dinner." She laughed at the memory.

I gathered the dishes and walked to the sink where the window overlooked the patch of yard bordered by tall pines. You would never have guessed that this postage stamp-sized area had recently been used as a landing pad. It looked both unassuming and undisturbed. The man who was already a legend in the world of collegiate football had come and gone without anyone noticing.

I thought about the monumental role my grandfather and godfather had played in Bryant's career, standing beside and behind him throughout, anchoring him as only those who know you and your earliest beginnings can. They had weathered personal and professional storms together, tethered by their love for and loyalty to each other. But their story would soon be lost with no trace of what had been a remarkable and historical journey. Someday, I thought to myself as I watched the helicopter vanish from sight, I'll write their story.

NOVEMBER 28, 1981
A YEAR AND A HALF LATER . . .

Fans watched and counted along with the clock on the scoreboard as it neared the end of the much-anticipated match between rivals Auburn and Alabama at the Iron Bowl. The thundering chant of "315 . . . 315 . . . 315!" continued unabated until the final seconds when the crowd rushed the field to celebrate Coach Bryant's record-breaking 315th win, making him the "winningest coach" in college football history. Sporting his signature houndstooth hat, Bryant strode off the field flanked on all sides by reporters and security. Fans swarmed in to get up close and personal and to congratulate the famed coach.

Small in stature, Verne Lundquist, sports reporter for ABC News, was able to muscle into the fray coming alongside the bear of a man. Positioning his microphone perfectly, Lundquist presented the first opportunity for Bryant to make what would surely be an historic post-game comment.

"It was, I know, a great honor for you to have so many of your former players and coaches here today," he said, thrusting the mic upward toward Bryant, who slowly made his way toward the locker room amidst the throngs of people surrounding him.

A statement haltingly delivered belied the carefully prepared words. "Yes. I'm real proud of all of them and real thankful," he said with his thick Southern drawl and signature mumble, "thankful I had the privilege of being associated with all of them." He paused slightly for emphasis. "But not only them . . . but people . . . good people. Fine people. Like Carney Laslie. And Frank Moseley. Who meant so much to me."

And with those final words he strode into the locker room. Later in official post-game interviews he went further:

"I'm thankful to the good Lord for the many wonderful people at Maryland, Kentucky, Texas A&M and here. Carney Laslie and Frank Moseley had as much or more to do with this as anyone. I wish they could have been here."[2]

Edy Moseley, watching the game on television from home, burst into tears when she heard his words. "Mama never cried," her daughter Alene told me. "No. Not ever. But when she heard Bear Bryant acknowledge my daddy like that . . . well, it meant a lot."

My mother's first words after hearing Bryant still resonate: "Not many in life get to say they lived out their dream like your grandfather and Paul Bryant did."

In the days and weeks that followed, my mother, Mary Lou Laslie Henry, heard from coaches and players around the country who wrote or called to say they had heard Coach Bryant acknowledge her father, and they, too, had not forgotten.

Sports pundits commented that Bryant had named only two dead, past assistant coaches in his post-game statement.

But they were much more than that.

Who they were and what they meant to each other is what ultimately underpins all heroes and successful endeavors: a loyal, trustworthy friend. Theirs was also a partnership of a shared vision. They were aligned with and understood what such a commitment to their goals required of them, a vital component needed to achieve the success they desired. As Laslie was fond of reminding his players, "To be the best . . . there is no substitute for work." He added in an interview with the *Charlotte Observer* in 1965: " . . . we [Alabama] are probably the smallest team in major football. But we always tell our boys that 'bigness is in your heart and not body.'"[3] In a televised interview not long after his "winningest game," Bryant was asked what it was that drove him to be a coach, to which he laughingly replied, "To be honest, I don't think there was anything else I could do."[4] Hard work. Huge desire. And, in the end, humility. The hallmark of a creed all three of these men embodied.

Many people today consider Bryant to be the greatest college football coach of all time. To those few who know the backstory of his trajectory to the top, Bryant's public comments about his friends at the most historic moment of his career was a balm of remembrance and an acknowledgment of their contributions to his rise to the top: that he, perhaps, would never have reached the pinnacle of the sport without them. He was indebted to them. And grateful to them both.

Their journey together unfolded amidst the fanfare and foibles of a sport, during its—and their—formative years. A sport that won their hearts as young men when they played together for Alabama in the 1930s, on through World War II and beyond when, after the war, the three joined forces and became the powerful coaching trio they knew they could be. Moseley, an integral part of their journey, would peel off from the other two, choosing the love of his life over his love of football. Bryant and Laslie would go on to coach together at three universities before the two finally arrived back at Alabama to coach the Crimson Tide. Their brand of coaching transformed both the boys they coached and the athletic successes of each school where they coached.

It was a game that consumed them till the end of their days. And like many who have played and coached this game, it was an addiction. "It's heady stuff to match quickness, speed, and physical violence with other addicts. The allure heightens until we cannot imagine living without it," Bill Curry wrote in his book *Ten Men You Meet in the Huddle*.[5] They were all three convinced that "football, in its right place, had the power to teach boys complete control of themselves, to gain self-respect, give forth a tremendous effort, and at the same time observe the rules of the game, regard the rights of others, and stay within bounds dictated by decency and sportsmanship."[6] They were convinced of this because the game had done all that for them and more. It can also be said they embodied the words of General Douglas MacArthur: "There is no substitute for victory." At Alabama, Bryant would go on to famously coin his own slogan: "There is no substitute for guts."

SPRINGFIELD, VIRGINIA
OCTOBER, 2011

The phone call from the University of Alabama was, in itself, startling. The purpose of the call even more so. "Are you Mary Lou Laslie?" the voice on the other end asked my mother. When she acknowledged that she was, the voice continued, "A ring was found. We believe it belongs to your father."

The ring—a University of Alabama, triple-bowl, National Championship ring awarded to each of the coaches at Alabama in 1965 after winning their third NCAA National Championship in three years—given to my brother after our grandfather's death, was worn night and day, a reminder of the grandfather lost and the legacy left behind. But in 1977, after absentmindedly leaving the ring on the side of a sink basin in the men's restroom at RFK Stadium in Washington, DC, despite his rushing back only a minute or two later, the ring was gone.

Five years later, Fred Martinez, a ranger with the US Army, was stationed at Schofield Barracks, a US Army post in Oahu. As he tells it,

> A friend and I were snorkeling and going down for coral to sell at the local flea markets. We were in about fifteen to twenty feet of water when we noticed sharks heading our way. We dropped everything and swam out of the reef as fast as we could. As I neared the beach, I saw something shiny on the bottom, about five to six feet down. It looked like it might be a gold coin. As crazy as this sounds, something told me to go get it, even knowing sharks were after us.[7]

It wasn't until he was safe on shore that he finally looked at what was embedded in the clump of sand he had scooped up from the ocean floor. Not a coin but a man's gold ring, with the words "Alabama 1965" encircling the large red ruby at its center. Engraved on the inside of the gold band were the initials "C.G.L.," faded but still legible.

Martinez wondered who "C.G.L." was. How had the ring come to be buried on the ocean floor? And for how long? Days? Weeks? Years? As soon as he got home, he locked it in his safe.

A few months later, in March of 1983, Martinez was transferred to Fort Rucker in Enterprise, Alabama, for helicopter flight school. Despite well-meaning friends who encouraged him to sell the ring, Martinez instead placed a couple of calls to the University of Alabama Athletic Department, which could find no player on the 1965 squad with the initials C.G.L. "They wanted me to send the ring to them," Martinez told my mother when he spoke to her years later, "but I was afraid it would never get to the family. So I kept it. When I first found the ring, my son was six years old. He asked me what I was going to do with it. I told him it wasn't my ring, and we must find the owner. I made a promise to God and to my son that I would continue looking."[8] It would take another thirty years.

In the fall of 2011, Martinez, now retired and living in Falkville, Alabama, decided to take one more stab at finding the ring's owner. This time he called the University of Alabama's Alumni Athletic Association (a.k.a. the A-Club). Once again, they could find no players on the 1965 team with those initials. He shared his frustration with his Men's Bible Study Group at Fairview Church of God. Much to his surprise, several of his co-members were also members of the A-Club, and they seemed to remember a coach by the last name of "Laslie." With a little bit more detective work, the university located my mother, and Fred Martinez made the call he had waited so long to make to personally speak to Coach Laslie's daughter and tell her the news.

Fred Martinez's son was now thirty-six years old.

The return of the ring awakened a memory of my own. With renewed interest, I spent countless hours rifling through piles of memorabilia, scrapbooks, and old photographs and diaries, housed in a literal treasure trunk, an old pine chest lovingly honed by my great-grandfather's hand, that had, for as long as I remembered, doubled as a coffee table in my parents' family room. The more I learned, the more intrigued I became.

In 2013, I flew into Birmingham, Alabama, rented a car, and charted a visit that would take me to Montgomery, Tuscaloosa, and Tuskegee, my grandfather's birthplace, to see for myself what had seeped into his veins at birth, creating a love for the South, and in particular Alabama, that never left him, despite the harsh realities that defined its time and place in history. Thus began my discovery of a story that had long been waiting to be told. My journey into the past armed me with an appreciation of what lessons can be learned from the land, the times, and from those with whom we experience life together. From this period of history, they were hard lessons wrought from hard times. But like my grandmother, Alice Laslie was fond of saying, "Ain't we got fun!" Indeed they did. This is their story.

PART I

THE 90-DAY WONDERS
1941 - 1945

"Upon the fields of friendly strife are sown the seeds that on
other fields, on other days, will bear the fruits of victory."

—General Douglas MacArthur, Superintendent,
US Military Academy at West Point, New York, 1919–1922

CHAPTER ONE

The Fighting Men of VMI

"You may be whatever you resolve to be."

—Stonewall Jackson's words inscribed over the Jackson
Arch Entrance to the present-day VMI Barracks

VIRGINIA MILITARY INSTITUTE
LEXINGTON, VIRGINIA, 1941

THAT SUNDAY AFTERNOON WAS looking to be like every other in the quaint, pastoral town of Lexington, Virginia. The white stone buildings comprising the hundred-year-old Virginia Military Institute (VMI) stood looming and fortress-like at its center. Most of the cadets were seated at their dormitory desks studying. Many families, having gathered for their traditional mid-day meal after the conclusion of Sunday church services, were in their kitchens washing up the dishes, while others had settled in for their Sunday afternoon naps.

On that day as well were two VMI assistant football coaches, Carney Laslie and Jimmy Walker, and Frank Moseley, an assistant coach at the University of Kentucky, who were waiting to hear from their friend Paul Bryant, an assistant coach at Vanderbilt University. Bryant was on his way back home to Nashville from Fayetteville, Arkansas, where he had applied in person for the job of the University of Arkansas' next head football coach.

The four men had formed a tight friendship during their college days as teammates playing football for Alabama.

Walker, the youngest of the four men, was tall and handsome, a collegiate star in both basketball and football. But he was equally held in high regard for his leadership abilities and congeniality. "Everybody was always talking about Jimmy," remembered Mary Lou Laslie, the Laslies' daughter. "They knew he would go on to do great things." Everybody loved Jimmy.

Coach Laslie got to know Walker well during Alabama's 1933 football season, when after graduating in 1933, he joined Coach Frank Thomas's staff as an assistant coach. That season, juniors Walker and Bryant, with senior Moseley, the co-captain of the team, played varsity.

By the time Walker was ready to graduate two years later, Laslie was in Arkansas coaching high school football, and encouraged his friend to follow his lead and take a job coaching high school football at a nearby Arkansas school. Walker heeded his advice, taking his first job at a school three hours from where Laslie was coaching. He was there only one year before they both moved to college football, joining the coaching staff at VMI in 1937.

Now college coaches themselves, they had a pact between them: whoever got a head coach position first would bring the other three along with him as assistants.

Bryant had long held ambitions to be a head coach. After four years of assisting under Alabama's head coach, Frank Thomas, he had spent the past two years at Vanderbilt as an assistant coach under Coach

Henry R. "Red" Sanders. He felt ready. But in the world of college football, he was, at twenty-eight, considered too young for the position. Nevertheless, he had the backing of his friends and ex-teammates Laslie, who at thirty-two was the senior member of the group, Walker, and Moseley, who all had confidence in Bryant's abilities, ambition and persuasive powers to convince Arkansas to hire him for the job.

It helped that Bryant himself was from Arkansas, born and raised. He had played football at Fordyce High School there before being plucked from obscurity by Alabama's Coach Hank Crisp. Bryant also had a strong calling card in the form of Carney Laslie, who was by now well known throughout Arkansas having produced three consecutive seasons of an unbeaten high school team in Blytheville, Arkansas, unprecedented at that time for a high school or college team. They all had high hopes that Arkansas would be where they would, as a dream team of coaches, showcase their skills and build championship teams. On the morning of December 7, 1941, Bryant had a good feeling. Some accounts relate he had been offered the job, while others that a formal offer would be forthcoming. Either way, Bryant, at age twenty-eight years of age, knew he had the job, and he was setting himself mentally to become the next Razorbacks coach. All four coaches had centered their hopes on Bryant's venture, optimistic about his success. None of them could imagine what the day would portend for all their futures— or indeed for everyone in the nation.

Suddenly, without warning, a shout was heard across the campus of VMI, breaking the stillness of the afternoon. Young men in every manner of dress, oblivious to the cold December air, streamed onto the school's open quad in the center of the campus. Townspeople out for an afternoon walk startled at the sudden outburst, rushing to find the nearest radio to hear the news. The time was 2:35 p.m., a mere thirty-five minutes after the surprise onslaught by the Japanese had begun 4,716 miles away at the naval base at Pearl Harbor, Hawaii. Casualties were certain. Exactly how many was yet unknown.

Two years earlier, a young and ambitious contingent of six former teammates from the University of Alabama had arrived in Lexington, Virginia to coach football. With the breaking news, each of the coaches made their way to the home of Carney Laslie, the line coach at VMI. The Laslie home, conveniently located near the campus, had always been the unofficial meeting place for the transplanted Alabamian coaches.

Coach Laslie, a natural-born storyteller with a reputation for weaving humorous tales, and his wife, Alice, who it was said never met a stranger, were natural hosts for the group. Eight years before, they had met as students at the University of Alabama, and were married in 1935, two years after Carney had graduated. Except for the addition of their adored young daughter, Mary Lou, now five and a half, their married life was a continuum of their college days where the football calendar reigned, and life was filled with the camaraderie of a close group of friends whose lives revolved around achieving a winning season.

Aside from the addition of new friends and coaches to the group, those first years in Lexington were like days of old when they were teammates at Alabama. Clarence H. Gilbert, the popular owner of Lexington's auto shop, was an honorary member of the group by virtue of being married to Alice Laslie's best friend, Edy Alphin Gilbert. Clarence, who everybody called "George" (by virtue of the saying "Let George do it!" made popular in the '30s and '40s), frequently joined in the lively evenings spent around the Laslies' pine kitchen table. Tall tales of hunting or fishing trips were told over games of penny ante poker, the evenings ending with a rousing rendition of a college fight song or two sung with gusto. Most of the time, Mary Lou listened from her bedroom, sometimes singing along to the tunes that had become so familiar to her. Other times, when awakened by the revelry, she would wander into the kitchen barefooted, dressed in her long flannel nightgown, sleepily rubbing her eyes. The men, hushed by her presence, would offer various apologies in chorus: "Oh my, honey, we're so sorry to be keeping you awake," sheepishly calling it a night.

On that Sunday in December 1941, the comfortable and safe world they all knew took an abrupt turn. As darkness descended, the mood grew graver and more somber with every passing hour, the usual fraternity-like atmosphere around the pine kitchen table replaced with a military-style seriousness. The men huddled together, heads bowed in earnest conversation with opinions offered about this plan or that. Anxious expressions combined with anger united them while they tried to keep abreast of the most current reports coming across radio airwaves. Coach Laslie's demeanor was remembered as being calm and measured, known for his authoritative air and distinctive bearing both on and off the field. The intensity of emotion was high as the reality of their country being attacked and the implications for them and the country became worse with each updated radio report.

The phone rang constantly. As soon as one call ended, another began as a network of coaching friends and colleagues from around the country sought to add their voices to the deliberations of the men assembled there. Paul Bryant, who heard the announcement over the radio just as he drove into Nashville, phoned in as well, checking in periodically to strategize along with the group about what might happen next and what their plan of action might be.

Mary Lou Laslie, a self-described quiet, obedient child, remembers that day sitting at the foot of the staircase close to the front door, having been given an important role: to listen for the door knocker or the bell to ring. Dutifully she sat, her hands folded in her lap, and waited to usher in the next visitor. The tall and boyishly handsome Coach Walker, a frequent guest and one of her favorites among her father's friends, didn't bother to knock. He rushed in, hat in hand. She leapt to her feet, breathlessly declaring, "Uncle Jimmy, something very bad has happened!"

Coach Walker gently placed his hand on top of her head.

"Everything'll be all right, honey, don't you worry," he reassured her before rushing off to join the others.

The men moved restlessly from kitchen to living room and back again as newcomers arrived. Ashtrays overflowed with crushed cigarette butts. The air, hazy with smoke, thickest in the kitchen, wafted through the small, modest home. Alice Laslie scurried to keep glasses and pitchers of water filled, a far cry from the customary beverage of choice imbibed on more festive occasions held at their home. Voices hushed whenever the red transistor radio crackled with the latest updates.

It seemed clear to all the country was headed to war. Auto shop owner George Gilbert, who had arrived at the Laslies' along with the coaches, declared unequivocally his intention to join the Army and become a pilot. Frank Moseley, who had driven immediately to the Laslies' from Lexington, Kentucky, voiced his personal admiration for the Marines. It was clear, though, that the coaches, despite their different opinions about which branch might be the best fit for them, were of one mind in their desire to defend the country. They became teammates once again, only unified in a higher purpose. Their goal was to defeat an enemy, not an opponent, an enemy on a battlefield, not on a gridiron. A tie wasn't an option. Their very lives and the future of the free world would be at stake.

The coaches who gathered at the Laslies' home on December 7, 1941, were unaware of an innovative training program that would be implemented by the Navy in a few short months. They had no idea that because of their experience and skills, they and others from athletic departments around the country would be recruited to participate in a fast-tracked officer training program at the Naval Academy at Annapolis: a group of coaches who would come to be known as "The 90-Day Wonders."

But on that day, it was only George Gilbert who left straight away and signed up to be an Army pilot. The coaches would wait. But not for long.

*VMI Coaches, 1939. L-R: Line Coach Carney Laslie,
End Coach Jimmy Walker, Head Coach Pooley Hubert, and Scout
and Backfield Coach Russ Cohen.*

CHAPTER TWO

Navy!
Football! War!

"The mission then is to train our pilots not only so they are more skillful in flying technique and knowledge but in one year and subsequent training to place them on the field of combat stronger and tougher, both physically and mentally. To accomplish this, our methods must be revolutionary as compared with our peacetime life. And the most intensive, rigorous and comprehensive program of physical and mental training that the world has ever seen should be installed. <u>Time is short.</u>"

—Original Plan for Pre-flight Training, V-5 Program,
presented by then Operations Officer Thomas Hamilton, 1941

"I think World War II was probably the greatest example of the magnificent cooperative effort of a nation that the world has ever seen, and I hope the US doesn't forget the lessons that we should have learned at that time."

—US Navy Rear Admiral Thomas J. Hamilton, 1978[9]

THE NEXT FEW WEEKS proved critical as the country mobilized for war.

Isolationist forces that had been holding back a more extensive training program not only for US troops but for all war preparations were swept away by the attack on Pearl Harbor. At the behest of President Franklin Delano Roosevelt, Congress declared war on Japan on December 8. Three days later, the allies of Japan, Germany, and Italy declared war on the United States. Mobilization ensued as the country began an aggressive campaign to prepare for an active role overseas. It was clear to many in the Navy that there was a shortage of qualified manpower for naval aviation. Modification and standardization of the existing Navy program was desperately needed to accomplish a quick buildup of troops.

The entire military force of the US swelled in numbers as the Army, including the Army Air Corps (which became a separate branch, the Air Force, in 1947), Marines, and Navy began immediately processing anxious men and women eager to answer the call to duty. On December 7, 1941, the Navy had an active strength of 337,349 men. By July 31, 1945, the number had swelled to 3,405,525 men and women on active duty. Part of the buildup occurred under the Department of Naval Aviation Training, which became one of the most transformative programs of the war effort.

Immediately following Pearl Harbor, the director of Naval Aviation Training, then Captain Arthur W. Radford, requested to meet with a man he deemed to be the best qualified to assess an idea he had: then Operations Officer Thomas Hamilton.

Hamilton was well known in the world of Navy athletics. He had played for Navy's 1926 National Championship team, coached at the Naval Academy in the mid-1930s and 1940s, and served as athletic director for the Naval Academy. But he was also a naval aviator, flying a variety of aircraft prior to the declaration of war, including torpedo, scout, patrol, and transport. Captain Radford wanted to get Hamilton's opinion on an idea he had been mulling over to prepare combat pilots for when the US entered the war. The time was now at hand.

Hamilton was summoned to Radford's office, where Radford explained his idea: recruit good coaches to join the Navy and use "competitive athletics and training in athletic skills to increase the abilities of Navy combat pilots."[10] Hamilton, who had fought in WWI, wholeheartedly agreed. The "use of various sports could quicken the eye, improve the judgment, the reaction time, get better mobility and precision"[11] to pilots. Swimming also could be taught since a great deal of the time, missions would be flown over large bodies of water. Before leaving Radford's office that day, Hamilton had given his unequivocal support for the captain's idea and "suggested he send someone to the joint meeting of the NCAA [National Collegiate Athletic Association] and the American Football Coaches Association to tell them the idea and find out who would want to serve."[12]

It didn't take long for Hamilton to be summoned, once again, to Radford's office. Radford had decided he would take Hamilton up on his idea of pitching the plan at the joint meeting of the NCAA and college football coaches coming up in Detroit. And he could think of no one more qualified than Hamilton, a well-known and respected coach who had developed a network of friends and acquaintances with other coaches over the years, to make the pitch. "I'm ordering you to go out and make this presentation to the coaches and NCAA," Radford told Hamilton.[13]

The plan was enthusiastically received by those in attendance. Coaches interested in serving were instructed to submit their applications to the Navy's Bureau of Aeronautics. Coaches Jimmy Walker, Carney Laslie, and Frank Moseley did so immediately. Bryant, however, took it one step further. After hearing the presentation, he drove straight to Hamilton's office in Washington the next day. "I heard your talk, and I'm ready to go to war," he declared. Hamilton told him he would see to it that Bryant's name would be one of the first to be considered, but for now to return to his coaching job at

Vanderbilt until he was called.[14]

The following week, Hamilton received new orders to join Captain Radford's staff at the Naval Air Station in Anacostia, Washington DC, and was put in charge of the Pre-Flight schools and the physical training section. Bryant showed up again less than a week after Hamilton was on the job.

"I haven't heard from you! I've left home; I'm not going back. I can't go back now; I've told all my friends that I've gone off to war," he said. Hamilton, admiring his zealousness and sympathizing with the young coach's plight, offered his home for the next three weeks while putting him to work as a civilian until such time as they could process his application and get him into the Navy.[15]

Hamilton would go on to craft the essential elements of the Navy's physical training program for naval aviation, as well as the establishment of the Navy's induction centers, where instruction would take place, forming the keystone of the entire physical program during the first months after Pearl Harbor. The tentative proposal included his additional observations on why it was needed:

> Our pilots to be inducted into the Naval service in general come from a soft, luxurious, loose-thinking, lazy, peace-time life in our homes and schools, and must be prepared physically and mentally to meet and defeat pilots and personnel of our enemies who have been thoroughly trained in a purposeful and wartime physical and mental system for years; in fact from childhood . . . To accomplish this, our methods must be revolutionary as compared with our peacetime life. And the most intensive, rigorous, and comprehensive program of physical and mental training that the world has ever seen should be installed. Time is short.[16]

Twenty-five thousand coaches and physical education professors applied to join the program. Of that number, 2,500 were selected. The process resulted in the top coaches and physical education professors in the nation leading the training at these schools. Commissioned into the Navy and given a rank commensurate with their age and experience ranging from ensign to lieutenant commander, they were then sent to the Naval Academy where they underwent intense indoctrination into the "Navy Way." The physical training and school routine design was also first tried out on the instructors there, so they could identify areas needing to be revised. The officer training program was initiated in early February of 1942 and consisted of five stages of intense instruction for the recruited coaches over a period of three months. That group of fast-tracked officers and those who came after them became known as "The 90-Day Wonders."

It was clear from Hamilton's written goals for the program that those selected to implement it would play a "vital part in the molding of" the minds and bodies of these newly recruited pilots. Thus, the coaches selected were, as Hamilton had outlined in his requirements, "examples of clean living, rugged manhood" and possessed "enthusiasm and a tough spirit." As far as possible, Hamilton emphasized, importance should be placed on "selecting men who are practical and experienced in teaching boys to face stern competition." The instructors selected also demonstrated the ability to "command the respect of the Cadets while working with them shoulder to shoulder," their brand of leadership aligning with the need to quickly equip the cadets to be able to accept responsibilities.[17]

It was not only the indoctrination to the comprehensive physical training regimen that needed to be taught to those coaches selected, Hamilton insisted, but also a deep dive into naval lore. This included being taught the background of "naval information, etiquette, and tradition" along with "wartime thinking, building hate for our enemies and their methods, teaching . . . it is a privilege to die for his country's cause, cultivating the reckless, devil-may-care spirit."[18]

Hamilton included in the plan he presented to Captain Radford his belief that this type of teaching, to embed the psychology of wartime thinking comprehensively and purposefully, should be "steadily built throughout the whole flight training course." He also believed that the Navy's current system was imbued with a singular focus of "unquestionably necessary technical subjects" but neglected to cultivate the student's mind to the "basic motives" needed to "destroy our enemies," leaving the student's basic emotions directed toward the enemy to "develop as they may."[19]

"Our nation's whole line of reasoning has been allowed to develop along this trend," he argued, "so that we find ourselves mere 'babes in arms' in this highly essential characteristic for war."[20]

Also recruited to staff the Pre-Flight schools were graduates of the Naval Academy who at the time were living as civilians. They were asked to return and serve their country by helping with the administrative roles and academic departments needed at each of the new schools and to model to the potential pilots Naval Academy culture and expectations. With the permission and assistance from the Naval Academy, many were located and eager to serve.

Not everyone was a fan of Hamilton's prescription for wartime training. From the beginning, Hamilton, a Navy football player, coach, and athletic director, saw the value of football as the sport that accomplished the most in achieving the goals outlined for the troops. After he had relocated his office to join then Captain Radford's staff, he was met with an unequivocal lack of support by fellow staffer Lieutenant Commander Gene Tunney, a former professional boxer, who was said to have been unsettled by Hamilton's presentation to the coaches and NCAA in Detroit. Inviting Tunney to meet him for a cup of coffee in the cafeteria, Hamilton tried to address his concerns.

"I understand you were disturbed by my making this presentation that Captain [sic] Radford wants to install in naval aviation, and I think that's needless," Hamilton offered.[21]

Tunney, ready for the debate, counter punched, telling Hamilton that he was, in fact, disturbed. "I just can't conceive of the Navy putting their training program in the hands of a bunch of fat and drunken football coaches," he said.[22]

His "ire raised" and not to be outdone, Hamilton replied, "Well, I guess you don't understand the whole concept is to use competitive sports in the training of these pilots. The greatest competitive teachers that I know of in the country are the football coaches, and I think they can do a better job than a bunch of punch-drunk boxers."[23]

The allusion was not lost on Commander Tunney, who had been a heavyweight boxing champion.

"Of course, that was the start of a beautiful friendship," Hamilton told an interviewer years later.[24]

Later, Tunney would again voice his doubts about the recruitment and training of coaches and cadets with so much of the focus on athletic ability. A naval pilot who got in a conversation with Tunney tried to explain why the emphasis on athletics at the Pre-Flight schools was important, to which Tunney replied, "Well, if I were to fly in combat with some pilot from a carrier, I'd much prefer not to fly with one who'd been up drinking coffee and cursing in the wardroom but would rather fly with a pilot who'd been in his room reading Keats and Shelley."[25] Hamilton later shared Tunney's reply at a breakfast given for legendary boxer Jack Dempsey and his illustrious manager Max Waxman. Upon hearing Tunney's comment, Waxman quipped: "Keats and Shelley. Who'd dem bums fight!"[26]

CHAPTER THREE

Pre-Flight, V-5 Naval Training

Lt. General Brett's inspection of Fleet Air Wing and Naval Air Station.

"It is the aggressiveness of the football field applied by our whole nation which will turn the tides of battle to success for our forces. The early part of this game has been spent desperately on our own goal line. Now it is our turn to have the ball. It is our determination that in this case the score will be overwhelmingly in our favor at the end, and there will be no enemy when we finish."

—FOOTBALL, The Naval Aviation Physical Training Manuals, 1943

ABOUT 800 COACHES WERE indoctrinated almost immediately. Their first order of business was to work out the syllabus of training for the system, building on the tentative proposal that Hamilton had already designed. Subsequently, some members of this group were then sent out to recruit cadets and others were assigned to Pre-Flight schools where they were to inaugurate the Navy's Pre-Flight Training (also known as the V-5 Program), and coach each school's Pre-Flight varsity sports teams.

In Hamilton's original proposal, he envisioned four schools (which he called "Induction Centers") strategically placed around the country: East, Middle West, South and West. The result was the four original Pre-Flight schools established at the University of Georgia at Athens, Georgia; the University of North Carolina at Chapel Hill; the University of Iowa at Iowa City; and St. Mary's College at Moraga, California. Each location implemented the newly standardized brand of naval aviation training known as the Naval Pre-Flight Training Program. Each school had the capacity to take about 1,800 to 2,400 cadets and give them a twelve-week training course in athletics and academics. Every two weeks, 200 new cadets would arrive and graduate fourteen weeks later.

Specialized recruiting for the program was implemented along with the regular recruiting service. During that first year, they signed up 80,000 cadets, a number so large that the Army gave Captain Radford an ultimatum: either the Navy had to release these new recruits as civilians to be drafted or put them in uniform. More Pre-Flight Training schools, a total of sixteen, and War Training Service schools, a total of thirty-two, located from Kansas, to California, Florida to Texas, were subsequently opened by Captain Radford.

The WTS schools were another type of flying school around civilian air fields. The goal of the entire program was to turn out a perfectly trained pilot along with the numbers of crewmen needed that Radford envisioned. Once graduated from WTS and Pre-Flight, cadets went on to advanced training at Jacksonville and Miami where they received their wings, becoming full fledged aviators, ordered to active squadrons and incorporated into the squadron organization as a whole. The total time it took a cadet to go from pre-flight to aviator was fourteen months.

Hamilton's part, in addition to the Pre-Flight schools, "was to put together the physical training of the whole structure of naval aviation which not only included the training bases, but also ships and tenders and bases where operating forces were working."[27] There was air crewmen training, done at the Memphis training center and in Norman, Oklahoma, and Jacksonville, Florida. Other bases, like the gunnery training at Clinton, Oklahoma, were training officers and men for carrier escorts. Hamilton's group of athletic instructors all were made part of the training and instructor personnel at those schools.

But it was the four initial Pre-Flight schools that led the way. The leadership assigned to the schools was made up of a group of preeminent retired commanding officers, whose skills were unparalleled in the ability to administer these schools, and they in turn were assisted by a group of the nation's most preeminent and respected coaches at these first four Pre-Flight schools.

They were looking for a few good men, a total of 30,000 to begin with. It was reported that one newspaper, *The World Behind The Headlines*, published in 1942, had an advertisement placed searching for qualified candidates that read, "Wanted: 30,000 eager young Americans yearly. Must be between eighteen and twenty-seven years of age, unmarried, American citizens, and graduates of high school or prep school. Accepted applicants taught to be naval aviators at best schools in the world."[28]

Candidates needed to be in top shape mentally and physically given the likely need for hand-to-hand combat skills and personal survival tactics should the graduates land on foreign soil in the middle of an active conflict. Excellent vision was also required; color blindness was an automatic disqualification. A full set of teeth was needed for oxygen masks to properly fit. Missing teeth, then, automatically disqualified the applicant.

In the official program, the purpose of the program's curriculum was summarized: "Thus the mental indoctrination required to prepare pilots for a vicious foe supplanting any romanticized idea of the fighting Navy pilot, along with the physical conditioning required is the program's central aim."[29] In addition, teamwork was highlighted as an essential component. In air combat situations, this was exemplified in the pilot-to-wingman relationship. Their survival depended on it.

This goal of teaching cooperation found its foothold around athletics. The Navy had already identified coaches from sports programs as being the best qualified to accomplish this goal within the troops, and among the different team sports considered to best exemplify teamwork was football, which they believed would foster not only a framework of cooperation between the troops, but the mental and physical toughness needed for war.

It was generally agreed that swimming was the most valuable sport in the Physical Training Program for naval aviators for obvious reasons, as most missions would involve flying over large bodies of water. But it was football, a rugged and combative sport, that was determined to have the most value overall in developing what would make the most effective battle-ready, fighting man. The sport embodied aggressiveness, physical fitness, coordination, alertness, discipline, toughness, and quick reaction. It was also considered to be the sport to best exemplify teamwork, which they believed would foster the needed framework of cooperation between the troops. Football players were known to "absorb the shock and pain of violent physical contact without wincing, and to rally strongly and courageously in the face of misfortune and adversity . . . [accepting] blows from Fate and his adversary as part and parcel of the game and stay[ing] in there swinging. He combines fortitude and strength with bodily skill and agility, and these factors with split-second thinking and reactions. These are the same qualities that make our fighting men the toughest and best in the world."[30]

Football's training structure—in non-war times, preparing the players for an upcoming fall season—seemed tailor-made for a military focus of preparation for war. It is during spring practice that fundamentals are stressed. Players perfect their knowledge of blocking, tackling, passing, and running with the ball. Basic plays are run repeatedly until they become routine. Techniques of offensive and defensive action are studied in "skull sessions" and plays displayed in "blackboard talks." Navy pre-flight training utilized all of these tactics.

Consequently, Navy "brass" established the value of having a football team at each Pre-Flight school, and football coaches who were already a part of the program were assigned to coach each school's team.

Varsity sports, where competitive drive was found to be experienced at its highest level, was considered critical to implement at each school. An overall standard of perfection could be applied to tests of both skill and character, the rules governing the latter desirably sterner. Morale was also boosted among the whole student body on the campuses where the Navy teams were formed. An infinitely valuable and not inconsequential benefit of the program.

However, once again, Thomas Hamilton and Gene Tunney found themselves at odds. An unintended lunch date with Eleanor Roosevelt proved to be crucial in removing the log that was jamming one of the most pivotal programs of the war.

Sometime early in the development of the program, Hamilton received a call asking him to go to the White House and pay a visit to Harry Hopkins, President Roosevelt's multi-faceted advisor. One of Mr. Hopkins's sons, Hamilton was told, was interested in naval aviation, and as a courtesy, Hamilton was asked to go and explain the program to the illustrious member of Roosevelt's inner circle, who also was a concerned father. Hamilton waited outside Hopkins's office for hours due to one of a number of unexpected crises predictably hijacking his scheduled meeting with Hamilton. By noon, with still no break in sight, Hamilton was asked if he would be interested in joining Mrs. Roosevelt for lunch. He readily accepted the invitation and was led to the second-floor dining room where he was "introduced to Mrs. Roosevelt, who had a lady guest who was a newspaper columnist" there as well.[31]

Charmed by the First Lady—which he admitted was not related to anything physically attractive about her, but rather "her presence and personality"—Hamilton had what he described as a "delightful luncheon." Toward the end of the meal, she turned to him, pointedly asking, "Well, young man, what are you doing?" to which he briefly gave an explanation of the training he was trying to execute for pilots. "Have you any problems that you haven't been able to solve?" she asked. Hamilton thought about this before he answered, wondering how prudent it would be to mention the current state of the problem he was facing with Commander Tunney, given his rank, but he decided to "bite the bullet."[32]

Hamilton explained to Mrs. Roosevelt that he had been struggling to establish football schedules with all the colleges in the country for the Pre-Flight schools, including the Army and Air Force service teams. All of the colleges had been willing to adjust their schedules to include Pre-Flight teams, and they had "top schedules." It was, Hamilton explained, the continuation of all their convictions that training and competitive sports events should be emphasized and kept going during the war years at all the high schools and colleges. Commander Tunney, however, was advocating cutting out all of these schedules to save transportation options if needed for emergency needs. Hamilton went on to explain that sporting events had been specifically targeted by the War Transportation Board with team travel to and from games prohibited. The ability to keep physical training going in the United States, he told Mrs. Roosevelt, would be severely impacted.

A week later, likely the result of the First Lady's prodding, an executive order signed by President Roosevelt cleared all the athletic schedules from the restriction. "It was a very notable thing in my mind to have that lovely lady go to bat for us, so to speak,"[33] Hamilton said.

Although the caliber and scope of inter-collegiate athletics predictably dropped, participation by the Pre-Flight schools in collegiate varsity sports went on to provide valuable publicity. Coverage of the Pre-Flight teams' successes by well-known sportswriters of the day generated interest for the public and also captured the interest of boys in schools around the country who were potential pilot material. It was not lost, however, on those who coached the game at these service schools that "things like football tended to dim in importance to men who, two or three months later, might be lying dead on some beach in the South Pacific."[34]

In mid-February 1942, VMI announced that graduation would be moved to May 15 from June 17 and the new graduates inducted into the US Army as second lieutenants. For the cadets at VMI, their future, like the nation's, was impossible to see. The graduating class was soon dispersed throughout all of the armed forces, and all of the VMI cadets felt how vital it was to cling to those principles and ideals that had been the mainstays of their lives. "We will not allow [these principles and ideals] to be disrupted nor lowered by conditions which we all hope and pray will be but a horrible memory within a short time," wrote the historian for the Class of '44.[35] He was right about the memories. But the war would go on for much longer than these brave young men could ever have imagined.

As VMI adjusted their academic calendar to the reality of war, so too did its athletic department. Coach Jimmy Walker left the coaching staff departing for Annapolis on March 22, 1942, citing his duty to join "the boys" that he played with at Alabama and coached at VMI. Laslie stayed on to assist in the reorganization of the sports teams, their rosters and game schedules for the remainder of the year already severely impacted by the war. He left for Annapolis sometime in April. Like all of those heading off to war, he said good-bye to his family not knowing if or when he would ever see them again.

CHAPTER FOUR

The Skycrackers

"This business of starting a team from scratch with high school, college, and pro players as my material is new to me," says the ex-Tarheel tutor. "I have no yardstick to measure our strength."

—Lieutenant Ray Wolf, Head Coach, Navy Pre-Flight Football Team the
Skycrackers, Athens, Georgia, September 25, 1942, on the eve
of their inaugural game against Penn State in Philadelphia.

FROM ATHENS, GEORGIA, TO THE ATLANTIC FLEET
1942–1945

OFFICIALLY OPENED FOR BUSINESS on June 10, 1942, the Navy designated their school at the University of Georgia in Athens as its Southern Center of the program. Campus facilities already existed at the school to accommodate both the training and housing needs for an influx of 2,000 cadets, designed to induct 30,000 pilots annually. Laslie arrived on campus not long after classes had commenced, completing his training at the Naval Academy and commissioned as a lieutenant in the Naval Reserve on June 13, 1942. (Among those in his newly commissioned group was future UCLA basketball coach John Wooden, who famously won twelve consecutive NCAA regional basketball titles and ten national championships between 1962 and 1975.) Two days after they were commissioned, the Navy announced that all Pre-Flight course instructors, including those newly commissioned, were also to be trained for combat duty.

Inducted into the Naval Reserves: First Row: L-R: 1. Carney Laslie, Second Row: L-R, 1. John Wooden. Noted on the back of the photo along with John Wooden is Raymond Kreick and Harry S. Harrison, both of whom, upon further research, were found to be avid golfers, which is perhaps why all three were identified—they made up a golfing foursome, which, other than football, was Laslie's favorite sport.

This was a new development, and Commander Gene Tunney, director of the program, explained the change in policy: "The Navy policy is to place these recognized warriors of the gridiron, the prize ring, and the baseball diamond into positions where their aggressiveness and leadership can be of value in actual combat. This new development is in accordance with the long-range policy of first having all shore establishments and training stations fully manned by instructors so that new recruits would undergo a competently supervised vigorous training before going into the fleet."[36] With that change the wives and family of these Navy coaches joined all of those around the country who were anxiously awaiting the news of where and when their loved one would be sent overseas.

Bryant, Moseley, and Walker, who had arrived weeks earlier in Athens, were on hand to welcome Laslie who arrived just in time for the first day of classes and the official opening ceremony held on June 18, 1942. Also among the coaching staff there was their beloved former coach from their playing days at Alabama, Coach Hank Crisp, who had continued in his role of mentor to each of them long after they had graduated.

These football coaches assigned to the Pre-Flight Program were charged with the implementation of the Navy's redesigned syllabus of training for cadets. They were to instruct cadets on how to become a fierce, battle-ready soldier, superior to any enemy they would encounter on the battlefield, by developing their mental surety and toughness and by focusing on the violence and aggressiveness that no other sport could provide as well as football. They would also work together to coach the Georgia Pre-Flight football team, the Skycrackers.

The Skycrackers' head coach that first year was Raymond "Bear" Wolf, a well-respected and renowned coach, his resume for the job including having played tackle at Texas Christian University before moving to Major League Baseball, where he played for the Cincinnati Reds in 1927. Later, he became head football coach at the University of North Carolina from 1936 to 41.

Included among the highly esteemed staff was the aforementioned Henry G. "Hank" Crisp, or Coach Hank as he was always known, now in the role of the official trainer and a physical fitness director for the Skycrackers. Crisp was a model of toughness. Handicapped after losing his right hand in a farm accident at age thirteen, he won eight athletic college varsity letters in basketball, and track, and also pitched on the baseball team. He was an example of what hard work and willpower could accomplish, and was known to sometimes be a harsh task master to the young men he coached.

His favorite known punishment from his days at Alabama when he was coaching these players now standing beside him as coaches in Athens was to have them run laps at the track starting at 4 a.m. One infraction remembered by Bryant as a young player that earned him the honor of Coach Hank's disciplinary ire was when he and a couple of other teammates were caught with a seventy-five-cent gallon of corn liquor in their room. Dropping the wayward group off at the track while a meet was in progress, Coach Hank had the last word on what he would or wouldn't tolerate. One hundred laps, he told Bryant and the other guilty boys. Don't bother coming back if you don't run every single one, he told them. They finished up around ten that night.

Infractions like these were few and far between, Bryant remembered in his autobiography. "A crisis consisted of a couple of guys getting caught smoking, or drinking some beer or something, that kind of thing. We all wanted to win so badly we never strayed too far off the line, and those who did would hide it from the other players."[37] The military culture of the new Pre-Flight football teams was that much more focused on discipline and intolerance toward any infractions. The country was, after all, at war.

The Skycracker football team of 1942 had a triumphant season, winning seven games, losing one, and tying one. Given the Navy's rule of coaches having only one season with a team, Bryant, Laslie, Walker, and Moseley were all deployed overseas by early 1943. The Pre-Flight Program continued to be tweaked and developed as the war effort gained speed. The following season saw 150 colleges around the country drop football, including Alabama and six more teams in the SEC. But at the end of the season of '42, both the Georgia Bulldogs and the Skycrackers were ranked among the top teams in the country by several polls.

Although the strict discipline and challenging physical activities of the Pre-Flight School left little time for anything else, some form of entertainment was needed to counterbalance the intensity of the training. Generally, no official leave was granted for the duration of a cadet's time at the school, although cadets were granted liberty on weekends, usually for several hours only on Saturdays and Sundays. This usually took the form of going to the Fine Arts Auditorium at the University of Georgia to watch a film, or seeing a celebrated comedian like Bob Hope, who made an appearance at the school in 1943.

Prior to the war, Coach Laslie had already established a practice of taking his players to the movies before a game to calm their nerves. And although most films shown on campus were purely entertainment, others foreshadowed the wartime world they would soon be entering. One cadet reminisced years later:

> When we returned late to our barracks, marching along the dark path through the pines, no one talked, but every once in a while someone would whistle or sing a phrase from "As Time Goes By." We were not so much thinking about the film as floating on its emotions, feeling the sadness of Humphrey Bogart, who had given up Ingrid Bergman for The Cause. We didn't really understand what The Cause was, exactly, what high principles linked the French at Casablanca to us at Athens, Georgia. But we felt the emotional link . . . As I fell asleep I heard one last cadet, alone in the shower, singing, "You must remember this, a kiss is just a kiss . . ."[38]

L-R, Bryant, Laslie and Walker having a farewell chat before each departs for their new duties, May 1943.

That Christmas of 1942, bachelors Walker and Moseley joined the Laslie family at their small home on South Milledge Avenue in Athens to celebrate the Christmas. Despite the uncertainty of the times and the financial frugality all had to practice, Alice Laslie was determined to make their gathering as festive as possible, insisting on their holiday traditions: a small, modestly decorated tree in the living room with presents stacked underneath for all, each box wrapped with bright bows and labeled with nametags no matter how small, mundane, or drab the gift inside.

In May of 1943, Naval Reservists Bryant, Laslie, and Walker, posed together for a publicity photo published in the Birmingham News. Wearing their dress navy blue uniforms, their faces turned toward each other, their smiles reveal their sense of accomplishment and the confidence born from men itching to get into the fray. They were, after all, three former and formidable Crimson Tide players, off to war.

Like all men of military age in the early 1940s, they were products of the Great Depression, when they had learned "to endure the cold, the heat, the hunger, and the pain of difficult times. They were hardened by the times and the elements even before they became football players, and they became good football players because of, and in spite of, those hard times."[39] It prepared them for their difficult years ahead and enabled them to ask of those they trained nothing less than what they had demanded of themselves and the risks they were prepared to take.

Awaiting their overseas orders together in Norfolk, when Bryant got word he was to be shipped out the next day, Walker was on hand to give him a proper sendoff: a seventy-cent bottle of champagne purchased at the PX to commemorate what they both thought was Bryant's last night stateside. Turns out, instead of immediately flying overseas, he landed at La Guardia airport in New York where he waited a few more days before being shipped out to North Africa to join US forces on the USS *Uruguay*. Walker departed soon after for the Navy's Fourth Fleet, Moseley to the Atlantic Fleet.

Laslie, however, was assigned to assist with the newly established Pre-Flight School at Williams College in Williamstown, Massachusetts, one of twenty additional programs opened after the success of the initial four schools. It would mean another move for the Laslie family if—and it was questionable whether it was possible—they could find suitable housing.

CHAPTER FIVE

Deployed

"Oh where, oh where, has his little mind gone?"

—Scrawled in the corner of a picture of Carney Laslie,
at the Panama Canal

WILLIAMSTOWN, A SMALL, PICTURESQUE town, was known as an enclave for artists of every sort. It was here where the renowned folk artist Grandma Moses began painting; her early works were regularly displayed and sold at local craft shows. It was also where, early in his career, famed songwriter Cole Porter had purchased an estate on forty acres. Fortunately, in addition to the Porters' main home, the property had an old, three-bedroom carriage house, which became available for the young family to lease. As it was located close to the college campus and a short walk to the elementary school Mary Lou could attend, the Laslies jumped at the chance.

Alice and Mary Lou arrived in late January 1943, just in time to experience the full force of winter. That year, the month's average temperature was nineteen degrees with fifty-one inches of snow falling. Snowed in for days on end, Mary Lou and Alice spent long days bundled up in layers of extra sweaters and huddled fireside to keep warm in the drafty carriage house. It became especially cold during the air-raid drills—a regular occurrence—with the electricity turned off and not even a candle allowed for light or warmth.

Carney Laslie standing in front of the guest cottage on the Porter Estate in Williamstown, Massachusetts, March, 1944.

With each move they made, the Laslies' small, red transistor radio, a valuable commodity in these times, remained firmly anchored in the middle of the pine kitchen table. There they would gather, listening for the latest war news as well as to their regularly scheduled popular radio shows of the day, a reminder of the life and friends left behind in their beloved Lexington, Virginia.

That spring, Carney Laslie received his deployment orders for Panama and Alice and Mary Lou returned to the bucolic college town where they settled into a second-floor, three-room rented apartment just off Jefferson Street in downtown Lexington, sharing a bathroom down the hall with another family (more of an inconvenience than anything else) and where they would wait out the war years.

Life felt peaceful and safe; the landlady, Mrs. Nicely, a widow remembered as friendly and loving. The prominent military presence of VMI cadets, participating in the traditional parades on the campus grounds, rifles at their side, and the college of Washington and Lee with statues of war heroes positioned around the grounds, enhanced seven-year-old Mary Lou's feeling of security and well-being. She never worried about the "Nazis." To her thinking, no one could overpower the mighty fighting squadron and cadets at VMI or the generals of Washington and Lee.

Many in the town shepherded the Laslies' young daughter through these tumultuous years, including Mr. and Mrs. Grossman, the Jewish proprietors of the women's dress shop, and the owner of the local movie house, both of whom offered small acts of kindness despite their own worries: an ice cream cone here, a walk down the street holding her hand there, the special treat of the latest Margaret O'Brien or Shirley Temple movie playing at the local theatre. The tragic casualties of war could not be avoided, whether in a small town or large city, with news arriving daily of loved ones lost in battle.

The dreaded telegram arrived mid-afternoon on a cold January day in 1945. Edy Gilbert, Alice Laslie's closest friend and companion and a second mother to Mary Lou, was unceremoniously delivered the news while at her desk at VMI where she worked as a secretary in the athletic department. Her husband, Clarence a.k.a. "George" Gilbert, the affable owner of the town's auto shop, honorary member of the group of coaches, who made the decision to go into the Army Air Corps right after Pearl Harbor, had been killed in action. Alice Laslie rushed out the door to be with Edy when she heard the news. Mary Lou, left with the household help, ran up the stairs where she found the maid on her knees, her back to the door as she cleaned the tub.

"George has been killed," she said breathlessly to the woman. Turning slightly, the maid gave Mary Lou a slight shrug before turning back to her scrubbing. Perhaps, like many in town, she had lost a friend or family member, grieving her own unspoken, unacknowledged, personal loss. Mary Lou, horrified at her indifference, picked up an empty glass milk bottle sitting just outside the door and hurled it, the glass shattering into the tub, milk residue dripping on the just cleaned tile. Not waiting for her response, Mary Lou fled to find their landlord, the appropriately named Mrs. Niceley.

The war raged on. British troops trained with Allied forces for an impending land invasion of Europe. The United States prepared for an invasion on its shores as well. It was anyone's guess as to when—and where—the landing might take place. The mission of protecting the canals in Panama, where invasion seemed likely, was the focus of Laslie's assignment.

He landed in Cuba in May 1944 direct from Williamstown and after a brief period of training was sent on to Panama. While there, the Department of the Navy sent official photographers on a mission to capture images of the hard physical labor the troops were involved in at this location. More importantly, in a PR campaign to contrast worrisome pictures of the conditions the troops were enduring overseas, they sought to provide images of humorous and positive activities.

Known for his dry wit and always a teaser, Laslie agreed to help in the campaign, posing for a variety of photographs. Scrawled above his head on one of the more serious photos from the collection of the copies he saved are the words, "Oh where, oh where, has his little brain gone?" as he scans the ocean's horizon on the lookout for an enemy

ship. In a series of lighthearted portrayals of R&R (rest and relaxation),
he can be seen in a group harvesting coconuts and in another posing
on a makeshift putting green on his hands and knees with a pool cue
stick to "shoot" a golf ball, many of which were published in various
newspapers and weeklies to show civilians what relaxing was like for
their men overseas.

Carney Laslie posing for the camera as he tries to make the putt.

CHAPTER SIX

The Boys Of Chapel Hill

"I know now why the Americans are the finest fighting forces in the world."

—Philippe de Gaulle, son of General Charles de Gaulle and a member of the French Army, upon visiting Pre-Flight School at Chapel Hill

CHAPEL HILL, NORTH CAROLINA, 1944

WHILE BRYANT, WALKER, LASLIE, and Moseley were overseas in, respectively, North Africa, South America, Panama, and the South China Sea, the Pre-Flight schools continued to churn out cadets trained by a roster of coaches, operations perfected, and training pushed to extremes as the war effort continued unabated.

Fifty years later, Col. Donald E. Marousek wrote of his experience as a young cadet assigned to the program at Chapel Hill in 1943. His memoir was discovered among his personal effects after his death in 2013. One of the most important lessons Marousek learned, he wrote, was this: "When you are totally physically exhausted and are convinced you can't go another step, will power can carry you as far again as you just came."[40] Memories were seared into his mind, including this never-forgotten moment when, met by seasoned cadets already immersed in training, the new, wide-eyed cadets disembarking from the Navy buses were greeted by strains of "You'll be soooorrryyy" that echoed throughout the station. Not an auspicious beginning. Marousek chronicles his experience and journey from pre-flight training at Chapel Hill to the next stage of pilot training:

> It was March, 1943, when the train took us to Chapel Hill—the University of North Carolina, the "Tarheels"—one of the [four] Navy pre-flight schools throughout the United States, but by far the most prestigious. This was the most organized, regimented, and disciplined operation I have ever witnessed. Everything was run by timing—not a wasted moment. As one class of cadets arrived for an event, the earlier class was just leaving. It was here that you developed your mind as well as your body. Classes in aircraft and ship recognition, Morse code, and blinker code, aerology, navigation—both dead-reckoning and celestial—and training films of all sorts, but not an airplane in sight!
>
> Then on the physical side was wrestling, boxing, basketball, and soccer (with no rules), marching, push-ball, swimming, hand-to-hand combat, and the dreaded obstacle course. We, at times, were also pressed into slave labor. Occasionally, a platoon would be marched out into the Carolina woods of red clay and small pine trees where a rock crusher was located and we fed boulders into the machine, which worked like an oversized food processor and broke up the boulders into gravel which was then graded into various sizes by passing over steel grates with ever-increasing hole sizes.
>
> The infirmary was kept busy with injured cadets. *Life Magazine* visited our campus for an article they were

doing, and we were to put on a show for the photographers, demonstrating push-ball. The ball is about ten feet in diameter, soft rubber, and inflated. Two teams of approximately thirty members per team tried to push the ball over the others' goal line. The demonstration got so violent that one cadet had a broken leg, and several others had broken arms or dislocated shoulders. Chapel Hill wasn't called "Cripple Hill" without reason!

... It was now July, 1943, and Pre-Flight School was over and most of us graduated! We were measured for uniforms—whites, this time, since it was summer, and, of course, we had to hold up the Navy tradition of looking our best. And so it came to pass that our orders came to go forward to our next level of training, "E Base."

The "E" stood for elimination, and here we would find out exactly who could fly and be recommended for more advanced Naval flight training, and those who were not adapting would fall into another class for disposition. Our Twelfth Batt. was broken into three classes, and we were given orders to proceed by train to either Olathe, Kansas, Great Lakes, Illinois, or Bunker Hill, Indiana. My orders read "Bunker Hill" for which I was pleased since this wasn't too far from Dayton, Ohio . . .

. . . We packed our belongings into green foot-lockers and suitcases, got all dressed up in our new Navy white uniforms, and boarded buses for our trip to the train stations. Remember, the War Effort was in full swing and all civilian men and women, whether exempt from military service or physically not acceptable were putting in long, hard hours in turning out tanks, weapons, ammunition, planes, food, clothing, and fuel for the war in Europe and the Pacific. In those days trains were the primary bulk carriers crisscrossing our nation. Freight trains were full, day and night. Passenger trains were few since travel was restricted only to those who were urgently needed for the war effort.

... It was the greatest industrial, all-out effort this nation or any other nation had ever seen in the history of the world! So when our "passenger train" pulled into the station that hot summer day in Chapel Hill, North Carolina, we were surprised to see it was an old-time, steam locomotive, not a stream-lined diesel. As it puffed and snorted past us on the platform belching white smoke, we then got a good look at the five or six cars it hauled behind. The railroad must have resurrected some old obsolete cars that had long since been replaced and that apparently had been sitting on a siding somewhere collecting dust. When the train finally clanked to a stop, we boarded this old dirty vehicle in our new, clean, white uniforms, and picked out our seats and tried to make ourselves comfortable. To say the ride from Chapel Hill to Bunker Hill was unpleasant would considerably understate the situation. First of all, it was hot, so we opened all the windows that would still open. Secondly, we all removed our white blouses with their high priest-like collars to try and keep cool. The train never achieved speeds greater than 35–40 miles an hour, whether this was because of its longevity or because of the excessive traffic I never did find out. But it was a long, hot, dirty ride. In the open country the engine belched thick, black smoke—no steam injection was used here as in the cities—so when the wind came crosswise to the train direction, the gases and carbon would swirl down into the open car windows and coat our new white uniforms black.[41]

Their white uniforms may have turned black, but their spirits remained unsullied. Their battle fatigues, however, would soon be covered with soil from foreign lands, and they would remain resolute in their pursuit of victory.

Although many cadets, like Marousek, regarded their experience at Chapel Hill as one they valued and never forgot, others swore Pre-Flight Training killed their interest in sports of any kind having a less-than-favorable view of the training overall, describing the methods as sadistic and brutal.

One naval doctor-turned-soldier, upon returning from the battlefield, however, expressed his point of view on the physical training at Chapel Hill in an interview in *The Cloudbuster*, the Navy's weekly published newspaper for Pre-Flight news at Chapel Hill. At one time, he confesses, he had made his opinions known, griping and complaining about what he felt was an unreasonably rigorous training. After his deployment to a Marine group that invaded Guadalcanal, he wrote he "wished to God they had been twice as tough in conditioning."[42] He described his change of heart in an article where he wrote of the necessity of a tough and hard mental and physical constitution for anyone who might come face to face with warfare and its life and death situations:

> Only men who have been well-conditioned and were in good physical shape could stand up under the grueling conditions which existed at the time of the landing and the following days. The tropical diseases were rampant and those in poor physical condition picked these up more rapidly, necessitating evacuation, in some cases, out of the area . . .
>
> A few men from time to time broke under the strain. It was always those who were in poorer physical shape. It finally came my turn to be evacuated and then it was that I wished I, personally, had been a tougher, better physically conditioned officer than I was . . . I am firmly convinced that an even more strenuous program of physical toughening and hardening will pay dividends in fewer men being evacuated . . .[43]

The soldier/doctor went on to relate a battlefield story that exemplified both the physical ability and mental toughness needed for war. He told of one Marine Capt. John J. Padley, a former all-Ohio football star, whose lightning quick action coupled with a cold steel mental resolve saved himself and his fellow Marines.

Hearing his men shout, "Look out, Captain!" Padley drew his bayonet with lightning speed, whirling around to find an enemy combatant rushing him with knife in hand. The force of Padley's move resulted in a thrust so powerful it brandished the enemy soldier in the air; the effect on those watching was electrifying as the Leathernecks sprang into action while the remaining enemy forces "elected to lie low and try sniping from the rear."[44]

Secretary of the Navy Frank Knox, in addressing the annual trophy dinner of Washington's Touchdown Club, declared his unwavering support for the Navy's use of football to train soldiers and pilots, pointing to the sport's involvement of aggressive body contact. "We are in a desperate war," he stated, "a war in which you kill or get killed. Nothing prepares a man better for that kind of war, especially in the Pacific, than the kind of training you get on the football field."[45]

Despite its detractors, there was no denying the success of the training. Less than a year after the inception of the program, the Navy reported a 22.7 percent increase in the average cadet's physical fitness from the time of entrance to graduation. In addition, every cadet completing the program could swim and support himself in the water for hours, the report said, with a focus on endurance, not speed.

It was also during this time, when Southern coaches sharpened their skills while serving at the Pre-Flight schools, that they observed the great potential of the Black athlete. Despite the integration of Black football players in the North, Midwest, and Far West during the war, the teams were forced to follow the dictates of segregation in the South, and Blacks did not play at Southern White schools. But Black players could not help but catch the attention of coaches at other bases.

Black Pre-Flight officers who composed an all Black marching band, and also played baseball and basketball on segregated teams, marched daily through campus and often performed at football games to boost morale. The Black military service team known as the Tuskegee Army Airfield War Hawks, in particular, which represented the future famed Tuskegee Airmen, posted a remarkable nine wins, one loss, and one tie in 1943. Although most coaches were focused on developing their skills within the social system that existed at that time, it opened their eyes to the possibilities that existed if and when segregation was abolished.

The Cloudbusters' upcoming season of '44 had its coaches worried. Head coach Lieutenant William G. "Glenn" Killenger could only hope that the latest arrival of the 59th Battalion to the campus would provide the manpower needed for the positions on the team he had identified as being the weakest: the line. He was looking for a few good men, guards and tackles specifically, to go up against a lineup of strong teams in the fall, namely the Naval Academy, Duke, and the Bainbridge Training Station.

Joining Killenger on his coaching staff was Paul Bryant, who had arrived at Chapel Hill from his tour of duty in North Africa in May of '44. The Cloudbusters had a brilliant showing, undefeated in their first four games, which included a powerful Navy team and one of the top teams that year, Duke, coached by the formidable Wallace Wade of Alabama fame, who had coached the Crimson Tide to three National Championships.

The 1944 season of college football produced another remarkable team, powered by two of the greatest backs in football history, Glenn Davis from California and Felix "Doc" Blanchard from South Carolina, and coached brilliantly by Earl "Red" Blaik at West Point. The Black Knights at West Point won twenty-five straight games between 1944 and 1945, crushing Notre Dame in a historical defeat, 59–0. Coach

Blaik would go on to be a pivotal figure in Coach Laslie's career and indirectly have a significant impact on Bryant's coaching.

With the success of the Cloudbusters' football season of 1944, Bryant was even more determined to secure a head coach position. He began a relentless campaign to convince the commanding officer at that time to let him take over the position from the soon-to-be-departing head coach Killenger. But it had been a tough sell, and he hadn't been able to convince the commanding officer yet. One reason may have been the one-season rule applied to the coaching staff implemented early on in the Pre-Flight regulations. But another could have had something to do with Lieutenant Commander William Madison "Matty" Bell, a Hall of Fame college football coach who coached Southern Methodist University to a national championship in 1935 and two Southwest Conference championships.

Bell was one of the directors of physical fitness in 1942 at the Athens Pre-Flight School, the man to whom Bryant was directly responsible to during his tenure at Athens. Known to run a disciplined and well-managed organization, Lieutenant Commander Bell didn't tolerate any type of misbehavior. Bell apparently believed the young Coach Bryant, who himself admitted he was a bit self-confident during these years but which others might have perceived as arrogance, was guilty of an indiscretion unbecoming of a naval officer. This reputation may have followed him to Chapel Hill, giving those in charge reason to doubt his being suitable for the position of head coach.

One person Bryant didn't need to convince that he had all the right stuff was Carney Laslie.

CHAPTER SEVEN

Victory And Loss

"I do not know how we are going to replace [him]. I doubt that it can be done."

—VMI Coach Pooley Hubert, coaching colleague and friend

LIEUTENANT COMMANDER GLENN KILLINGER, head coach of the naval Pre-Flight Cloudbusters, submitted his resignation in February of 1945. Included in the Cloudbuster news article officially announcing Killenger's resignation was the official appointment by Lieutenant Commander James P. Raugh, commanding officer, to instate Coach Bryant as the Cloudbusters' new head coach for the fall season of '45. Bryant, who described himself as a nuisance with his persistent requests for the job, was also quick to request Laslie as line coach, and upon his arrival to the Chapel Hill campus of Pre-Flight in May of '45, it was formally announced that joining Bryant would be Coach Carney Laslie. The Cloudbusters' opening practice game was set for the middle of August, and their season opener, against the Athens, Georgia–based Pre-Flight School's Skycrackers, was scheduled for September 23.

Victory in Europe was declared on May 5, 1945, and the end of the war with Japan was believed to be close. A shift in thinking began to occur for those troops far from home: an eye toward the future instead of day-to-day survival. Much had changed over the past four years. Families who had endured long separations looked forward to reuniting. But many friends and loved ones would never return. The entire country had been restructured economically during those years, and challenges abounded, not the least of which included housing shortages and food rationing. Despite this, dreams sidelined at the beginning of the war were once again put into play.

The long-awaited partnership finally realized between Laslie and Bryant at Chapel Hill, however, proved bittersweet. The two had not seen each other since word had reached them about Jimmy Walker's death.

In a crucial partnership during the war, the United States Navy used bases on the coast of Brazil to establish surveillance operations of the South Atlantic where they were on the lookout for German submarines who used the route to ship war supplies to and from Italy and Japan. The Fourth Atlantic Fleet was deployed there to provide both armaments and training for the Brazilian soldiers.

First reports inaccurately stated that Walker had been killed in action. Later facts confirmed that the tragedy happened in Brazil, Walker's Navy plane having just landed in Recife, Brazil. On his way from the airport into town, the Jeep he was riding in crashed into a trolley. The details of the freak accident, which occurred on December 20, 1943, were not revealed until many months later. The young and handsome Walker was mourned by all, described as "the type of boy who had no enemies"[46] by his coaching colleague Pooley Hubert, head coach at VMI.

Laslie and Bryant bitterly grieved the loss. It seemed inconceivable to many that the young man who had such a bright future and seemed destined to survive would have been lost so tragically. Bryant wrote in a letter to Jimmy's mother, "To all of us who were close to Jimmy, there can be no compensation for his loss."

Pooley Hubert wrote in a letter to friends in Tuscaloosa, "I do not know how we are going to replace Jimmy. I doubt that it can be done,"[47] his death symbolic of the senseless loss of life in wartime.

Jimmy Walker would never be forgotten by Bryant, Laslie, and Moseley. His influence on them, both as a teammate and coaching colleague, was one that made an indelible mark both personally and professionally. Losing Jimmy did not deter or dim their vision of what they could be together; rather, it inspired them. These three had survived and would continue to aspire to create a dream team of coaches. It could be said that Jimmy Walker would have wanted nothing less.

Anticipating a sooner than later end to the war, college athletic departments were anxious to restart their football programs, and a fall schedule of 1945 was slated. Schools began in earnest to scout for head coaches among the Pre-Flight schools. Harry Clifton "Curley" Byrd, president at the University of Maryland and a powerful member of the NCAA, was one of those who began to scan the landscape for a qualified head coach for his program. He contacted Carney Laslie to gauge his interest in coming to College Park as his head coach. Laslie knew Bryant would accept nothing less than a head coach position. Laslie's goals and Bryant's differed in this way: Laslie had no aspiration to be a head coach. Bryant would settle for nothing less. Laslie knew with the synergy of their talents and ambitions theirs would be a winning combination.

Laslie had long ago recognized Bryant as a man who, like him, not only had a drive to win that fueled his passion for the game, but who possessed a propensity for hard work that matched his own. He also exemplified many attributes Laslie found important: love of family and love of country, loyalty and honesty, and the important role the sport and good coaching could have on equipping athletes for life after football. Bryant's confidence and ability to inspire those around him were not lost on him, either.

The pre-war pact made between him, Bryant, Moseley, and Walker—that whoever secured a head coach position first would bring the others along with him—still stood, and Laslie had no doubt that together they could create championship teams. Laslie was also aware that Bryant was perceived as young and not having the experience needed or a record that would inspire confidence among those colleges that were then hiring for the head coach position. Universities had a pool of eager coaches with more experience than Bryant who were also readily available. But Laslie saw an opportunity with Byrd's offer: he knew he wasn't Byrd's man for the position of head coach. Bryant was. Their dream team of coaches was within reach. But before deciding on a plan of action, Laslie went first to the man he "never made a move in the coaching business without first consulting,"[48] his former coach at Alabama, Wallace Wade.

Laslie's admiration and respect for Wade lasted far beyond their days as a freshman/sophomore player and revered coach. "I can't express the admiration I hold for Coach Wade," Laslie said in an interview in the *Charlotte Observer* many years later. "He is one of the great figures of football." The two had remained close even with Wade's move from Alabama to Duke University in 1931. Over the years, their relationship had transitioned from player to colleague. Always reticent, Laslie had a reputation of knowing much more than he ever disclosed—a trait that earned him the nickname of the Silver Fox for both his thick head of prematurely white hair and discreet ways—his friendship with Wade downplayed and portrayed to colleagues as being one based solely on his one year of play under the famed coach in 1930.

Bryant, too, revered the former Alabama coach. Wade's last game at Alabama, the 1931 Rose Bowl game in which Laslie played, had been pivotal in Bryant's decision to attend Alabama and play football. The day the Rose Bowl was played, Bryant was visiting the campus of the University of Arkansas, having been invited by those interested in recruiting him. Bryant found a way to slip away and listened to the game on the radio back in his room. It had been a thrilling game with Alabama victorious. Afterward, he knew he wanted nothing more than to play for the Crimson Tide.

Wade's reputation at Alabama continued to be legendary well after his departure from Alabama in 1931. Bryant, who knew Laslie kept in contact with Wade through the years, had long been after his friend to personally introduce him to the former Alabama coaching legend. Wade, who at this time was still the head coach at Duke, was also intrigued by Bryant. Bryant was the offensive line coach on the 1944 Cloudbusters team that beat Wade's Duke team that year. The Associated Press, which had begun its now traditional and revered first football poll that year, called the Cloudbusters' performance impressive, catapulting the Navy Pre-Flight team into second place among the country's best college and service teams.

The timing for a meeting with Laslie and Bryant couldn't have been better. Coach Wade was known to be able to quickly assess a man's character and work ethic. Even more critical, Wade knew Laslie better than anyone and could evaluate the coaching partnership overall with an eye toward Laslie's ultimate goals. With Coach Wade agreeing to a visit, Laslie could accomplish a thrill for Bryant as well as have Bryant engaged enough to get Coach Wade's opinion on whether the plan Laslie was considering was a wise one or not.

Of course, as for the real purpose of the visit—an evaluation by Wade—Bryant was unaware. On the surface, the meeting was nothing more than a casual get-together between a former player and his old coach.

Bryant recalled the meeting in an interview with Al Browning, sports editor of the *Tuscaloosa News*, many years later, after Laslie had passed away. "I expect I know Coach Wade better than his players ever did because they were all so scared of him," Bryant said. "The first time I really got to talk to him was when he was at Duke. Carney Laslie and I went to visit him. Carney never said anything, but I talked a lot. I had never played for Coach Wade."[49] Laslie had, of course, let Bryant do all the talking.

When Laslie conferred with Wade later in private, Wade gave

Laslie his respected opinion. Bryant never did learn of the real nature of his first meeting with Coach Wade. But it did serve to confirm in Laslie's mind what he would do next about President Byrd's offer at the University of Maryland.

Cloudbuster Coaches

L-R: Lt. Frank C. Albert, Lt. Ray R. Bray,
Lt. Comdr. Paul H. Bryant, Lt. Carney G. Laslie, and Lt. John F. Druze.

PART II

CARNEY GRAHAM LASLIE
1909–1933

"The early places, the first places, seep into the skin and mind and heart like humidity into a salt box until the salt cannot be dried nor the water extracted, and both remain, for better or worse, in a bonded clump."

—Julia Gregg, *Wild Sweet Orange Ride*, "Montgomery"

Carney Laslie, 1910

CHAPTER EIGHT

Beginnings

" . . . beautiful little town, with a high and healthy location . . . a town such as one rarely sees in the South. Its quiet shady streets and tasteful and rich dwellings remind one of a New England village."

—Booker T. Washington, July 14, 1881

TUSKEGEE, ALABAMA
1909–1919

CARNEY LASLIE WAS BORN in 1909 in the cotton-producing and historically important town of Tuskegee, Alabama. In its earliest days, Tuskegee had been part of the land comprising the Creek Nation. When European settlers, Black freemen, and White tradesmen discovered the area's abundance of natural resources, the Creeks' way of life was systematically destroyed by their slow and steady invasion. Despite the Indian nation's early and repeated diplomatic attempts to halt the infiltration, the US government opened the land to American settlers in 1830. After an aggressive campaign that would be characterized as a relentless policy of extermination, the remaining Creeks were "removed" to Oklahoma by way of the infamously named "Trail of Tears," its path leading right through the center of town.

The Laslies, a Scottish clan, emigrated to east-central Alabama and Kentucky in the late 1700s. Angus Laslie's name is found in Macon County court records dating back to 1798. No official records were kept for anyone in the state during that period except for the wealthy. Inclusion of the Laslie name in the state's records reflected the fact that they were considered highly prominent citizens of the area at that time with a significant amount of land owned located approximately forty miles east of Montgomery in Macon County where they grew acres and acres of cotton.

Today included on the historic registry of homes in the city limits of Tuskegee is an antebellum home on the corner of Martin Luther King Boulevard and Laslie Street known as the Cobb-Laslie House, home to four generations of Cobbs and Laslies where it was said the "finest hunting dogs in the County"[50] were raised. Restored to reflect its earlier days of grandeur, it is now a bed and breakfast serving tourists and locals alike. Likewise, a two-story brick home located across the street, also a former residence of the family, is known as the Laslie House. To the best of family knowledge, Carney never returned to his birthplace after departing at age ten, other than for his mother's burial and a brief visit to settle aspects of an aunt's estate many decades later. He rarely, if ever, spoke of the town or his early childhood there. Likewise, he never mentioned the town to his daughter, Mary Lou, as being of any significance, other than it being his birthplace.

Laslie had a strong affection for his father who had passed along many of his legendary hunting and fishing skills to his youngest son. Despite this, Mary Lou has no memories of ever meeting William Laslie, Sr. He died of a heart attack in 1953 when Mary Lou was seventeen years old, a traveling salesman whose residence at that time is listed on the 1950 census as a rented room in a boarding house in Knoxville, Tennessee.

In 1913, however, W. T. Laslie, Sr., was known as a "gentleman farmer" managing his family's cotton plantation located on the outskirts of the town of Tuskegee. For generations, most of Tuskegee's poor Black families worked on the farms and plantations located throughout the county. However, in 1913, Tuskegee was also the epicenter of intellectual life for Black Americans due to the presence there of the Tuskegee Institute (now Tuskegee University).

Booker T. Washington, a twenty-five-year-old teacher from Hampton Institute in Virginia, arrived there July 14, 1881, becoming the first principal at one of the nation's first African American colleges. He remained at that position until his death in November 1915. A letter written to his family shortly after he arrived at his new position described his being pleasantly surprised with Tuskegee's overall picturesque appearance, which belied the ugly reality of the pervasive racism that existed there. Like elsewhere in the South, it was inescapable in Tuskegee, and on a level that was shocking and murderous. Violence bred by generational attitudes and hatred was rampant in the area. In the February 1913 issue of the NAACP's monthly journal, *The Crisis*, "a harrowing tally of the names and hometowns of blacks lynched or burned for supposed crimes, sixty-three documented cases in 1912 alone" in cities across the South was published. In response to the horrific report, Booker T. Washington wrote a letter to the then news editor of the Associated Press, condemning American cities like Atlanta where "a man could be punished for beating a horse or killing birds," but it was impossible "to prevent a mob from burning and torturing a human being."

It was into this cultural reality that Carney Laslie was born.

For the next ten years, with economic upheaval threatening the livelihoods of both Black and White, Tuskegee braced for the inevitable invasion of a common enemy: the boll weevil. During these years of uncertainty, Carney's father traveled across the country to compete in sharp-shooting contests, often bringing home prize money. Tuskegee, known for its "bountiful game, many 'sweet' water streams, rich agricultural lands, great forests, and an agreeable climate,"[51] was a sportsman's paradise. Over the years, hunting became a passionate hobby for the elder Laslie, who became a skilled marksman. He was a regular at shooting competitions throughout the state of Alabama and beyond, including the prestigious Pinehurst Country Club's famous skeet competitions in North Carolina and in contests held in places as far away as Colorado.

During the early 1900s, "Wild Bill" Hickock and "Buffalo Bill" Cody traveled and entertained throughout the country with their Wild West show. Shooting competitions and displays of marksmanship were a common part of the program. Great feats of skill using rifles, shotguns, and revolvers were a popular part of the show. The troupe's performers, which included the famed female markswoman, Annie Oakley, were all excellent shots. But its top billing went to the famed Buffalo Bill. It was said that nobody could top the illustrious man whose long hair, mustache, and goatee made him a recognizable figure as he sat astride a galloping horse, aimed his rifle, and easily hit his target. The show traveled to Alabama a total of seven times between 1898 and 1912, specifically to Montgomery and Opelika.

W. T. Laslie, already known as the best shot in the region, entered the show's traditional challenge to local sportsmen. When Laslie, Sr., beat Buffalo Bill in the skeet shooting competition, his name became synonymous with the gun he had used to defeat the famed shooter: Remington Rand.

W. T. Laslie, far left, at Pinehurst in 1911.

These contests, at times, carried a purse for the winner and provided necessary funds to support his family. The work that was required, however, to sustain an annual cotton crop to support his wife and five children required field hands, and it was getting harder and harder to pay his workers. Meanwhile, the scourge of the South— swarms of small, gray beetles with "impressively long snouts"[52]—crept closer and closer to their doorstep, having already devoured cotton crops in Texas, Louisiana, and Mississippi. It seemed inevitable that Alabama would not be spared. Yet the farmers continued to be hopeful.

Whereas the family had enjoyed prosperous beginnings, by the time of Carney's birth, the Laslies were in financially dire straits. A record of a handwritten demand of payment dated July 13, 1909, was filed at the Macon County courthouse as an exhibit of evidence that a man named Dr. Johnston had failed to pay Carney's father William for an outstanding debt. It reads,

You will please send your check for Sixty ($60.00) dollars to me today by R.P. Harris without fail else I will be compelled to give up. Expense is too great for me to go any farther without the little help you promised. It is enough to get hands [farm workers], and advance them taking much risk in and then can't get horses. Let me hear from you today.

Respectfully,
W. T. Laslie[53]

With the collapse of the international cotton market in 1919, cotton prices plummeted, along with any hope of rescue for the Laslies. With nothing yet discovered to combat the boll weevil's advance and infestation, there was no saving the Laslic plantation.

"We are but one step from the poor house," William lamented to his family on a regular basis.

The threat of being "sent to the poor house" was no idle one for those in Macon County. In February of 1919, an act was passed by the Alabama legislature that gave county commissioners the power to decide the fate of the county's poor.

Depending on their circumstances, [the county's poor] shall be maintained inside or outside the County poor house; That those who are entitled to live outside the poor house shall be given a monthly or quarterly allowance as deemed necessary by the Court, provided that all persons seeking permission to reside outside the County poorhouse shall file a petition with said court, to the effect of filing proper affidavits, and proof showing it would be just, meritorious, and economical for the County to make the allowance and grant the petition.[54]

With William unable to pay his taxes, no money to settle outstanding debts, no crops to sell, no future in cotton production, and no horse trading, which he had hoped would save them, he saw no way out. The courts would soon be demanding some accounting. He had exhausted his options for continuances. Even William's two brothers, Edward and Carney, who were sympathetic to his plight, were unable to loan him any more money to keep the plantation in operation. It was a desperate situation. The next step for him and his family would indeed be the poorhouse. But as irony would have it, instead of the land robbing him of his livelihood, it provided him a way out.

The same year that the Laslies' crop was wiped out, the Remington Arms Company was looking to utilize the excess manufacturing capacity it had created during World War I. The company officially incorporated a new direction of product in Delaware in 1920, and plans were made to open an office in Charlotte, North Carolina. William took pride in saying he had never had a "real job," which is taken to mean that he never had a "desk job." He managed the farm. Along with those responsibilities, he possessed skills of hunting and sharpshooting along with a wealth of knowledge about guns and the widespread reputation of being the best shot around. He used this resumé when he applied for a position with the renowned company. That was sufficient for the original purveyor of rifles, Remington Rand. William was hired and saved from a path that he saw would bring shame and dishonor to him and his family.

The W.T. Laslie children with their grandparents and cousins. First row, left to right: Lester, Carney, and a first cousin. Second row, left to right: Florence, "Brother Bill", "Fanny", and a first cousin.

William Laslie organized a hasty departure for his wife, Frances, and their five children: two sons, Bill, sixteen; and Carney, ten; and daughters Fanny, fourteen; Florence, twelve; and Lester, five. It had been decided that everyone but Carney would go to Charlotte. Carney, however, would travel to Montgomery and live for a time with his favorite uncle for whom he was named, his father's beloved brother, the highly esteemed Dr. Carney Graham Laslie, a practicing physician.

The few livestock they owned were sold, the workers given their final wages. The stately plantation, emptied of most of its furnishings (many of them sold to cover debts) had survived the Civil War and

Sherman's March, but it was no match for the devastation wrought by the boll weevil. They fled Tuskegee ahead of the debt collectors. However, the Laslies did not leave empty-handed. The extensive collection of heirloom family silver, including William's collection of silver trophy cups from shooting contests won over the years, was packed and cherished, a reminder of earlier, prosperous days. In later years, though the exact date is not recorded, the plantation burned to the ground under unknown circumstances.

Life in Charlotte was different from the rural, farm living the Laslies had led in Tuskegee. There were, however, similarities: William was away from home for months at a time as a traveling salesman, and the family enjoyed a celebrity-type status in the region, where he was still famed for his sharpshooting skills.

For the next fifteen years, William showcased the company's guns, including the newly designed Miracle Trap, and also household wares that Remington had added to their company's offerings. He continued to travel extensively, entering shooting contests around the country, maintaining a celebrity-type status for his abilities. By 1934, the trap became a "standard in the industry . . . used exclusively at the 1934 Grand American Handicap—the premier classic trapshooting event."[55] And although his shooting prowess earned him fame in North Carolina, it did not include fortune; his new occupation barely provided enough to support his wife and five children.

Carney Laslie's love of the outdoors came to him naturally, his father having unparalleled skills in shooting and fishing, which he passed on to his youngest son. In later years, Carney's reputation for being a skilled marksman and fisherman, winning competitions in his own right, revered for his talent among friends and colleagues, can be attributed to both his love of the sport and to his father's teachings.

CHAPTER NINE

Family Ties

"No one knew who exactly that man was up in Washington, DC that Coach Laslie knew. He never would say."

—Dr. E. C. Brock, Orthopedic Surgeon, Team Physician, U of A, and personal friend

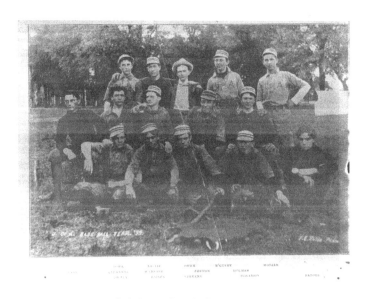

U of Alabama baseball team, 1899.

MONTGOMERY, ALABAMA
DR. CARNEY G. LASLIE
1919–1923

IN THE FALL OF 1919, Carney's uncle, Dr. C. G. Laslie, and his wife, Isabelle, along with their two young sons, John Lewis, aged two, and Carney G., Jr., four years old, welcomed their ten-year-old nephew and cousin into their home. He was fondly nicknamed "Buck" while living with the family and was known by that name by that branch of the family from then on. Dr. Laslie was one of Montgomery's most affluent and influential citizens at the time, the epitome of a beloved family physician. At the time of his death in 1953, he was said to have delivered more babies in Montgomery than any other physician in the state for five years in a row. He was described as a man whose "qualities of mind and heart were such as to make him . . . impossible to dislike," known for being "generously imbued with the quality of sympathy." His "warm and gay nature . . . endeared him to everyone."[56]

Dr. Laslie's career is one worth noting as it speaks to his drive, discipline, and passion for his work. He graduated in 1903, at the age of twenty-five, from the University of Maryland's medical school at a time when there were very few post-graduate training opportunities in the new and upcoming specialty of obstetrics, his primary field of interest. There were some dramatic discoveries made within the practice of medicine during these years. Surgery could be performed more safely and painlessly through the understanding of disinfection methods and their use and the development of anesthesia techniques. All of this had implications for the ambitious young doctor and fueled his academic desire for continued study.

While attending the University of Maryland, he impressed his colleagues and professors with his ambition and talent, winning a coveted award for his pursuits, which carried with it an appointment for an internship at Baltimore's Lying-In Hospital. It was one of the very few post-graduate, clinical training programs in the country at the time, the teaching hospital providing care and skillful attendance to all women needing a home during their pregnancy. Dr. Laslie quickly accepted the invitation, eager to broaden his clinical knowledge and experience in the field of obstetrics.

For months, Dr. Laslie worked tirelessly, the hours sometimes stretching into days. But it wasn't long into his training that he received word that his father, Carney Laslie, Sr., was near death. Even though Dr. Laslie was not the eldest, he was the favored son and favorite brother. He quickly made the decision to abandon the prestigious appointment, returning home to Tuskegee in the latter part of 1903. In addition to caring for his ill and dying father, he took over the family affairs as well as practicing his profession in Tuskegee as a family doctor with a specialty in obstetrics.

His father died two years later in 1905. After his death, with the advances in medicine continuing to be made, Dr. Laslie felt a calling once again to pursue his education further and strengthen his skill set. Being unencumbered with a wife or children, and with his father's affairs in order, he traveled, not back to Baltimore but to London, England. It was then a common practice to go there for post-graduate study in medicine. He spent extended time in Scotland, where he availed himself of some of the world's most learned teachers in the field of obstetrics. It is not known exactly when he departed US shores and made his way to Europe or exactly how long he stayed. But the record shows his return in August of 1908. By 1910, the twenty-nine-year-old bachelor physician was well established again in Montgomery, "to the delight of its citizenry."[57]

Isabelle Cobbs, a distant cousin, knew of the sophisticated and successful physician if not by family connection, then by reputation. Born and raised in Montgomery, the two were in the same social class, living in adjacent neighborhoods (also known as wards). Even though she was twelve years younger, she may have had her mind set on him long before they met. She was known to have a high-minded and vivacious personality, and sometime after Dr. Laslie's return home to Alabama, the two became reacquainted. Now thirty-one years old, the eligible doctor was ready to settle down. When the two met, Isabelle was in the middle of obtaining her college degree at Hollins College, in Roanoke, Virginia, with two years left to graduate. Shortly after she received her diploma, they married.

At twenty-two, Isabelle was known to be adventurous and, like her husband, had a love of travel. Dr. Laslie booked passage on a ship from Philadelphia to France for their honeymoon, and they left right after their wedding, spent a month touring, and arrived back stateside in July. Their first child, a daughter, was born a year later but died at birth. One year later came a son, and eighteen months later, their second son.

Isabelle was ill prepared for the demands of being married to the city's busiest family doctor. She was an ambitious woman who was noted to have a desire "to make meaningful contributions to society,"[58] chairing committees for social and industrial improvements and lending her time and talents to improving the "conditions of women in employment and welfare of prisoners."[59] She actively pursued women's right to vote, and when the Nineteenth Amendment was ratified in 1920, she must have felt a personal sense of satisfaction.

But all was not well. As a liberal-minded woman in the South, her discontent with the demands of young children and an absent husband contributed to her unhappiness. She struggled to run a household with two rambunctious boys under the age of four and a husband never at home due to his long hours taking care of patients.

By the time Carney arrived to live with the family, the marriage was well into the throes of dissolution. Isabelle warmly welcomed her nephew. There were clearly advantages of their young nephew coming to live with them, one being his ability to help her keep her brood entertained. Given the circumstances that existed in the household at this time, it is hard to imagine the environment provided the additional care and attention needed to allay Carney's fears and insecurities and the desperate state from which he'd come.

But despite his uncle and aunt's ongoing marital problems, the years the young boy spent in Montgomery were a needed respite during which time a close relationship was forged between Carney, his uncle and cousins which lasted a lifetime.

Under the influence of his uncle, Carney learned many of the manners and decorum he would later become associated with among his peers. He found himself living in a household whose life and style of entertaining were, in all probability, more formal than in Tuskegee, and in later years, he would remember the regular use of "finger bowls," a small china dish, placed at each place setting which held just enough water to rinse off one's fingers so as to avoid staining the cloth napkins, during the evening meal in Montgomery.

His uncle's social circle, which included various politicians and business leaders and other members of the social elite throughout Alabama, would also prove helpful to him in the future. The two also shared a love of hunting and fishing, a passion of Dr. Laslie's that at one time had him in the company of the writer Ernest Hemingway on a fishing trip in Cuba. Overall, the home further engrained in Carney what many associated with a Southern upbringing: strong on manners with a gentle demeanor. These qualities combined with Carney's Southern drawl led many to later describe him as true Southern gentleman.

One year after Carney's arrival, Isabelle left her two sons and husband for Frank Mahoney, a civil engineer from Wisconsin, who was listed in the1920 census as living in a boarding house in Birmingham. He later became a utilities executive as President of the Cuban Electric Company, as well as a Vice President of the American and Foreign Power Company. At the time he and Isabelle met, however, he was neither wealthy nor powerful.

Her sons, then ages three and five, were left bereft, and they looked not only to their father but to their older cousin Carney ("Buck") for support and comfort. A scandalous divorce followed. Isabelle assumed she would secure custody of the children. But Dr. Laslie refused to relinquish them to her care, fighting to keep them in Montgomery. The courts sided with Dr. Laslie in a particularly surprising ruling given the times. Meanwhile, Carney's mother, Frances Laslie, continued to decline, her health deteriorating to a point the family needed him back home in Charlotte sooner than later.

Dr. Laslie's overall influence on Carney cannot be overstated, his fondness for him regularly expressed in the many letters he wrote to his nephew along with his continued pride in his accomplishments, including a congratulatory note on his decision to attend the University of Alabama:

Dear Buck (Carney):

I am glad you decided to go to Alabama . . . I am enclosing two clippings from *The Montgomery Advertiser*; they seem to think you can play football. Had a letter from each of my boys, they report having a wonderful time, John Lewis is wild about Havana, says he is catching some fine fish. You know it [is] not very long until school time. I wish you could come down and visit me for some time before going to Tuscaloosa . . . Write to me often. Love to all the family, Uncle Carney

Dr. Laslie would eventually remarry. Amelie Hill, an elegant and accomplished woman sixteen years his junior, was the twin sister of Lister Hill, longtime Alabama senator. Dr. Laslie and Amelie married in 1932. Dr. Laslie's sons, John and Carney, Jr., remained close to their mother, Isabelle, spending time with her and and their stepfather, Frank Mahoney at times in Havana, Cuba, and at their homes in Mannhatten, and Maine. Dr. Laslie died in 1953. Amelie never remarried and died at the age of ninety-five.

CHAPTER TEN

Family Woes

"Charlotte boys are high-minded;
They get hit and they don't mind it!"

—Charlotte Central High School Fight Song

CHARLOTTE, NORTH CAROLINA
1923-1929

THE LASLIE FAMILY'S REVERSAL of fortune impacted the two brothers differently. Carney, by all accounts, was kind and gentle as opposed to William, Jr., called Bill, who was known as a merciless bully. Carney's sisters adored their younger brother. Florence explained later in life that she never married because in her words, she never found anyone as wonderful as her brother, Carney. Family dynamics notwithstanding, the family's financial troubles left deep emotional wounds and fears.

As an adult, Carney had a reputation of being tight with money, the result of a subconscious threat of the poorhouse that never left him. This fear served him in his subsequent roles in successfully managing budgets and programs but also strained his closest relationships. Bill, referred to as "Brother Bill" by his siblings, also suffered from the financial hardship. But he would handle his fears and insecurities in a more degenerate fashion.

Brother Bill's jealousies, fear of the future, and overall dislike of his younger brother played out in his mean-spirited behavior toward Carney. Six years older than Carney, Bill was relentless, the older sisters remembering his taunting of Carney starting when Carney was very young and becoming physically abusive whenever he got the chance. Fanny and Florence intervened whenever possible, keeping an eye out for the predatory ways of their older brother. Though the sisters would threaten Bill with telling their father about the beatings Carney suffered at his hand, Carney begged them not to, for it led to retaliation and more brutal attacks when their father left again on business trips.

The acrimony between the two brothers lasted a lifetime, culminating when Bill finally left home for good, taking with him a portion of the family silver and treasured shooting trophies and then selling them to support himself. Forever after he was referred to by his siblings as the black sheep of the family, and they rarely spoke of him again. When Brother Bill died in 1945, Carney refused to go to his funeral, despite his sisters' pleading. Even Carney's closest friends never knew he had a brother.

Carney reunited with the rest of the family at 5 Hawthorne Lane in Charlotte at the age of thirteen after living with his uncle and family in Montgomery, Alabama, for two years. He couldn't know it yet, but it was a perfect location for a future star football player as it was situated within view of the high school stadium.

The adjustment of moving from a financially secure household to one living literally hand to mouth was a difficult one. Although Carney's two older sisters doted over him, and his younger sister, Lester, adored him, having a lackadaisical, hostile older brother in the household proved to be a major problem. Two years of additional physical growth on Carney's part helped stem his brother's bullying, but the household he had left as the favored nephew of his beloved uncle and aunt, supplemented by two adoring young cousins, was in stark contrast to the family unit he rejoined. His mother was not well, took to her bed often, and was known to rage unpredictably, assailing the household with her angry outbursts. His father was away from home most of the time. This was not unlike the household from whence he came, where his uncle was a busy physician. But unlike Carney's uncle, who had provided a huge level of emotional support despite his busy professional life, his father was both physically and emotionally absent.

By the time Carney arrived in Charlotte, school had already started. He was two grades behind his peers academically due to his years in Montgomery. His larger-than-average size for his grade level immediately caught the eyes of the school's athletic coaches. They encouraged him to play football, and he quickly excelled at the sport.

Two years after arriving back home, Carney's mother died at the age of forty. Frances Laslie had succumbed to a chronic kidney ailment that had plagued her for many years. Though her invalid condition itself was a hardship on the family, the loss left the Laslies now grief-stricken and motherless, and the state of the household worsened. Sometime after her death, Frances's body was taken back to Tuskegee, home to five generations of Laslies, where she was buried in the family plot.

Entering his first year of high school at the age of fifteen, Carney endured an understandably tumultuous and painful time. His grief manifested itself in wholehearted pursuit of excellence in his own area of strength: athletics. It proved to be the young boy's salvation. Football served as an outlet for the anger he felt on so many levels: toward a brother who tormented him, a father who deeply disappointed him, and a mother whose death he mourned but who had abandoned him long before. He could blast through the opposing team's line with a ferocity and passion that one could only imagine served a purpose on multiple levels. He was also a successful member of the track team, a surprise to many who knew him as a top lineman in football, as those playing in that position are generally not known for their running speed. But excel he did as a member of the four-man team for an event in track and field called the Weightman's Relay at Charlotte's Central High School in 1927. Their track division won the South Atlantic Division Championship where they met the best interscholastic talent in that region.

He performed well in track, but certainly not as well as in football, where his reputation grew and his appetite for winning increased with every game. He was relied upon to score points with his foot, as newspaper articles pointed out time and again, his kicking abilities attributed to securing the winning point or a crucial field goal. He later imparted his love and abilities for the kicking game wherever he coached and was instrumental in developing a game strategy in his future role as a coach.

The years at Central High School provided opportunities for Carney's athletic abilities and his confidence to grow as well as relief from some of the stress and feelings of failure off the field. But it did not eliminate them.

The constant threat of authorities discovering there was no "official" parent at the Laslie home made Carney's situation even more precarious. With the help of his older sisters, he made sure he arrived at school on time, his clothes cleaned, his hair cut, homework in hand. They all made sure there was food on the table at home. All the while he dealt with the shame he felt at his situation. At this young age, he was the man of the house, his older brother having abandoned the family not long after their mother passed away. He took seriously his role of protector and guardian of his two older and one younger sisters. It was a heavy load for a young man to bear.

Known for his ferocity of play, a leader who could be counted on to "hold the line," Carney's four years at Charlotte High School saw the

Hawks win three state championships.[60] When the announcement was made at the sports banquet at the end of his junior year that he had been elected captain of the team for his senior year, players, parents, coaches, and invited dignitaries of the city gave him a long and rousing standing ovation. No doubt their pride and applause was not only to acknowledge the athletic accomplishments of the talented player, which included being ranked a top lineman of the South, but also that his success was achieved in spite of the many sacrifices, pain, and hardships that he had endured even though most were hardly aware of the extent of his difficulties. He was admired for the caliber of person he was: a leader who inspired others to face their own challenging circumstances because he personally had overcome so much.

With accolades for his playing and leadership abilities from all over the state and beyond, the star high school lineman soon caught the eye of the University of Tennessee's famed head coach General Robert Neyland, who personally wrote to Carney during the second semester of his junior year at Central High. "You have been recommended to me very highly as a football player with a great deal of ability," wrote Coach Neyland. "From the reputation which has been given you, we are more than anxious to have you decide to enter the University of Tennessee next fall."

It was an offer that any young man with dreams of playing big-time college football would have been ecstatic to receive. But what Coach Neyland didn't know about the boy from Charlotte, North Carolina, was that he was Alabama born and bred. Both his father and uncles were alumni of the University of Alabama as well as proud members of Alabama's Sigma Nu fraternity. It was always assumed the family tradition would continue with Carney. After all, he had been raised to "hate those Vols," and he imagined nothing more satisfying than to be on an Alabama team that beat the Tennessee Volunteers.

But there was another reason why Carney wanted nothing more than to attend Alabama: the Rose Bowl of 1926.

CHAPTER ELEVEN

The Religion Of the South

"And in the South, football is a religion,
and Saturday is the holy day."

—Marino Casem, Athletic Director at Southern University, 1986–1999

ALABAMA'S WIN AT THE Rose Bowl of 1926 was described as nothing short of a miracle. A miracle indeed. The Crimson Tide wasn't given much of a chance against the Washington Huskies, a team that came into the Rose Bowl undefeated. In fact, the invitation for Alabama to play at that year's Rose Bowl had been grudgingly extended when Rutgers University, the first choice for the championship game, turned down the invite. Inviting Alabama was a second thought. Despite the team's record of finishing the regular 1925 season undefeated, the South's play was considered overall inferior to the game as it was played in the West and the East.

On Alabama's first possession of the game, in what seemed to be a validation of the famous Will Rogers label for the team from Tuscaloosa as "Tusca-losers,"[61] they were stopped cold by the Huskies

at Washington's fifteen-yard line. In the next two consecutive plays
by Alabama, they suffered a total ten-yard loss. On third down, the
Huskies intercepted an Alabama pass and scored a touchdown. A
brief hush may have fallen over all the South as the thought of total
humiliation was contemplated. When the Huskies failed to convert
the extra point on the field goal attempt, one can imagine the feeble
cheer and rallying of the mostly Huskies fans who filled the stadium.
Little did either team realize at the time that it would be this botched
kick that would be the Huskies' demise.

At half time, Washington led 12–0, two touchdowns against
Alabama before the first half, compared to only one touchdown
scored against the Tide all year. When reports of the score were
announced over the Associated Press wire, the crowds that stood
outside on cold streets like Dexter Avenue in downtown Montgomery
and in packed auditoriums like the city's Grand Theater, or who were
gathered with family and friends around radios, tried not to despair.
In the locker room at halftime, Pooley Hubert, who Coach Wade in
later years called "the best field general I ever coached; he could lead
men like no other player I ever had," railed at his teammates, rallying
them with an emotion and level of fervor as they most likely had
never experienced before. Coach Wade, seeing the frenzy his team
was being whipped into, simply walked into the locker room, made
an adjustment to his lineup, then said in a low voice, "They told me
boys from the South would fight."[62]

On Alabama's first possession of the second half in that Rose
Bowl of '26, Hubert exploded through the middle for a gain of
twenty-seven yards. He ran the ball three more consecutive plays
and was stopped at the one-yard line. The next play, and fifth carry
in a row, he bulldozed across the Washington goal line, and after the
extra point was kicked, the score was 12–7 for Washington.

Though the game was far from over, it was redemption for a
dismal first half, and fans in the streets and in homes and businesses
across the South from Montgomery to Atlanta to New Orleans

went wild. Alabama scored again on its very next possession with a spectacular catch by all-star Johnny Mack Brown and a sixty-three-yard play, putting Alabama in the lead 14–12. Another touchdown, a total of three in seven minutes—unheard of in that era—and they widened their lead, 20–12.

The Huskies, with plenty of time left, tightened the spread with a touchdown in the fourth quarter, the score now a one-point difference, 20–19. With the clock ticking, the game had the sports world holding its breath, but the import of the game had already been realized: Alabamians could hold their heads high. Win or lose, Alabama had proven its mettle. And although Alabama had only completed four passes out of the thirteen attempts, they were such dramatic catches resulting in touchdowns by fullback John "Hurri-" Cain and quarterback Allison "Pooley" Hubert that fans of both sides leapt to their feet cheering wildly with every aerial display. So thrilling was the game that one can almost imagine the rumble of the ground as an entire nation of sports fans stomped and jumped in both exhilaration and frustration.

When the Crimson Tide clinched the game with an interception, fans throughout the South erupted in jubilant celebration. Even fans in the West were thrilled at the spectacle of achievement. Sports fans, young or old, listening to the game over the airwaves that day remembered the experience for a lifetime. Carney Laslie was one of them. When he listened to the amazing plays being reported, he had no way of knowing then that quarterback Pooley Hubert, forever remembered as one of Alabama's greatest examples of a champion, on and off the field, would be his first mentor as a college coach.

The next year was Carney's sophomore year at Central High, and the University of Alabama was invited to make a second consecutive Rose Bowl appearance. With the popularity of Alabama's appearance in the Rose Bowl the previous year, the National Broadcasting Company decided to broadcast the game nationally; the first-ever game to be aired on television coast-to-coast. On January 1, 1927, Alabama went

head-to-head with Stanford, and the final score was a 7–7 tie. The
game would be the last Rose Bowl to end in a tie without an overtime
period. The outcome resulted in Alabama and Stanford sharing the
National Championship title.

Alabama's stellar performance that year shocked the West of the
sport. Many in the West were of the belief that Alabama's win the
previous year was a fluke. But with a second appearance, the South
was now on the map of regions to be taken seriously in the world of
big-time college football. The streets of Montgomery and all around the
state of Alabama flooded with celebratory fans thrilled at the validation
of their place alongside well-regarded colleges and football programs.
It was then that college football became the vehicle that Alabamians
and residents of other states in the deep South could rally around,
the performances of their teams for the next fifty years and beyond
an accomplishment they would use to showcase their superiority and
domination of one of the country's most popular sports.

Southern historians later would reason the pedestal Southerners
put college football on was due to their desire for national relevance.
The Northeast and Midwest had grown in economic dominance, the
industrial revolution transforming its economy. The South's agrarian
economy was still in the throes of a reset dating back to the devastation
of the Civil War. Also, manufacturing on a scale the North enjoyed
was all but impossible in the South in the years prior to the arrival of
air-conditioning. The South's success in the sport of football, historians
would argue, served as emotional redemption and reclamation for
their inferior status since the Civil War.

Up until the burgeoning success of their football players and
teams, the sport had been railed against from the pulpit, church
leaders decrying its violence and the ill effects it had on the academic
focus of students at colleges and universities. Shortly after the national
success of their teams, however, the tone changed, and religious leaders
embraced football, noting the many character-building aspects of
the sport. With the sport given a stamp of approval by the religious
community, it quickly grew in popularity, with football coaches and

players alike revered on their membership rosters, the sport overall described by many as the "religion of the South."

Listening to Alabama's Rose Bowl win of '27 on the radio had conjured up images of valor and glory for the young high school football player at Central High in Charlotte, North Carolina. Someday, he vowed to himself, he would be on that field playing for Coach Wade and Alabama. It was a goal that fueled his discipline and play for the next three years at Central High.

In November of Carney's senior year, as a star lineman and captain of the football team, he was selected to play on the state's All-Star Team, the only one on Charlotte's multi-talented team at Central High to achieve that honor. That year, he also was selected as their football team's most valuable player. He was unable to travel to the All-Star game, however, either because of injury or personal financial hardship.

Carney announced in July his intention to attend Alabama, officially—and it can be said, delightedly—turning down Coach Neyland and Tennessee. (Neyland would later figure prominently in the trajectory of Laslie's coaching career, a twist of fate that most likely neither would have believed in 1928.)

Arriving in Tuscaloosa in August of 1929 to begin practice with the freshman squad under the tutelage of then assistant coach Hank Crisp, Carney's dream of playing big-time college football at Alabama had finally arrived. His performance on the freshman team caught the eye of head coach Wade, and by the end of his freshman year Wade saw a player capable of competing on the varsity level. Elation at being tapped by Wade turned to bitter disappointment when Carney learned Wade would be leaving after the 1930 season. But he and the rest of the players on that team, known as the "Wademen," gave their coach the satisfaction of going out in a blaze of glory with an unexpected appearance and win at the Rose Bowl on January 1, 1931.

CHAPTER TWELVE

Coach Wallace Wade

"On the importance of athletics, a field which sends healthy, intelligent, loyal leaders to take up citizenship cannot be over emphasized."

—Coach Wallace Wade

UNIVERSITY OF ALABAMA
1929–1931

IN THE FALL OF 1929, the campus in Tuscaloosa buzzed with all the normal excitement mixed with the anxiety one associates with being a college freshman. Alabama's stellar Rose Bowl performances in '26 and '27 for their seasons respectively in '25 and '26 had earned them national attention. The then thirty-nine-year-old Wallace Wade was at the top of his profession, having built Alabama's football program and with it a respect for Southern football among the nation's elite programs of the East and West, attracting more students than ever to the university, a record-breaking 3,500 students having enrolled that September. The new 12,000-seat Denny Stadium (named for the university's president, George Denny), financed by the proceeds of Rose Bowl appearances in 1926 and 1927, had only just been completed and opened to great fanfare in Tuscaloosa that September.

As a freshman in 1929, Carney Laslie's goal was to do what he could to make sure Alabama added another Rose Bowl appearance during his time of play there. It was an exciting time to be a football player for the Crimson Tide. With the start of classes, a general mood of optimism prevailed, and the national economy seemed robust and healthy. However, in late October after soaring to new heights one month before, the nation suffered a serious jolt when the stock market collapsed.

In the South, the effects of the crash were not felt as dramatically as in other parts of the country. Though over sixty years had passed since the end of the Civil War, many parts of the rural deep South remained in the grip of an economic stranglehold due to its long-lasting effects. The impact of the Great Depression on families across the country that we associate with the most extreme of economic circumstances—displacement, desperate hardship, and working long and hard under extreme circumstances to survive—was a continuation of what many Alabamians had long experienced due to their overall chronically depressed economy.

At the University of Alabama, however, life continued in the usual manner—or at least one would assume from reading the pages of *The Corolla*, the university's yearbook, which reflected upon student life at that time. On a page with the heading "Chronology of What Happened During 1929–1930," eight events of October 1929 were listed, summarized in one or two sentences. Listed between the entry "Mr. Edison, the inventor, re-enacted the original experiment at Henry Ford's Museum" and "A child was born in an airplane while it circled twelve hundred feet above Miami, Florida," the nation's catastrophic event "Stock market smashed downward" is included with no allusions to its devastating effects on the country or even on the state. Everywhere, however, its effects were felt by the halting of expensive building projects. Some large construction plans were abandoned permanently, casualties of the national banking and funding crisis. Construction on The Empire State Building in New York City, for example, was halted and remained vacant, nicknamed the "Empty" State Building, during this time. Fortunately, Alabama's new Denny Stadium had just been completed or it too could have been a casualty of the times.

Despite all of this, it seemed to be perfect timing for Laslie, who arrived on the Alabama campus excited to play in the school's new stadium and for a coach who had led the school to two Rose Bowl wins. But as Bill Curry, former head coach at Alabama wrote in his book, *Ten Men in a Huddle*, "The life of a college freshman football player is a jarring mixture of excitement and fear. . . . That's true of any step up in class—say, from junior high to high school, from sophomore to junior to senior. But for an athlete, going from high school to college is a real jolt. Bigger? Stronger? Faster? Way more than you could possibly have guessed during your senior season of high school glory." Laslie had a chorus of accolades, awards, and praise for his play during high school to bolster his confidence. But he lacked the confidence in an area that Coach Wade deemed important to those who played for him: academics.

It was with this in mind that Coach Hank Crisp, longtime member of Alabama's athletic department who had recruited Laslie, assigned Frank Howard as Laslie's roommate. Howard, then a varsity player, went on to achieve legendary status when he took Clemson University in South Carolina "from football obscurity to the ranks of the national elite"[63] over the span of his thirty years of coaching there.

Howard and Laslie were almost the same age, both born on cotton farms in Alabama in 1909. They were both linemen, also known as guards, who in that era played both on the offensive and defensive lines. It may have seemed a compatible pairing for those reasons alone. But

Crisp also knew that Laslie, who was two years behind in school due to family hardships, struggled academically whereas Howard was at Alabama on an academic scholarship.

Howard, like Laslie, was known to be "a storyteller who could entertain listeners way into the night."[64] The two were also known for spontaneous quips and a dry sense of humor, an example being this reported exchange between Howard, when he was athletic director at Clemson, and a group of students who asked him for money to make competitive rowing, or crew, a varsity sport. Coach Howard leaned back in his chair and let these words slide slowly out of his mouth: "Klemptzin . . . will never sponsa . . . a sport . . . where men sit on their fannies . . . and go backwards!"[65]

Howard had exhibited great leadership skills since arriving at Alabama: president of his freshman class and in his senior year president of the A-Club, the illustrious association for athletes at Alabama. It was clear Coach Crisp, who always was of a mind to guide and influence his young charges, saw promise in pairing these two.

Crisp's instincts proved right. Laslie followed in Howard's footsteps, becoming vice president of the A-Club his junior year. They remained close friends and colleagues well into their careers. In an interview about their early years as roommates, Laslie joked, "Frank Howard was a junior and I was a freshman when we were roommates at Alabama, which proves Howard is a lot older!"

Coach Wade noticed the talented freshman tackle right away. At the end of the '29 season, Wade's worst season since arriving at Alabama, he moved the freshman Laslie from the "Baby Tide" frosh team to varsity. It was there the young player had the opportunity to be influenced by one the greatest mentors in the sport.

Wade exemplified over and over what he held as the gold standard of behavior he expected of all his players. On November 16 of the '29 season, Alabama played against a highly favored Georgia Tech. The Crimson Tide wrecked Tech, 14–0. As soon as the game was over, Coach Wade rushed across the field to shake the hand of Stumpy

Thomason, Tech star, and later made the following statement to the press: "Thomason is one of the cleanest players Alabama has faced in my seven years at Alabama and is better liked by Alabama players more than any other star we ever played against. One of the most pleasant things I have to remember about the three years he played against us is his fine fighting spirit and clean sportsmanship."[66]

Despite Wade's six seasons of coaching at Alabama, which included two Rose Bowl appearances, the dismal season of '29 had both the alumni and the board of trustees at Alabama disappointed with the team's performance. With his bosses grumbling in the background, Wade made the decision at the end of the season to take a serious look at Duke, which had made overtures earlier in the year. Duke was looking for someone who was known not to sacrifice academics to athletic process. Still another attraction was its "spectacular new Gothic campus with new athletic facilities."[67] By the end of the year, Wade had had enough. He made the decision to leave prior to his contract running out in 1931, and announced his decision on March 31, 1930. The season of '30 would be his last. He would use his last months before departing to help in the selection of a new head coach and prepare the players for his departure.

The news of Wade's planned departure was met with overall dismay, but none were more broken-hearted than Laslie. Despite his disappointment, there was still incentive for him and the rest of the team to persevere. They would make it a never-to-be forgotten season.

The 1930 Crimson Tide football team, with its record number of sophomores, was considered the dark horse of the Southern Conference (SoCon) with little chance for a championship given the dismal record of the season before. Historians often refer to the team of 1930 as the finest Wade ever coached and one of the best in Alabama's history. A veteran number of tackles led the way, the All-American "Freddie" Sington being one of them. However, it was the team's dependable group of sophomores—including Carney Laslie—that, despite one newspaper's report early in the season to be simply "satisfactory enough,"[68] astounded most every Southern football expert. No one was looking for Alabama to be a force to contend with in 1930. But by mid-season, "On to the Rose Bowl!" was a cry heard everywhere until finally the invitation came for Alabama to play the Washington State Cougars in the football classic of the year in Pasadena on New Year's Day 1931.

When the whistle blew sounding the end of the final season game, it also signaled Coach Wade's last game played at Alabama. Rising to its feet, "the vast crowd . . . cheered long and loud for the man who had done so much for Alabama and Southern football."

And then, it was on to the Rose Bowl!

Coach Wade had groomed Laslie all season long to step into the shoes, if needed, of "Freddie" Sington, Alabama's All-American tackle, or Charlie "Foots" Clement, captain of the team and an All-American honorable mention. He boarded the train in Tuscaloosa bound for California to meet the best team in the West at the Rose Bowl with the rest of the varsity team which included former roommate Frank Howard, Jess Eberdt and J.B. "Ears" Whitworth (who would go on to be head coach at Alabama many years later). The train, nicknamed the "Crimson Tide Special," was loaded not only with players and coaches, but a stockpile of barrels containing drinking water from Tuscaloosa in order to reduce any chance of players coming down with intestinal illness due to drinking strange water.

"The spectacular triumph of the Wademen by 24–0 at the 1931 Rose Bowl took the football world by storm and the Alabama team was immediately placed on par with the famed Knute Rockne's Notre Dame Eleven,"[69] after its "versatile attack was deemed superior to any displayed in the country."[70] When Laslie went in for lineman John Miller during the game, he became one of the first sophomores to play in the Rose Bowl.

During Coach Wade's last year coaching at Alabama, Laslie played with such ferocity and passion that it earned him the attention of the revered coach. But it was Laslie's underlying strength of character and work ethic, combined with his quiet and congenial manner, that won him Wade's admiration. He recognized in Laslie a level of grit he knew was born from adversity and difficult circumstances and saw in his play and manner a man who had the potential to take adversity and shape it into a powerful tool for good. To that end, Wade made himself personally available to Laslie. Wade's role as a trusted mentor and colleague to Laslie lasted for their entire careers.

Carney Laslie, second row, third from the right.

CHAPTER THIRTEEN

Team Play

"When you get out between those white lines, everything is fair. Everything is equal. It doesn't matter what your last name is. It doesn't matter how much money your daddy makes. It doesn't matter what kind of house you came from. All that matters is what's inside you, and maybe this is the only place left where that really can happen anymore."

—Bear Bryant

Carney Laslie, Tackle, University of Alabama, 1929.

TUSCALOOSA, ALABAMA
UNIVERSITY OF ALABAMA
1931–1933

THE FALL SEMESTER OF 1931, Carney Laslie's junior year, the University of Alabama celebrated its centennial. When President Denny gave his address before the crowd of students, faculty, and alumni that filled the stands of Denny Stadium, he did so at a podium on the field surrounded by hundreds of students dressed as Indians, early settlers, Confederate soldiers, and an array of livestock used to depict the changing times and symbolizing the passing years of history. Alabama has "taken its place as a university of the people, by the people and for the people, which is the proper role of a university in a democratic society,"[71] he passionately told the crowd. His words, however, applied exclusively to white citizens, as Jim Crow laws, state and local statutes enforcing racial segregation in the South, prohibited Black Americans from attending.

President Denny concluded his address with: "To all who love the University of Alabama and are striving to keep its commandments, this is a day of memories. It is a day of prophecy. It is a day of renewing our vows."[72]

Denny also used the opportunity to introduce the Crimson Tide's new coach, Frank Thomas. It was a new era of football without Coach Wade who had left behind a legacy of winning. One that all hoped would continue. His speech was a rallying cry even as the Great Depression cast its shadow.

Tragedy struck shortly afterward. With Coach Thomas fresh on the job and players ready to rally around him, they suffered what would be Alabama's greatest loss in their history.

James Richard Nichols, an eighteen-year-old, 200-pound center, who was "unusually heavy and strong despite [being short in] stature," was reputedly one of the freshman squad's most promising members. As reported in the *Tuscaloosa Times*, "On November 11,

1931, during a freshman/varsity practice scrimmage played in Denny Stadium, Nichols dove underneath varsity interference when a play was directed over his position in the center of the line. He suffered a dislocated vertebra and was immediately carried off the field and rushed to Druid City Hospital in Tuscaloosa. He died six days later, the first major accident in the thirty-nine-year history of football at the University."[73]

Laslie and Moseley, both members of the varsity team, would have been at practice the day of Nichols's fatal injury. Bryant, though not yet officially enrolled, regularly practiced with the freshman squad. James's death traumatized the entire university community—a shocking loss of a well-liked and promising young athlete and student and a tragedy for his family. University officials and the local press sought to divert some of the inevitable backlash always swirling around about whether the integration of athletics within an academic environment was misguided and should be banned.

That year, among all levels of play, thirteen deaths of young men around the country were directly attributed to lethal contact sustained on the football field. Two of those happened in the SEC: James Nichols and another college freshman in Florida whose fatal play occurred coincidentally on the same day. University officials knew academic purists would rush to point out that overzealousness on the part of players and coaches on college campuses would always result in serious injuries and deaths and that the loss of even one life never justified the rigorous pursuit of such an aggressive sport as football. Accounts, however, also included comments made by the father of James Nichols, a college graduate himself and a prominent businessman. James Nichols, Sr., noted that "he believed college athletics constituted one of the most important phases of a college education," and expressed gratification that his son had taken part in them while he was at the university.

At the NCAA convention in 1931, concern was expressed at the rise in the number of casualties attributed to football from the 1920s, the number first reported in some newspapers as being forty-nine before being corrected to thirty-one. This was a wake-up call for those who had thought the reformation of the rules in the pre–World War I era had solved the problems of the sport for good. Of the thirty one deaths reported throughout play at all levels (including professional, college, high school, and sandlot football players) only eight were the result of play at the college level. The majority of the remaining deaths happened at the high school level of play. It was determined it was not the rules that failed to protect players, but rather the financial effects of the Great Depression. High schools were hit harder than the colleges by the effects of the depression, as budgets in school districts were cut, allowing less money for coaches and equipment. The consequences proved tragic as football required a higher level of supervision, training, and equipment than other sports.

Football at the college level had always been far less prone to the most common causes of death such as concussions, spinal injuries, and heat stroke given higher levels of coaching skills and bigger budgets to purchase the best protective equipment available. Most of the deaths and serious injuries during this time always occurred at the high school level. The concern over a spike in deaths at the college level in 1931, however, "played second fiddle to a society plagued by the desperate problems of unemployment and bankruptcy."[74]

The day Nichols died, Coach Hank Crisp, their mentor, task master, and hard-as-nails coach, whom the players called "Coach Hank," gathered them together at the old gym and broke the news that the young freshman center had died. He did so with great calmness and stoicism. Later, Laslie, overcome with his own emotion, walked into the restroom down the hall where he found Coach Hank, himself in a stall, blowing his nose as he tried to hide his grief from his players. But, as Laslie wrote in a letter to his beloved coach on the day of Crisp's induction into the Alabama Hall of Fame in 1970, the evidence of his compassion and sorrow was too obvious to be concealed. "That day," he wrote, "I learned that you were not so tough after all."

Carney Laslie never forgot James Nichols. A freshman from

Indiana who died in an accident caused by a play involving the varsity line. The remorse was crushing to all those involved. Three of those known to be on the field that day—Laslie, Moseley, and J. B. Whitworth—would go on to coach, the tragedy a reminder of the perils of the sport and the importance of their role as coaches.

The Great Depression continued to devastate the economy, and attendance at college football games lagged. Many believed big-time college football was on its way out for that reason alone. Others, however, saw the decline and renewed their efforts to reform the game. In 1932, college officials joined forces by implementing a variety of policies at their schools they hoped would restore amateurism to collegiate athletics. One such action was abolishing so-called training houses or athletic dorms in order to encourage a more balanced relationship between academics and athletics.

For the most part, however, many of the standards set forth by the report, known as the Gates Commission, were ignored by the major institutions of the day, and the "systematic evasion of the NCAA's amateur code took place just barely out of sight."[75] Athletic dorms continued to be commonplace for most if not all of the programs in the South, valued for what they contributed to the creation of a team through camaraderie, friendship, and opportunities for mentorship.

Coach Hank recruited Paul Bryant after watching him play high school football in Fordyce, Arkansas. Arriving at the University of Alabama in 1931, he stayed with Coach Hank at the bunkhouse on his property until he was able to complete a language class required to earn his high school diploma and qualify to move on campus. During this time, Bryant attended Tuscaloosa High for part of the day and practiced with the university freshman team in the afternoon.

After Bryant successfully completed the courses needed, Coach Hank placed the rough-around-the-edges freshman farm boy into room 9 in 1932 in what was then called the Athletic Dormitory (actually the old gym which the athletes nicknamed "the BO House"), and like Crisp's other roommate assignments, it was no accident.

As the story goes, Coach Hank pointed to the room and growled to Bryant, "Maybe you can learn something from these guys."[76] "These guys" were three trusted upperclassmen football players, one of whom was Frank Moseley, also known as "Chesty," and by this time, one of Carney's closest friends. "Coach Hank didn't exactly have pets," wrote Bryant in his autobiography, "but he almost did and I was one of them." Laslie and Moseley, too, were on that list of pets, with Coach Hank's fingerprints all over each of their careers. But it can't be said it earned them special privileges, just extra attention. For Bryant, that meant getting extra jobs, like cleaning the toilets and showers on his floor.

The question of subsidizing athletes for play at universities was also controversial in the 1920s and 1930s. Alabama was competing with programs like University of Pittsburgh, which was then known to produce some of the best teams in the country. Muckraking journalist Francis Wallace exposed the history of subsidizing players with his reporting about Pittsburgh's football program. Although Pittsburgh's practices went through varied phases due to struggles between coaches and administration, as well as the state of the national economy, Wallace's reporting in the *Saturday Evening Post*, as well as Robert C. Alberts' *The Story of the University of Pittsburgh, 1787–1987* does give a window into what would have been common practices at other schools at the same level of competition.

Prior to 1933, players received cash payments, the amounts based upon their abilities and bargaining power. In industrial Pennsylvania, this could average $50 a month, from which players paid their room, board, and expenses. By 1933, with attendance at football games at their lowest point, this dropped to $40 a month.

It was well known that athletic officials at Eastern and Midwestern colleges were uncompromising in their push for strict rules to be applied to an amateur athletic system. However, Coach Wallace Wade speculated that players at these schools received additional amounts from alumni and boosters, which would have provided some athletes with a healthy income, contradicting the efforts to keep athletes in an "amateur" category. Since there was no effort to accommodate the unique challenges of the amateur athlete in the deep South— namely that many couldn't afford to attend college and play football without financial assistance—little effort was given to disguise the widespread financial support for football players in the deep South. They chose instead, as the *Washington Post* characterized it, to be more inclined to "adopt a 'ho, hum,' and 'well, what of it?'" attitude toward subsidizing athletes.

For most players, money was a constant issue. This was certainly true of Laslie, Moseley, and Bryant, by now fast friends, during these years. Each carried the pressure of supplementing their financial support from the university in whatever form it came, whether it was cash, tuition, room, board, or work placement. Along with their scholarship money, which after living expenses didn't amount to much, they were supposed to cut the grass and clean the gym. But during the summers, they would be assigned summer jobs with the University. Coach Hank was also known to slip a few dollars into the hands of a boy when he knew they were short on cash.

Carney, known to be tight-fisted with money, was haunted by the fear of not having enough money as a result of the trauma over the loss of his family's fortune and their financial troubles. A member of the waiters' union, he, along with fellow teammate Don Hutson, waited on tables during the off-season to make up for any shortfall in funds. Occasionally, Carney would accept a gift of funds from his favorite uncle, Dr. Carney G. Laslie, who also happened to be an alumnus, booster club member, and fellow Sigma Nu at Alabama.

Frank Moseley, a known pool shark, plied his talent on the unsuspecting to make extra money. Conveniently located adjacent to his dorm room in the BO House was the A-Club Room, where he had full use of the pool table from which to earn a few dollars. The varsity lettermen were privileged to have exclusive use of the social gathering place with its sparse furnishings, which consisted solely of a pool table, some benches, and a couple of chairs.

Bryant would make a few dollars by placing a bet here and there, noting in his autobiography he "probably shouldn't say this, but it's true" that the one bet he made on a game was on Alabama, the underdogs in the game. The night before their game against Tennessee in 1935, he and some other players anted up a chunk of change between them totaling five dollars and bet on themselves to win, which they did, pocketing about one dollar apiece in winnings.

Financial pressures were a common experience for many college students during the Great Depression. But Bryant, Laslie, and Moseley also shared a personal struggle caused by the emotional pain of having fathers who were an overall disappointment to them for a variety of reasons: shiftlessness, alcohol problems, emotionally disconnected, or a combination of all. They also shared the common experience of how sports, and particularly football, helped to compensate for the lack of male leadership in their homes growing up, an outlet for any unresolved anger fostering a kinship between them despite coming from very diverse households with unique hardships and backgrounds.

Bryant, born and raised in Fordyce, Arkansas, was from a hardworking, poor farming family. He was an average student, and his teachers when asked about their impression of the young boy said there was nothing they could remember from that time that really stood out about him. He struggled in school academically but experienced success in athletics. In his autobiography, he shares the shame he felt at not having enough money, summarizing his childhood in a few sentences: "The one thing I disliked most about growing up was getting up every Saturday, hitching up our mule to our wagon, and going to Fordyce with Mama. I didn't mind the work . . . what I hated about it was coming face-to-face with the people we met along the way . . . I didn't feel like I was as good as those people. I thought they looked down on me."[77]

"Paul never forgot how that felt," his sister Louise said in an interview for a video produced celebrating the coach's hundred-year birthday.

Frank Moseley grew up in the White working-class section of old Montgomery, Alabama where his father was a career police officer, the family home located on the edge of a Black neighborhood. From a very young age, Frank, the oldest of four, and his younger brother Max, spent their days playing sports—baseball, football, whatever athletic team of the day they could find—in the sand lots nearby. Their teammates were primarily the Black boys of the neighboring streets. Every minute they could find—after school, after chores, on the weekends when they weren't working—they played ball. His mother, a former teacher, was dedicated to her children getting an education and saw to it that their studies were attended to. At the time, policemen commanded a very modest salary, and with a family of six, the Moseleys were among the working poor. The brothers took on extra jobs to help. It was during this time that Frank developed into a successful pool shark, dutifully contributing his winnings to help support the family.

The Moseley children attended Sidney Lanier High School in Montgomery. It was then as now a premier high school institution. The school was considered the best in Alabama—state of the art for the times. The number of award-winning athletes from Sidney Lanier who later rostered championship teams in the South is likely unequaled. Frank thrived there, his natural athletic abilities blossoming into a disciplined, focused athlete, and he soon got the attention of the recruiters in Alabama. Max Moseley was equally talented in sports, but was not the athlete Frank was. He dropped out of school to help send his older brother to college.

Over the years, Max became a good friend of Laslie's and Bryant's by virtue of his older brother Frank's close relationship with the two men. In later years, his shared passion for golf contributed to their ongoing friendship. But it is Max's impact as a sportswriter, and more importantly his contributions to the civil rights movement, that makes his influence noteworthy.

At the age of sixteen, Max knew he wanted to be a sportswriter and started full-time as a copy boy at the *Montgomery Advertiser*, working his way up to a full-fledged sportswriter by the age of eighteen in 1932, a reporter there for the next forty-seven years. It was said that "Max was just color-blind" when it came to sports and good coaching. He kept up with their childhood friends from the sand lots, many of whom had gone on to be coaches at Black junior high and senior high schools and colleges in the region. He knew there was a high caliber of play being exhibited at these schools and it wasn't getting reported.

Appointed sports editor at *The Advertiser* in his late twenties, he became well known—sometimes infamously so—within the SEC. He always had an Associated Press college poll vote, served on the Heisman Committee several times, and was awarded what his family considered his highest achievement, the Man of the Year, by Thurgood Marshall in 1940. The award was given to the first sports editor in the Southeast to put Black sports in the paper, the result of *The Advertiser* approving his request to make the last page of the sports section an all-Black sports page including junior high, senior high, and Black colleges. It was a huge step for a newspaper whose circulation was decidedly White and of the Jim Crow–era mindset. In 1954, the Extra Point Club, an Atlanta Black sports organization, gave a special citation and silver plaque to Max, presented at the Tuskegee Institute, for his consistent and fair reporting. Family members wondered how it came that they didn't ever have a cross burned in their yard.

Like Max, Frank was colorblind when it came to sports, a cultural anomaly at the time. It was during Frank Moseley's tenure as its head football coach and athletic director at Virginia Tech from 1951 to 1978 (then known as VPI) that the university joined Duke, Wake

Forest, University of North Carolina, and other surrounding schools actively recruiting Black athletes in 1966 while the State Office of the NAACP and Virginia Council of Human Relations publicly accused the University of Virginia of racial discrimination in athletics.

Similar to his brother, Frank also embodied leadership qualities that were further developed during his years at Alabama. He was vice-president of both his sophomore and junior class, member of the Honor Council, and successor to Carney Laslie as vice president of the Alabama A-Club, an illustrious organization composed of men who have achieved varsity playing status (the "A" team) in the various sports played at the university.

After Alabama's Rose Bowl win in 1931, the team wouldn't return for a national championship title game until its next Rose Bowl appearance in 1935. During that span, however, the team was still a force to contend with, their talent was deep, and their coaching was some of the best regarded in the sport. Carney's record at the tackle position during his subsequent years of play in '31 and '32 was recorded as among the finest in the South, playing alongside some of the notable greats of the game, including teammate Don Hutson. In addition to his stellar performance at tackle, Laslie's adeptness at kicking off and converting the extra point after touchdowns was relied upon as Alabama finished out its last year in the Southern Conference, a record of 8 wins and two losses. The next year would find Alabama a member of the newly formed SEC, beginning a tradition of great football rivalries between what was then referred to as big-time football programs of the South. His performance was spotlighted when Alabama defeated St. Mary's College in Moraga, California, in what was described later as a brilliant intersectional game played in San Francisco, though it can be assumed the number of 'Bama fans present to witness his play was severely diminished due to the financial constraints of the Great Depression.

With his last season of collegiate play behind him and graduation looming, Laslie spent the final months of his senior year enjoying fraternity life, waiting tables for extra money, and hitting the canteen where regular dances were held for the A-Club athletes. Sometime before June, Coach Thomas and Coach Hank offered Laslie the opportunity to join them as an assistant on the coaching staff, a position the senior had no doubt been eyeing. With a degree in physical education under his belt, Laslie joined his teammate J. B. "Ears" Whitworth on the assistant coaching staff for the fall season of '33.

Assigned as an individual instructor for the tackles, Laslie was reassigned to coach the "Bama Rats" or the "Baby Tide," by Coach Thomas early in the season, taking over as the "Frosh Mentor." The '33 Alabama freshman team won every game played and was reportedly "one of the best drilled Freshman teams to represent the Capstone, its blocking and hard tackling attributed to the careful, painstaking tutelage"[78] of Carney Laslie.

Alabama's '33 varsity team included senior Frank Moseley, co-captain, sophomore Paul Bryant, and sophomore Jimmy Walker. That season, the Crimson Tide had a remarkable record, garnering the very first championship title of the newly formed Southeastern Conference (SEC), posting five wins, zero losses, and one tie. The team of '33 paved the way for the '34 season, with a roster of rising juniors and seniors that led the team to another Rose Bowl victory in 1935.

With the impressive success of the freshman team, Coach Thomas looked to Laslie with an eye toward capitalizing on his ability to motivate young men to play football. Years later, Paul Bryant described in his autobiography Laslie's ability to bring out the best in players: "You could win him just by trying like hell, fight as hard as you could. Some people have that, and some don't. Carney Laslie had it." True, Laslie was known to demand a player's best effort, but there was another side to him that made players want to give him 100 percent, a connection he was able to make with players to communicate he cared about them even when he was pushing them hard.

Bryant's son, Paul Bryant, Jr., who was particularly close to Laslie, knew this softer side better than anyone. Fond of nicknames, Laslie affectionately called the Bryants' only son "Pablo." Bryant, Jr., related the following story when asked to describe his uncle Carney:

> At a dinner honoring General [Norman] Schwarzkopf, many years after Uncle Carney's death, I sat next to a General who I thought may have been at West Point at the same time Carney was there coaching. I leaned over and asked the General if he happened to have known Coach Laslie when he [the general] played football at West Point. He paused a moment then shook his head and said no, he didn't recall him. A couple of minutes later, he looked up from his plate, turned towards me shaking his head knowingly, and chuckling said, "As a matter of fact I do remember Coach Laslie. He was a mean son-of-a-bitch," he told me. I realized then he didn't know him at all.

During the years Laslie coached at West Point, then cadet James Henry experienced his future father-in-law as quiet, gruff and aloof. However, one afternoon in 1955, when the young lieutenant joined Coach Laslie and the commandant of West Point's young son on the golf course, he observed then Army coach Laslie in a totally different light. He was thoroughly impressed with his father-in-law's ability to be both firm and instructive as well as encouraging and patient, a manner and skill not lost on the soon-to-be platoon leader. From that point on, Lt. Henry never passed up the opportunity to observe the man, whether it was on the golf course or joining a cadre of coaches to hunt and fish at Laslie's favorite hunting camp and retreat, Dollarhide. It was no less than an art, a masterful way of interacting with young men, that drew his respect and admiration for the formidable coach.

PART III

FROM ARKANSAS TO MARYLAND
1933–1941, 1945–1946

*Coaches Carney Laslie and Herb Patchett observe the William & Mary and
Richmond game from the sidelines. Richmond-Times Dispatch. Nov 25, 1937.*

CHAPTER FOURTEEN

The Blytheville High School "Chickasaws"

"Ain't We Got Fun" Lyrics

Ev'ry morning, ev'ry evening ain't we got fun?
Not much money, oh, but honey, ain't we got fun?
The rent's unpaid dear, we haven't a bus
But smiles were made dear for people like us
In the winter in the summer don't we have fun?
Times are bum and getting bummer still we have fun

Bing Crosby and Rosemary Clooney
Bing & Rosie, The Crosby Clooney Radio Sessions, 2010

BLYTHEVILLE, ARKANSAS
1933–1936

EARLY IN THE UNIVERSITY of Alabama's history, athletes from
Arkansas high schools were recruited to play on the football team—

indeed, talented players were delivered annually to Alabama's team roster through a virtual pipeline from Arkansas. Many of Laslie's Crimson Tide teammates hailed from Arkansas, including Don Hutson, Jess Eberdt, Paul Bryant, Tilden "Happy" Campbell, and J. B. "Ears" Whitworth. It was no surprise that Alabama kept a lookout for high school coaching opportunities in Arkansas where their newly groomed assistant coaches could get hired. It improved the opportunity to pluck promising talent from the ranks of graduating seniors.

City leaders in Blytheville, long frustrated with the high school's poor athletic standing and achievement compared to other schools around the state, were ready to make some changes when, in 1933, the school's basketball program rose to prominence after winning the district title. Aspirations soared, and a state championship now seemed not so much but rather well within their reach. Basketball players were often also on the football team, and Blytheville movers and shakers saw an opportunity for their football program as well. Such success, they believed, could move the school into the upper echelon of sports programs in Arkansas.

The chairman of the alumni athletic committee in Blytheville, Fred Saliba, pushed for an infusion of new blood into the Blytheville High School athletic program to help them reach their goal of having powerhouse high school sports teams. The search was on for a new head football coach for the Blytheville Chickasaws, "the Chicks."

Carney Laslie wasn't the only Alabama player to apply for the job. Friends and former teammates Jess Eberdt and J. B. Whitworth, both alumni of Blytheville High School, were also candidates. Along with that bit of rivalry came the potential to derail their friendships. In the end, it was Laslie who prevailed, the hiring committee impressed with the recommendations, experience, and his winning record as head coach of the freshman team at Alabama. For Laslie, the widely touted new spirit of cooperation between the community leaders and a local booster club focused on increasing attendance at football games was likely appealing to the young coach. He was looking for the opportunity to build a program from the ground up. He had confidence that he was the man to do it. The enthusiasm and community support meant he could get the resources he needed to be successful. He accepted their offer. As far as any hard feelings among the three former teammates and coaching assistants: there were none. They remained close friends for a lifetime.

Much rested on the new coach's shoulders. Not only was the community looking for Coach Laslie to remake the football team, but they were banking on its success. Although 1934 began to show signs of reversing itself as the economy stabiliized, college football attendance, a baraometer used to predict ticket sales at the high school level, had hit rock bottom the year before. It was anybody's guess. Something exciting needed to happen to draw fans, which was averaging just a few hundred a game, to come out on a Friday night to watch their high school team play during such an economic downtown. Blytheville was looking to the talents of their new young coach to create that excitement. The stakes couldn't have been higher.

Fans, parents, and sports pundits alike took to guessing the strategy that Coach Laslie would employ. Would he adopt Wallace Wade's system, which placed power and strong line play at a premium? Or would he utilize Frank Thomas's approach of a modified Notre Dame style, which also demanded power, but depended more on speed and an open game? Six lettermen from the prior season were gone, leaving Coach Laslie with a squad of seven seniors and three juniors. By the time he finished trolling the area for boys to play on the team, he had nineteen players to work with and "compared to some of the squads in larger cities, the material seemed pitifully inadequate. What they knew about football was almost zero."[79]

To bolster attendance and gain attention for their new football coach, the city's business leaders began a creative campaign to lure fans back into the stands for home games. The license numbers of twenty cars spotted randomly on the streets of Blytheville were included somewhere within the pages of *The Courier News*, the local newspaper. A variety of stores such as the downtown drug store, radio and shoe repair shops, cleaners, and others embedded the car tag numbers into their individual ads placed in the paper the week of the home game, making the owners eligible to receive a free ticket. To claim their free ticket, winners then simply had to drive their car to the merchant in whose ad their license number appeared. It was the first but not the last of such contests designed to help bring new life to the sluggish football program.

On the eve of his first game, reporters teased the new varsity head coach about the superstitious charms he was known to carry around. Apparently, he carried several with him on a regular basis. One reporter for the *Blytheville Courier News* teasingly warned residents not to be surprised if they saw Carney Laslie, Chick's head coach, out in the graveyard some night, trying to run down rabbits in the moonlight since he'd likely be needing quite a collection of rabbit foots, and before the season was over four-leaf clovers and totem poles as well, alluding to the overall weakness of the varsity squad. "So any of you wizards who brew a magic potion (not the kind that makes you forget troubles but wards them off) start the pot boiling for Carney Laslie," he added to his humorous caricature of the new coach. Such superstitious habits marked the beginning of his tradition of wearing what he considered his lucky hat, a black fedora, to every game he ever coached.

One wonders, if Laslie also added a rain dance to his superstitious routines, as the Chicks defeated their opponent, Osceola High School, 39–0, in a driving rain, playing their first game of the season in what was described as a sea of mud. Despite the conditions, the win was met with the most enthusiastic support the team had received in a very long time, though it is safe to say there weren't the numbers in the stands the booster club had hoped for that Friday night in September. The weather certainly kept most away—likely even those who had won a free ticket. Coach Laslie declared the team to have looked "pretty good," adding that the line played a major role in the victory, the unsung heroes of the game. Hershel "Herky" Mosley, the oldest of the four Mosley brothers (no relation to Frank Moseley) who went on to famously play football at the University of Alabama, played quarterback for the Blytheville "Chicks," and reportedly carried the ball "in good fashion."[80] Mosley went on to become one of Alabama's greats, known as the Blast from Blytheville, achieving football fame for his performance as quarterback in the 1938 Rose Bowl under coaches Thomas, Crisp, and a young assistant coach named Paul Bryant.

To temper the unbridled enthusiasm that followed their first victory of the season, Laslie quickly squelched any idea that the score over Osecola was something to be proud of. He emphasized to his young team that the many mistakes they made would ordinarily have lost them the ballgame.

Their second game was no less challenging weather-wise, played entirely in a fog that overhung the field, frequently becoming so thick that despite the powerful stadium lights, it was impossible to identify the players or at times the direction of plays. More than once "the football disappeared into the low-hanging fog as it took flight off a kicker's toe and came down like a ghost ball yards away." Such would be a good excuse for poor performance or lackluster effort by any team. By the time the official barked an end to the game, however, the Chicks had crossed the goal line thirteen times and successfully kicked seven field goals, making the final score 85–0.

It is safe to say that the new coach wanted to prove a point (no pun intended) to fans, opponents, and his own players: that they could indeed play football.

One of the hardest tasks to face Coach Laslie at this point was keeping his players from becoming overconfident in their abilities given their first two games were such blowouts. He picked the game to pieces and showed his players the faults in such a one-sided victory, but he also knew his players would likely hear what their upcoming opponents were saying about the win, which would also serve to temper their overconfidence. "Blytheville always looks good early in the season," the coach of the Shawnee High School Indians in Joiner, Arkansas, was reported as saying. "They'll drop to their usual level before long." And though happy with the unusual trouncing, fans said they would rather see a good, competitive game. "I'm satisfied with what the Chicks can do when they're ahead. Now I want to see what they can do when they're behind," commented the school superintendent.

"So do I—but not too far behind," countered Coach Laslie.

The opportunity came soon enough. In their next matchup on October 19, Laslie's Blytheville Chickasaws went against the Forrest City High School Thoroughbreds in what was considered their first big test of the '34 season. It proved to be what the fans were looking for: a nail biter that kept them on the edge of their seats.

The Thoroughbreds scored first with a touchdown in the second quarter, but Blytheville was able to tie it up with a seventy-five-yard run to the goal line after an intercepted pass on Forrest City's twenty-five-yard line. Blytheville scored another touchdown in the third quarter and pulled ahead. Forrest City then rallied, bringing the ball to their seven-yard line, threatening to score, but Blytheville turned it into a fumble and touchback. The Chicks made a third touchdown to which their opponent answered with a touchdown in the final quarter. But it was not enough to overcome Blytheville's lead.

The final score, with Blytheville on top, was 21–13.

The national rhetoric at the time echoed the fierce competition and striving that was taking place on high school and college football fields across the country. On October 20, 1934, President Franklin Delano Roosevelt spoke at the inauguration of the new president of William and Mary College. Sounding much like a coach in a locker room at halftime, FDR said, "The necessities of our time demand that men avoid being set in grooves, that they avoid the occupational predestination of the older world and that in the face of the change and development in America they must have a sufficiently broad and comprehensive conception of the world in which they live to meet its changing problems with resourcefulness and practical vision."[81]

No doubt Coach Laslie was also preparing his team with a philosophy that had the same strains of Roosevelt's exhortations: know your opponent, be ready to change the game plan when needed, and most importantly, be prepared.

By that November, the Chicks remained undefeated and went up against the undefeated Walnut Ridge High School Bobcats for the regional championship at the Bobcats' home stadium. Every car and storefront around town displayed signs aimed at the demise of the Chicks: "Crush Chicks," "Beat Blytheville," "Execution of Chicks Starts at 2 p.m." And in Blytheville, railway and town planners alike had capitalized on the excitement, procuring a special train to bring what was projected to be a minimum of 350 Blytheville fans in for the game. They festooned the train in the team colors of maroon and white, commissioned local bands to provide music on board, and offered a special discounted one-dollar fare.

A few days before the big game, the editor of Blytheville's *Courier News* received a letter from the publisher of Walnut Ridge's newspaper: "We are glad to know you are bringing a special train," he wrote, "but bring plenty of substitutes as those bone crushers of ours are a hell of an opposition. We are closing up the town for the game leaving nothing running but the water and the electricity. The hospital and staff will be ready to give emergency service on the field. You can do anything you like over here except beat our Bobcats," he warned. "You can parade, root, buy hot dogs—and those that wish may get drunk— the four officers being detailed for duty only on the sidelines to keep spectators off the field."

Despite the threats and bravado, the Blytheville Chicks prevailed on game day, the only incident requiring medical attention reportedly being that of a Chick fan being hit over the head with a wrench by a disgruntled Bobcat fan. The first undefeated team in the school's history[82] attributed its success to Coach Carney Laslie. His ability to keep his players in top physical condition while nursing his meager squad along with as few injuries as possible was seen to be a crucial factor.

His role as athletic director for the high school also required his coaching on the basketball court. As soon as the last game of football was played, he pivoted his attention to hoops. Many of the same boys who played football played basketball. He put them all "through the mill," focusing on the fundamentals of the game so they would all be ready for their first game of the season to be played on Saturday, January 5, 1935.

Adjacent to the January 4 article heralding the Chicks' basketball game opener on the sports page of the town's paper was a report spotlighting the Nazis' preparation for the summer Olympic Games of 1936. Adolf Hitler's rise to power had occurred after Germany had been awarded the Games. Incidents overseas began to be reported nationally to substantiate the growing wariness that some politicians had of Hitler and his regime.

One such incident was reported on December 29, 1934, when Miss Elsa Sittell of New York disappeared at the French border after last being seen waiting for her train in Germany. She had been arrested after she made a disparaging remark about Hitler's storm troopers while dining at a restaurant in Germany. Though she was eventually released, it made front page news in major city papers and more than a few rural Southern publications, one of many disturbances that were momentarily spotlighted then faded into obscurity. These events were isolated and random enough to only disturb the collective American conscience instead of awakening it.

The increased reports of incidents involving Hitler's supporters and his storm troopers was sufficient for the US to demand a pause in the building taking place in Berlin for the Olympics. US diplomats sought to pressure Germany to publicly denounce what the Germans characterized as inconsequential behavior by a few, not a statement of their overall politics. It was not until Germany gave several assurances to the International Olympic Committee that there would be no racial prejudices against Jews competing in the Games that there was any certainty the Games would be held in Berlin. Construction continued for what would become the largest stage ever built in the history of the Olympic Games.

The United States had its own domestic worries. Though Blytheville was mired in the nationwide economic woes, the high school sports mania provided entertainment for both Black and White, distracting them from social issues, like racism, and the unsettled international climate. The Chickasaw basketball season of 1935 saw only two losses. Still, the story continued to be the phenomenal success of its undefeated football team.

Back at the University of Alabama, Jimmy Walker and Paul Bryant, both juniors, also had tremendous success during the '34 football season as members of an unbeaten Crimson Tide, also known as the Red Elephants. Alabama claimed both the SEC and National Championship that year, beating Stanford in the Rose Bowl, 29–13. The two ended their college playing years in 1935 with Walker as their captain and a 6–2–1 record.

At the end of the season of '35, Paul Bryant was now married with a baby on the way. With a family to support, he considered playing in the pro league (he'd had a few offers), but was dissuaded by Thomas who told him if coaching was ultimately his goal, then playing pro for the money was a waste of time. With a family to support, his first child due March 1936, Bryant left Tuscaloosa his last semester, taking a paid assistant's job at Union University in Jackson, Tennessee, under head coach A. B. Hollingsworth. With the season of '36 ready to begin in the Fall, Frank Thomas offered Bryant the opportunity to come back to Alabama and join the coaching staff. With one more semester to go to get his degree, Bryant knew if he was to have a future coaching college ball, he needed to graduate. As Bryant relates in his biography, a student assistant position would have meant low or no pay. Bryant accepted Thomas's offer on the condition that even though he would be enrolled as a student, he would be paid at the higher pay grade of an assistant rather than a student assistant, as he had a family to support. Thomas agreed.

At the end of his senior year in 1935, Walker, too, reportedly had several overtures to coach from both pro football and basketball teams (the Boston Redskins and Boston Celtics, respectively). Instead, with the encouragement of Laslie, and one can presume Coach Hank and Coach Thomas as well, he accepted a head coach position at El Dorado High School in El Dorado, Arkansas, located approximately 300 miles from Blytheville. One can imagine the good-natured rivalry that was spawned within the state between the two schools following Walker's appointment.

Just in time to give their rival teams an opportunity for a matchup came the decision by the executive committee of the Arkansas Athletic Association in Little Rock to adopt a plan for a new high school state football title playoff. With Blytheville's undefeated record in 1934, the argument about who had the best football team in the state grew louder, and pressure on the Arkansas Athletic Association to do something about it escalated as well. A state championship was adopted to settle the annual argument in the State about which high school football team was truly the best. It was also a way to increase the revenue possibilities of the sport. The Executive Committee was given full authority for matching the teams and selecting the time and place for all championship games, as well as selecting the officials. Proceeds of the game were to be divided 40 percent to each team and 20 percent to the Arkansas Athletic Association. The winner was to be declared the state champion and presented with a trophy.

Coach Laslie and his Chicks continued their record-breaking winning streak through 1935 and 1936, remaining undefeated for three consecutive seasons. In what was billed as the biggest game of the 1936 season, the only two undefeated teams in the state, Blytheville and Searcy High School, met on Searcy's home field. The game became one of the state's most legendary high school games ever played, pairing the Chicks' 195-pound lineman Byron Walker, also known as "the Ripper," against "Five Yard" Evans, Searcy's towering fullback.

A 210-pound giant, Evans had pummeled Searcy's opponents that year, earning a reputation that painted him as almost superhuman. Rumors circulated in locker rooms and on bleachers around the state that "he could tuck a football under his left arm and run through a brick wall." Coach Laslie walked into the locker room the day of the game and gathered the players around him. "If Searcy receives," he warned, "Evans will hit the center of the line on the first play. When he does, I want the line to open up and let the Ripper have the first shot at him."

As predicted, Evans hit the line on the first play. "The obedient Chick forwards politely allowed themselves to be removed from his path. As Evans charged through the opening, a human thunderbolt in red pants met him with a cruel crash of bone and muscle. When the dust cleared the dazed 'Five Yard' Evans came slowly to his feet and went back to the huddle, but he was not the same tearing, slashing demon of Searcy High who had crushed his opponents all season." "The Ripper's" vicious tackle ended the image of Evans being invincible. The game that had been billed as one that would be the best in the state, with fans and players in a high pitch of anticipation, ended with a score of 57–0, Blytheville on top. The win was attributed to a smart young head coach named Carney Laslie and the incredibly talented athlete Byron "the Ripper" Walker.

With an uninterrupted winning record, the Chicks were invited to the Tri-State Regional Championship in November of '36, where they suffered their first loss in three years after a streak of twenty-eight wins. They played the championship game in front of 5,500 fans, one of the largest crowds recorded at that time for a high school game in Memphis, Tennessee. In what was described as a "nip and tuck game," the final score was 7- 0, a thriller that was not decided until the final seconds as a frantic Blytheville tried to score but was unsuccessful, giving the unofficial Tri-State Championship title to Lee High School from Columbus, Mississippi. It was a disappointing loss for the Chicks, one that even their rivals back in Arkansas may have mourned.

With the conclusion of the football season, the celebrations to honor their home team and coaches began in earnest. Blytheville women's social club, known as the Red Pepper Club, hosted their annual dinner for the football team and faculty on December 5, 1936. The program included football player Calvin Moody sharing his sentiments in his address titled "Why I Like to Play Football," a commentary on "What Authorities Think About Football" by an invited guest speaker, "The School and the Team" by the former head coach of the Chicks, W. D. McClurkin, and closing remarks by Coach Laslie, which was titled "Reviewing the Season and Business." The three years had brought a phenomenal display of cooperation as well as player development. The undefeated streak was a record-breaking accomplishment—one that Coach Laslie ascribed to the hard work of the players.

Laslie's record had not gone unnoticed by his peers. When famed 1926 Alabama Rose Bowl quarterback Pooley Hubert, who is now considered one of the best defensive backs of all time, was offered the head coach position at Virginia Military Institute in Lexington, Virginia, the first man he called to join him was Coach Carney Laslie. A meeting was scheduled with Hubert and VMI athletic officials on January 15, 1937, in Lexington. It was the day after the year-end sports banquet at Blytheville High School.

Ninety players, coaches, parents, and booster club members of Blytheville High School gathered at the city's grand Noble Hotel for a formal celebration that included dinner, awards, and speeches. "Above all, don't neglect your education," advised Ralph Clyde "Shorty" Probst, a physically gigantic man who was the head coach at Southwestern University, in his keynote address. "You will need it for your future." He also spoke about the subsidization of players, a controversial but present condition of football recruiting. Like many, he saw the virtue of subsidizing players in college. "It gives many a boy the opportunity to secure a college education who would not otherwise be able to do so," he told the crowd. The speech, full of advice for a life after football for the young athletes, encouraged them not to make the mistakes that so many football stars, including All-Americans, made after leaving grid iron play. "You can't eat football," he warned.

Coach Laslie may well have glanced nervously at his watch as the evening wore on. He made a surprisingly brief speech given the occasion, but it was not out of character as he knew the occasion was not about him but the players. Although Coach Laslie's focus on fundamentals, physical condition, and development of a strong line were winning combinations that took the Blytheville football teams of 1934, '35, and '36 to unimagined heights, Laslie was also quick to remind them it took not only physical execution, but heart. This underlying factor had the power to make a team extraordinary. Coach Laslie had succeeded in motivating this small-town team of high school boys to give their hearts to the game, and in doing so, they discovered the strength of character and athletic discipline that would serve them well for a lifetime.

The brevity of his speech can also be understood given one more fact: he had a train to catch.

Laslie had a ticket on an 11 p.m. train leaving that night from Memphis, Tennessee—a good sixty-seven miles away, and well over an hour and a half drive from Blytheville. The train's route would first take him to Birmingham and then up to Lexington, Virginia, where he had an interview with the newly hired head coach at VMI the next day. As the evening wore on, two booster club members, Frank Whitworth, and Carl Ganske, made the offer to drive Laslie from Blytheville to the station in Memphis. Emmet Maum, a sportswriter from Memphis who was in Blytheville to cover the banquet, hitched a ride back home with them. As soon as the banquet ended, the merry band of four sped as fast as they could go up the highway so Laslie could catch his train.

The train was just pulling out as they raced into the station. All four dashed out onto the track where the *Birmingham Flyer* was slowly but steadily gathering speed. Undaunted, they took off running after the train, yelling and shouting to the conductor to hold up. Ganske clutched Laslie's suitcase in his hands and ran ahead to pitch it onto the train. Just at the crucial moment, the suitcase popped open, and its contents went flying. Watching it all from the back platform, the pullman porter, who was authorized to pull the brake cord in case of an emergency, did so, and the train screeched to a stop. He ran to the aid of Ganske and asked him, who he assumed was the traveler, what was his destination. Ganske stared at him blankly and turned red with embarrassment while he stammered that he had no idea. Laslie came up from behind huffing and puffing and climbed onto the rear of the train. The three men left back on the tracks watched as the train gathered speed and disappeared into the night. Their last image was of Laslie stuffing his clothes into his suitcase.

Laslie's years at Blytheville produced players who went on to make exceptional contributions to Alabama football, notably the Mosley brothers, who were outstanding stars on the team during their years there. Coach Laslie hand-picked James Nisbet, a teammate on the '31 team, to be his successor at Blytheville. The pipeline funneling top athletes from Blytheville to Alabama remained intact after his departure.

CHAPTER FIFTEEN

The Fighting Squadron

"In football you get to rehearse life before you play it out for mortal stakes, which is part of what makes the game as valuable as it is."

—Mark Edmundson, "Why Football Matters: My Education in the Game," 2014

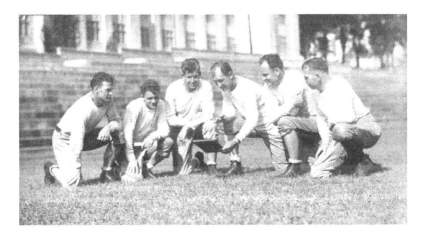

VMI Coaching Staff, L-R: Jimmy Walker, 3rd from Left Carney Laslie, 4th from Left, Pooley Hubert. 1940.

LEXINGTON, VA
1936–1942

ON THE INTERNATIONAL STAGE of sports, triumphant performances by Team USA at the '36 Summer Olympics in Berlin thwarted Hitler's hopes for German dominance. Jesse Owens's very presence as a Black member of the American track team drew stern pushback from racist attitudes most prevalent in the South, and Germany's racist policies toward both Black and Jewish athletes had been a point of contention between the two countries, causing many in the US to support a boycott of the Games altogether. But others on the Olympic Committee pushed for Owens to compete, arguing that his undeniable superiority in track and field, made him a gold medal contender.

The United States' track and field athletes broke world records and overall won an unprecedented number of gold medals. The crew team from the University of Washington beat the German team in the eight-man rowing race by an eighth of a second to win gold, an event in which the Germans fully expected to dominate. Jesse Owens became the star of the Games,winning four gold medals in the track and field division. Yet even after the close of the Olympic Winter Games in December that year, with the athletic achievements of the US heralded around the world, it was not enough to lessen the unease that many in the United States felt as tensions abroad increased. The clouds of war over Europe were hard to ignore.

Spectator sports, especially football and baseball, continued to grow as a favorite past time, an emotional distraction from the country's problems. Sports competitions produced a flame of pride to stoke the hearts of Americans across the nation. With the last victorious game of the 1936 football schedule one for the books, "Chick Fever" in Blytheville was still robust and healthy.

The Sugar Bowl in New Orleans, which came on the scene in 1935, was almost instantly popular. By 1936, in the wake of college football's growing popularity, many saw the potential of success in any business enterprise associated with bowl games, despite the Orange Bowl still not having gained the status of being a so-called "full-fledged affair" after its third year of existence. But it did not discourage the rise of other regional contests such as the longstanding Cotton Bowl held in Dallas, Texas, which emerged in 1937. By the late thirties, bowls with names like Celery, Dixie, Eastern, Flower, Fruit, Glass, Grape, Orchid, Pineapple, Salad, and Silver sprang up all over the country. The East-West and North-South All-Star games were particularly popular, an outgrowth of the entrepreneurial endeavors of a New South that pushed the boundaries of football competitions beyond those traditionally played between schools located within their same state.

The evolution of sports as an entertainment platform also spawned an evolution of what schools looked for in the leadership of their athletic programs. College football programs in the Southeast sought a new breed of coaches. By the start of the 1936 season, four out of the nine teams in the region were still seeking a head coach. Not so at VMI, where players were welcomed back by not only a new head coach but an entire new coaching staff.

VMI's football program had languished for years. The ever-influential hand of Alabama's Coach Hank Crisp, who had played basketball and football in Virginia at Hampton-Sydney University located just south of Lexington and also for Virginia Tech in Blacksburg, came into play once again. Allison T. "Pooley" Hubert, who Wallace Wade described as the greatest quarterback he ever coached, was hired to rebuild the football program.

Hubert was given carte blanche to hire his staff. With pay less than that of other private and state-supported universities, Hubert would have to rely on his own power of influence, as well as the lure of a town nestled in the beauty of the foothills of the Blue Ridge and the historical tradition of football at one of the nation's premier military institutes to attract a prospective coach and his family. Hubert was looking for a collegial group of men to coach alongside him: like-minded in their coaching philosophies as well as men who shared his values of hard work, discipline, and honesty.

Laslie's meeting with Hubert went well, and he accepted the position of line coach at VMI. He quickly recommended Jimmy Walker to fill the position of end coach. Walker, still in his first year as head coach at El Dorado High School in Arkansas, gave his notice in March 1937 that he would not be returning for the fall season. Coach Hubert then turned to Albert Elmore, a teammate of Laslie's from the 1930's Rose Bowl team, and offered him a post.

Paul Bryant, too, was contacted to join them. On the surface, it looked like a perfect move for the Bryant family. Riley Smith, who had just arrived in Lexington to coach at Washington and Lee, was a roommate of Bryant's at Alabama. Bryant's wife, Mary Harmon Bryant, and Riley's wife had also been roommates, and the four were the best of friends. It certainly must have been tempting because Bryant initially indicated interest. But at that time, in his first year as an assistant coach under Frank Thomas at Alabama, Bryant was not ready to move. It wouldn't be the last time they tried to recruit Bryant to the fold at VMI. Hubert tried again in 1940. Anxious to join Laslie and Walker and the rest of the staff there, Bryant informally accepted an assistant coach position. But when Henry "Red" Sanders, the new head coach at Vanderbilt, asked Bryant if he'd like to be his offensive line coach, Bryant didn't hesitate. The job paid more than what VMI could offer and money was not an insignificant consideration given the times.

The Alabama contingent of the coaches at VMI were well suited to each other for another reason. Both Hubert and Laslie were "brothers," members of the collegiate fraternity Sigma Nu, as was Paul Bryant. Known as the first "honor fraternity," this brotherhood of men prided themselves on adhering to a core of values: their slogan of "Love, Honor, Truth" and vision statement of "Excelling with Honor" were words they lived by. Many years later, Hubert reflected on Bryant's almost joining them in 1940. Bryant would have been a good fit for VMI, full of patriotism, and a believer in the virtues of military discipline for the benefit of young men, Hubert told an interviewer. "He was also truthful," added Hubert, "a believer in the honor system—something [I was] too."[83]

With his coaching staff now complete, Coach Hubert turned his attention to VMI's alumni, whose interest in the school's football program had all but disappeared. He traveled to regional alumni chapter associations, laying out his plans for the upcoming year, a makeover that included a change of the team's name from Flying Squadron to Fighting Squadron and new uniforms. His rallying cry for support created a renewed sense of enthusiasm and vision for the program, his popularity soaring among alumni before the season even started.

In their inaugural year, the Fighting Squadron tied for the state title. The team was said to have been characterized by hard charging and sharp blocking, a signature influence of Coach Wallace Wade on the Alabama coaches. As significant was the contribution of Byron "the Ripper" Walker (no relation to Coach Jimmy Walker), Blytheville's star tackle who had followed Laslie to VMI. Byron Walker went on to captain the squad his senior year, continuing his reputation of being an outstanding athlete likened to a raging bull on the field, with a quiet and modest persona off the field.

General Charles E. Kilbourne, the superintendent of VMI, held a reception for the team at his home, which was festooned in the school's colors of red, white, and yellow. Coach Laslie stepped in for Coach Hubert who was out of town and could not attend, greeting guests as they came through the reception line.

Alice Laslie, along with Coach Hubert's wife, Mary Nell, pitched in as well. They served sandwiches, cake, ice cream, and punch for the reception. Though its purpose was to celebrate the players, for the women it was also the celebration of another year of employment for their husbands, and a toast to their own successful adjustment to life in the college town where they were now comfortably situated. The 1938 edition of *Kitchen Kapers*, an annual publication of recipes collected from Lexington's Junior League members, included Mary

Nell Hubert's Pin-Gin Punch (the nonalcoholic version), Alice Laslie's Scandinavian Cookie recipe, and Coach Elmore's wife's recipe for Scotch Shortbread, noted to be "excellent when served with tea."[84]

Russ Cohen was added to the coaching staff for the upcoming season and rounded out an illustrious group of coaches. His story is worth mentioning for the enduring connection of friendship that developed among the coaches there during these years. The distinguished Cohen, who with his small, rounded tortoiseshell glasses looked more like a college professor than a football coach, was known as one of the finest scouts in Southern college football as well as a sound and excellent head coach himself. Personally, however, he didn't find the head coach position to his liking. He also was a man known for having impeccable habits. He neither smoked nor drank, and it was said that no one had ever known him to utter a swear word. He was forty-five when he joined Hubert at VMI, making him the senior member of the coaching staff.

Cohen had had an illustrious football-playing career at Vanderbilt. He was the captain of the team in 1915 under none other than Wallace Wade. When Wade moved over to Alabama as head coach in 1920, Cohen joined him there as an assistant coach. It was there that Cohen made the acquaintance of then player Pooley Hubert. It was Coach Cohen (along with ever-present Coach Hank Crisp) who personally worked with Hubert to help him achieve his All-American ranking. It was also there that Cohen and Hubert began their life-long friendship.

How he found himself coaching at VMI speaks to the loyalty and friendship between the two men. In October of 1937, when Cohen was in the last season of his three-year contract at the University of Cincinnati, he suddenly and unexpectedly made the decision to resign. His entire varsity squad, which had dwindled to fewer than twenty-five players that season, had met on campus and decided to strike. The players had been plagued with injuries ranging from sprained ankles to pulled muscles, one player leaving school altogether because of repeated injuries.

Many blamed Cohen's rigorous practice schedule and demanding drills. But it was also reported Coach Cohen had little regard for players he felt were not up to the task required. When Cohen learned of the planned strike, he gave them a dire warning: if players didn't show up for practice, he would promptly resign. The players went through with their strike. They didn't show up, and Cohen immediately sent his letter of resignation to the university president. Hubert had never lost touch with Cohen. When he heard of his friend's recent calamity, he offered him a position on the VMI '38 staff as a scout and backfield coach.

L-R: Carney Laslie, Jimmy Walker, Pooley Hubert, scouting a game at University of Virginia, 1939. From VMI.

At the end of the season, the college's athletic council renewed the contract with Hubert for another two years, with one-year contracts for all his assistants. Those four seasons, from 1936 to 1940, put VMI football back on track and Hubert and his staff were credited with not only raising the level of respect for their program around the state and conference but across the nation. Molding a top-notch football team at a military is not an easy task. Cadets have their time strictly appointed for study, meals, classes, drilling, and sleep. Coaches must adhere to the given time allotted for practice. There is no ability to call for extra practices and game prep meetings as is often the case in non-military programs. The VMI coaches were also noted to have trained the athletes with an emphasis on fair play and sportsmanship, which was always of the highest priority with these men.

Cohen and Hubert remained at VMI till 1946. Cohen left to join Clemson University's longtime and highly successful head coach Frank Howard, Laslie's former roommate at Alabama. He remained at Clemson until retiring a few years later to Waynesboro, Georgia. Hubert went on to coach at the University of Southern Mississippi till 1951, after which he joined Cohen in Georgia, where they collaborated once again—this time buying a peach farm together. They revisited their football glory years one year when they agreed to coach the local high school team, successfully leading the team to a state championship.

Bryant and Cohen stayed connected as well. The Cohens grew peaches and bred dachshunds. It was to the Cohen farm that the Bryants traveled when young Paul Bryant, Jr.'s, beloved dachshund, Fritz, died. "Little Paul," heartbroken after the loss of the family's pet, was able to pick out a new puppy from the Cohens' latest litter. And when Cohen died in 1972, a big man with a houndstooth hat was seen standing at the back of Waynesboro Presbyterian Church in Georgia.

Russ Cohen and his son Russ, Jr. would always remain close to the Laslies due to the familial connection they shared. When Russ, Jr., was looking for employment, Laslie helped him secure a position at his brother-in-law's pharmacy, and drugstore on St. Simons Island in Georgia where Russ, Jr., worked alongside Dr. Williard "Billy" Backus, Alice's brother, as his pharmacy tech for well over thirty years until Dr. Backus's death in 1998.

*Alice and Mary Lou at their beloved
St. Simons Island, Georgia, summer 1940.*

CHAPTER SIXTEEN

University of Maryland's "Terps"

"I'm not your man. Paul Bryant's your man."[85]

—Coach Carney Laslie when offered
the head coach position at Maryland

COLLEGE PARK, MARYLAND
SEPTEMBER 1945–JANUARY 1946

UNIVERSITY FOOTBALL PROGRAMS LANGUISHED during the war years, but in 1945, with the war in Europe ended in May and the end of the war against Japan imminent, universities began to search again for coaches. So did pro football owner, George Marshall, of the Washington Redskins, who approached both Laslie and Bryant with separate offers. Pro football was not as popular as college play, didn't draw the crowds that a college game did, and subsequently was not as profitable. Playing at the colllege level meant more fame and admiration and commanded more press coverage, all the measure of big-time college football at that time. But above all, Bryant and Laslie were more interested in mentoring young men at the collegiate level than they were in managing and directing seasoned, professional athletes.

When the war ended, it was an opportune time to pursue a head coach position at the college level, and Bryant was more determined and confident about his prospects than ever. Though Bryant had been the head coach of the Cloudbusters at the Pre-Flight Training School in Chapel Hill for its upcoming season, the war's end had deprived him of the opportunity to coach a regular season game in that capacity. By his own admission, he was not an experienced coach, a child by coaching standards. A risk that many, including University of Maryland's President, Harry "Curley" Byrd, a former football coach himself, was not at first ready to take.

Instead, Byrd, the indefatigable and enterprising Maryland president, approached Laslie with the offer of the head coach position. But Laslie had another idea, one that he wanted to run by Coach Wallace Wade before he gave Byrd an answer. After arranging a meeting between Wallace and Bryant, Laslie came to his decision. "I'm not your man. Paul Bryant's your man," Laslie told Byrd. Laslie had no doubt Bryant would accept President Byrd's offer and bring Laslie with him to College Park. "How can I reach him?" Byrd asked.

As Bryant related in his autobiography, he was at the annual All-Star Game in Chicago. George Marshall was also in town for the game, and he and Bryant attended the *Chicago Tribune*'s annual press party Thursday night before the game on Saturday. It was at the press party that George Marshall offered him a position with the Washington Redskins as an assistant coach. Bryant turned him down and told him why. "What the hell do you want, a head coaching job?" Marshall demanded.

Bryant gave a brief but emphatic response. "Well, yessir," to which Marshall then instructed Bryant to go to his room. Bryant walked into his hotel room to the sound of the phone ringing. It was President Byrd.

"Are you interested in being my football coach?" Byrd asked. Bryant did not hesitate.

When Bryant reportedly told Laslie he had been offered the position, he added, "I won't go without you." Laslie immediately contacted Frank Moseley, who was still serving in the Atlantic on the USS *Lexington* aircraft carrier. "I'll only take the job if you agree to join us," Laslie wired. At thirty-two years of age, Bryant finally had himself a promising head coach position with Laslie and Moseley as his senior assistants. Bryant never knew what had transpired behind the scenes that culminated in the prearranged timeliness of President Byrd's call.

Once again a group gathered at the Laslies', including Alice and Mary Lou who had joined Carney in Chapel Hill in June, and they listened to the news being broadcast over the red transistor radio: the Japanese had officially surrendered. It was September 2, 1945. WWII had ended. Immediately upon hearing the news, Alice declared, "That's it. We're going home." Home was in Lexington, Virginia, where best friend Edy Gilbert and the known comfort of a small town and good solid friends beckoned. Alice packed up the red radio and other personal items from the small apartment in Chapel Hill, moving back to Lexington into a rented room in a private home— and waited for word when she and Mary Lou could join her husband in Maryland.

Meanwhile, Laslie, Bryant, and Moseley and the rest of the newly formed coaching staff worked night and day to pull a team together for the '45 season of football at the University of Maryland.

Crucial to understanding the controversies which plagued football teams in the coming decade was how to assist the financially challenged athlete, a plight which all three coaches were personally sympathetic to.

How to regulate this among a diverse swath of universities and athletic programs was the job of the National Collegiate Athletic Association, the NCAA.

Prior to the US entering the war, the NCAA (National Collegiate Athletic Association) had risen considerably in influence, its governing body strengthened by a change of attitude associated with the expansion of the role of the federal government in the 1930s. To avoid a possible federal intervention into college sports, the NCAA (formerly, from 1905–1910, known as the the Inter-Collegiate Athletic Association), like many other groups and associations during this time, saw the danger of losing control over their entities if their oversight appeared to be lax. To address this, the NCAA expanded their power by adding a number of additional policies by which to govern their member colleges and universities.

One of the more controversial pieces to the NCAA's newly expanded role was the addition of policies for reprimanding and punishing their members who were out of compliance with their existing regulations. It gave the NCAA room to admonish the now five-year-old Southeastern Conference (SEC), which included Alabama, for what the NCAA viewed as its blatant thumbing of the nose at the association's stance on athletic scholarships. The NCAA's view of any scholarship given to athletes, no matter what their economic need, was "pay for play", and they supported the notion of subsidies and work programs put in place at universities to help financially challenged athletes at their institutions. These were abundant at Eastern and Midwestern universities where the more powerful leadership of the NCAA resided.

However, member schools of the SEC contended that the smaller Southern cities and towns did not have the jobs or the wealthy citizenry to support their players. Because of this, those SEC members viewed the parameters defined by the NCAA as irrelevant to their conference and not policies that could be applied to them in general. They continued to utilize scholarship programs to recruit talented athletes. Particularly at those universities of the Deep South where these traditions were most deeply rooted, they didn't take kindly to rules imposed by schools who had jobs for their own athletes and wealthy alumni to support their players. The NCAA, however, saw it as a move to mock them, raising the ire of its members.

The NCAA finally reached consensus late in 1939. Bylaws were added that defined the criteria to be met for an athlete to be in good standing and eligible to play at the college level: scholarships based on need while the athlete played at their institution, the athlete only receiving aid from their athletic department except in the case of legitimate employment. And, finally, the most important change involved enforcement, which authorized the NCAA to examine the practices of prospective members and, by a vote of two-thirds of the membership, expel offenders."

The hardline taken by the NCAA served to fuel the differences between the North and the South rather than uniting them. As the war progressed, many football programs were suspended across the country. What type of pay disqualified a player from being classified an amateur sportsman in the world of collegiate football was tabled.

Little could this band of coaches—Bryant, Laslie, and Moseley— foresee how this policy, which would be reinstated postwar, would impact them in the future.

The line between what defined an athlete as an amateur or professional was particularly blurred on those teams at military training schools, such as those at the Navy's Pre-Flight Program. The players on these teams were obviously paid, as they were enlisted in the Navy, which by default also was considered a type of scholarship. Despite every program challenged by either a lack of students or a curtailed schedule because of the comings and goings of players called up for service overseas, the sport continued to be popular. Even with all the obstacles, teams found a way to compete during the regular season.

When the war ended in September of '45, the NCAA resumed

where it left off: testing its muscle of oversight and addressing the ongoing tensions between academic elites and athletic football directors and coaches. Big-time football, which defined itself by the "gate receipts and glory" measurement that rose in the late 1920s, was pointed to time and time again by those who found its pursuits distasteful and unaligned with a university's goal for its students: an education.

Coaches, boosters, fans, and players alike continued to fight for the survival of the sport on college campuses. They were aware of what a football experience, big-time or not, could provide a young man's education beyond academics. The availability of scholarships, work programs, and subsidies, they argued, was crucial to their ability to attend college, and to football's survival as a collegiate sport. To eliminate financial assistance meant the game would effectively be played by the wealthy who could afford to attend, a debate that had been resolved nearly a hundred years prior in the sport of rugby in England when the governing body of that sport sided with the poor manufacturing communities in Wales to allow players to be subsidized in order to compete with the wealthy, privileged classes in England, thus catapulting rugby into the mainstream and the world.

When Dean Hobbs addressed the NCAA convention in 1945, he identified both what would be a boon to college football games, but also a bust: "Recruiting, subsidization, athletic scholarships, and the like are sure to be just as prevalent as ever, if not more so. There are hundreds of good athletes in the armed forces who were not in the colleges before the war, but who will be sought after with great vigor when it is."

There were plenty of young men who returned home from the war anxious to get both a college education and to play football. Coaches, too, waited with open arms for those veterans and were eager to afford them that opportunity. These prospective football recruits were, as a group, older players and in most cases physically larger than their non-GI counterparts. Many were in top physical condition due to the rigors of war. The stage was set for conflict between football enthusiasts and those dedicated members of the NCAA who took amateur athletics seriously, believing that the job of the organization was to protect their students and institutions from win-at-all-costs professional coaches and corrupt alumni and associated alumni booster clubs. Not only were football enthusiasts opposed to the NCAA's approach, but so were many university presidents who championed the game's virtues.

Bryant, Laslie, and Moseley began their post-WWII coaching careers with this controversy swirling. The Navy's Pre-Flight football team players were in high demand by college football programs all around the country. Their athletes were the cream of the crop. Bryant and Laslie quickly hand-picked seventeen players and two managers from their existing roster. Coach Bryant, without official authorization from the University of Maryland, brokered a deal with the players. If they chose Maryland, Bryant promised all seventeen GIs full scholarships. Combined with what they qualified for under the GI Bill, that meant extra spending money in their pockets. According to Bryant's autobiography, there was immediate talk once they arrived at College Park that the players would be declared ineligible by the NCAA. Bryant took it up right away with President Byrd, who told Bryant not to worry. "I make the rules here," Byrd, a former football coach, reportedly told him.

Byrd's influence was undeniable. His reach was extensive not only into the politics of the sport but into the regulatory arm of the NCAA. Bryant had no worries and was grateful to be aligned with someone so powerful within the sport. What he couldn't foresee was that Byrd's attitude extended to a legion of other areas, which would soon not bode well for the ambitious Bryant. But at this stage, there was only excitement and confidence in what he and his stellar group of coaches could bring to the university. They were poised to bring winning back to the Terps in historic fashion.

Just in time for their first game of the '45 season, the group of ex-servicemen from Chapel Hill joined what remained of the Maryland football lettermen from the previous year at College Park. The Terps kicked off the season with a crushing victory over Guilford College, 60–6. Despite having the home field advantage against a notably overall weaker football program, the opening game was seen to be a great victory, showcasing the team's potential and the skills of the new head coach.

The task of the coaches physically relocating their families to College Park was a hurdle yet to be crossed.

CHAPTER SEVENTEEN

Dashed Dreams

"A lot of us wanted to go with him," Bonk said. "We had a team meeting, and he told us what had happened. He was crying, some players were crying."

—Harry Bonk, Fullback, University of Maryland, 1946

COLLEGE PARK, MARYLAND
LEXINGTON, KENTUCKY
1946

THE NEW JOB AT College Park proved to be a rough start for the coaching staff as they sought to create stability both in the football program and within their individual families. The housing shortage was at crisis proportions across the entire US. There were no homes available to rent in this small, rural college town that the university could offer the coaching staff and their families. The men had to once again be satisfied with living apart from their loved ones for what they hoped would only be a few more months.

Bryant's wife, Mary Harmon Bryant, and their daughter Mae Martin Bryant, stayed in Birmingham with Mary Harmon's parents while university officials worked hard to find a house suitable for their new head coach. During this time, Alice and Mary Lou lived with their friends the Millers, who also had a daughter the same age as Mary Lou, named Mary Anne. By this time, Alice and the recently widowed Edy Gilbert had become inseparable. Though it had only been a short time since George Gilbert's death, Alice had already been dropping hints to Edy about Carney's bachelor friend and fellow coach in College Park, Frank Moseley. Edy and Frank would eventually meet but not under the circumstances Alice had hoped.

Frank Moseley arrived in College Park in mid-October, direct from his twenty-four-month tour of duty aboard the *Lexington*. He and Carney were to share a dorm-sized room in an old, abandoned building on campus until something more acceptable could be found. It wasn't much of a change for Frank, who had spent the last two years on a carrier, sleeping in a hammock, one of many slung row upon row in the cavernous bowels of a ship, where every shred of luxury had been removed. That they were the best of friends made it more tolerable. That the two men were rarely there except to sleep also helped. They, along with Bryant, worked night and day. They had high hopes the state of their housing would soon improve.

All the coaches held out for the promise made by President Byrd that he was doing everything in his power to find appropriate housing for them. Everyone was struggling through the shortage, anxious to be together again with their families. But it was only due to the strength of their friendship, the passion for their work, and the promise of a future that enabled them to concede to the conditions with a polite tolerance. This, though, had its limits.

Not long after Frank's arrival at Maryland, Alice Laslie, in the early stages of pregnancy, was rushed to the hospital for emergency surgery. Carney learned of her medical crisis in the middle of a home football game. At the sound of the game-ending whistle, he jumped in his car and, with Frank at his side to help keep him calm, drove frantically to Lexington. Edy, who had never left Alice's bedside, was there when Carney and Frank arrived late that evening.

With Alice resting for the night, the three left the hospital in search of a meal. Though Frank and Edy had never formally met, Frank was no stranger to Edy. She had heard Frank's name bantered about many times over the years. It was only in recent months that the Laslies had hoped to introduce their two closest friends, Frank, the confirmed bachelor, and Edy, the war widow, who they thought would be a good match.

That night over a late dinner, Frank and Edy helped Carney process the news the Laslies had received—that Alice would not be able to have any more children, and commiserated into the wee hours of the morning. One drink turned into two, then three and four. Noting the lateness of the hour, and that they were in no condition to find their way back into town, Edy offered the exhausted, well-watered men the guest room at her family's farm a short drive away. She was apologetic about the accommodations as there was only the one spare bedroom, which consisted of a bed with a three-quarter-sized double mattress. The men assured her they were grateful for a soft bed to collapse into, telling her not to worry. They had been sharing a room for a month and sharing a bed wasn't that much of a stretch.

The next morning, while the two men slowly awakened to their surroundings, Frank, disoriented, turned to Carney, asking, "Where the heck are we?"

"We're at Edy's farm," Carney said groggily.

"Who the hell is 'Edy'?!" Frank replied.

On December 1, 1945, the Terps played their last game of the season, ending in a "height of glory" with two intercepted passes resulting in touchdowns, a final score of 19–13 against the University of South Carolina. The result: a winning record of six wins and three losses. Everyone had high hopes for their future there.

Despite the professional success, living apart from his young daughter and wife began to take a measurable toll on Coach Laslie. The drive from Lexington and back to College Park to the "little cubby hole in a deserted building on the outskirts of campus" was so depressing even the long hours of work weren't helping.

When President Byrd was finally able to offer a house to Bryant, he passed on it, offering it instead to newlyweds Ken Whitlow, the younger of the assistant coaches, and his wife Cotton to rent. It was a kind offer, and the Whitlows gladly accepted it. When Mary Harmon came for a visit, the Whitlows invited them over for dinner at their new home. It was a cold November evening, and the four huddled around the coal stove where a dinner of hot dogs and beans was cooking. Bundled up in their overcoats, boots, earmuffs, and hats, Bryant described it as being the coldest place he'd ever been. "We were more interested in the stove than the food," he recalled in his autobiography.

Time went on and still no homes became available for the three coaches. Bryant never regretted his decision to pass on the house.

Finally, the waiting was over. At the team's annual sports banquet, President Byrd made an unexpected announcement. From the podium he called on Bump Watkins, a well-known building contractor and Maryland alumnus who was in the audience, to build the "Bryants one of the finest homes in College Park. Over by the chemistry building." Bryant didn't have any idea where the chemistry building was, but the rest sounded just fine to him. The season ended on a high note with hopes for the program, their careers, and a brighter future for them all.

Plans to spend the holidays in Lexington with Alice and Mary Lou couldn't come soon enough for Carney. Extending an invitation to Frank, he joined the family for the Christmas and New Year holiday.

In his first letter to Edy written not long after his visit, Frank wrote how anxious he was to have another opportunity to be with the woman he described as being "serious minded, thoughtful, and independent," telling her he planned to "break through" her protective shell. In his second letter to her dated four days later, he wrote to say she should "feel pretty good about [him]" as it is "the first time in many a moon that I have written to the same person twice within any one ten-day period." Further on in the letter, he laments that though it seems he "made a rather favorable impression" on everyone else, he wasn't sure whether he made one on her at all. And she was the only one he had really tried to impress.

Their friendship, however, quickly blossomed. With Edy living in Lexington and Frank in College Park, he shed his "man of few words" persona and took up pen and paper. Daily he wrote, expressing his devotion and longing for the day when they could spend more time together.

Bryant spent his time during the Christmas break with his wife and daughter in Birmingham, but not before he had secured a home to rent in College Park while waiting for the large home President Byrd had promised to build him.

Laslie and Moseley were not so confident in the promises made by Byrd. They appeared to be no closer to better living arrangements. Much of their time over the holidays was spent crafting an alternative plan to deal with their abysmal and unacceptable living quarters. They conspired on a plan B to put into play if things didn't improve as promised. Plan B involved the University of Kentucky, where Frank had spent his coaching years after leaving the University of Alabama in 1935.

At the end of the war, Kentucky had been actively recruiting for its head football coach position and offered Frank the job. Frank had turned it down to go to Maryland with Bryant. Perhaps, Frank and Carney thought, they were still interested.

There was good reason Kentucky would be anxious to get Moseley back into its fold. Moseley had a long history with Kentucky dating back to his senior year at Alabama. With the football, baseball, and basketball seasons behind him (he played all three sports) and graduation looming in '34, "Chesty" Moseley, as he was known then, was approached by the University of Kentucky, which had identified the not-yet-graduated physical education major as the man to help develop UK's languishing baseball and football programs. The university needed a strong, no-nonsense leader who could help foster the development of players and organize the programs of both sports. With Kentucky guaranteeing Moseley a diploma, it was enough to lure the well-regarded and confident Frank O. Moseley onto its staff of coaches. He departed Alabama after the last game in '33, and received his diploma from Kentucky in June of 1935, signed by newly elected Albert Benjamin "Happy" Chandler, the governor of Kentucky and a University of Kentucky alum.

Moseley also was able to pursue his baseball dreams during that time—though for 1936 only—on the semi-pro team known as the Kitty League (short for Kentucky-Illinois-Tennessee). Moseley's stats were respectable, but not enough for a viable career option as a baseball player. He maintained his role at Kentucky, coaching both baseball and football during that time, and remained at Kentucky until the outbreak of the war.

When Moseley arrived at Kentucky in the spring of 1935, he quickly became an invaluable addition to the athletic program which remained short-staffed until 1936, when Thomas "Kitty" Gorman, former freshman football coach at Notre Dame, joined the coaching staff. The addition allowed Moseley, whose other nickname "Bully" came from his skills in the boxing ring, to take over the boxing team at Kentucky that same year. He had a profound love of the game and is attributed to his tireless effort to raise the status of the sport at Kentucky, which succeeded when boxing came into its own as a major sport at the university in 1939. By all accounts, he conducted boxing under the highest of ideals. He saw the sport as a means of developing mental and physical skills in those youngsters who enjoyed the fighting ring. He was not a fan of boxing as a career, and never encouraged his boys to seek a professional path. On the contrary. He discouraged it.

Boxing had a long history—since 1894—of using film to study for an upcoming match, the first sport to do so. It is likely that this tool was also being used during this time at Kentucky. It may have been the catalyst for Moseley's implementation of the use of football game film in his high school football recruiting programs. Moseley's commentary of football game film was always a popular draw when he spoke to audiences, particularly at Kentucky high schools when speaking to scholastic football stars, a successful recruiting tool during those years prior to World War II.

University of Kentucky coaching staff, 1938. L-R, Frank Moseley, Bernie Shively, Ab Kirwan. Used with permission. University of Kentucky, University of Kentucky general photographic prints.

It was at these events when he would tell his audience of All-Star players, coaches, and luminaries of the sport that the half dozen or more colleges and universities in the state, including the University of Kentucky, was equal to any in America. "Boys who pass up our schools for what appear to them to be attractive offers elsewhere learn too late that the sunshine of recognition is brightest near at home, and a name made at home means a name established for life. I don't say go to UK, I say go where your heart dictates, but stay in Kentucky."[86] His feelings about this would never change, a difference of opinion that at times put him at odds with Bryant.

Laslie and Moseley returned to College Park on January 2, 1946, and despite the success of their first season, the relationship between the assistant coaches and President Byrd was even more strained as Byrd's promises to make their housing issues one of his top priorities fell flat. One of Frank's letters to Edy included his thoughts on their situation: "I think the man [a.k.a. President Byrd] that Carney and myself were planning to have the big fight with in regards to real estate must have gotten word that we were on the way because he pulled up and shoved off for Florida early this morning. We are planning to look elsewhere." Plan B was set in motion. Unknown to Bryant, they began to consider their options.

Bryant understood his assistants didn't have adequate housing and were not happy about it. He was sympathetic to their plight, though he also understood much of it was out of his control. But added to the housing issue for his senior coaches were other reasons that Maryland had become a problem for Bryant.

President Byrd's reputation for stirring up controversy was well known. He and Bryant had already butted heads earlier in the season. In one instance, Bryant had fired a star player who Byrd then, without Bryant's knowledge or permission, reinstated. Bryant, who had been on the road on a recruiting trip, was unaware of the development. Laslie had been contacted by Byrd with his decision and, knowing there would be hell to pay, waited on the athletic building steps for Bryant, ensuring he was the first person to break the news to him when he returned.

When Bryant pulled up and saw Laslie sitting there, he knew something was wrong. "It's not good," Laslie said as Bryant stepped out of his car. Curley Byrd, he continued, had reinstated the fired player. Summing up an explanation for the move, he did so using five words: "His daddy," he drawled, "is a politician." Bryant was incensed.

A second crossing of the proverbial line occurred not long after. It was Byrd's unauthorized and unilateral decision to fire one of Bryant's own coaching assistants, Herman Ball, which he also did without Bryant's knowledge. It cemented the message to Bryant from President Byrd: he would always have the last word in Terp Country. But it was the housing problem for his assistant coaches, still no closer to being resolved after three months of promises, that made the situation immediately and hopelessly untenable. After the separations from family suffered through the war, it was hardly what they all envisioned the next chapter of their lives would look like.

With the unannounced departure of the man (a.k.a. Curley Byrd) to Florida solidifying their suspicions that housing wasn't a priority for the assistant coaches, Frank placed a call to the University of Kentucky. Kentucky, still on a hunt for a new football coach, was thrilled to hear from their pre-war coach.

Over the years, their program had yielded little stability, with twenty-four different coaches over fifty-three years. Their current search had produced no takers. Several well-known coaches had been offered the job, but each demanded, among other things, a ten-year contract, a condition Kentucky was not willing to provide. When Moseley contacted President Herman Donovan, he was immediately offered the position once again. However, Moseley wasted no words. "I'm not your man," he told Donovan. "Paul Bryant's your man."

Up to this time, Kentucky had never considered anyone as young as Bryant. With an endorsement by Moseley attesting to Bryant's coaching abilities, Moseley also made assurances to Donovan that despite his age and lack of overall experience, Bryant's chances of being "successful at Kentucky [were] extremely high." Both he and Laslie had, Moseley told him, the utmost confidence in the young, charismatic, talented coach. With that ringing endorsement, Donovan immediately sent a telegram to Bryant: "IF YOU WANT TO BE HEAD COACH AT KENTUCKY CALL ME COLLECT. DR HERMAN DONOVAN, PRESIDENT."

According to Bryant's autobiography, the telegram languished on his desk for four days. Whether Bryant ever did learn about the conversation Frank had with President Donovan is not known. But the public record, including his account in his autobiography, was that he could only wonder at how Kentucky got his name at such an opportune time.

His senior assistants, confident as they were Bryant would accept Donovan's offer, knew that if Bryant failed to negotiate a contract to his liking at Kentucky, and opted to stay at Maryland, he would do so without them, and they would go to Kentucky without him.

On Friday night, January 11, Bryant arrived in Lexington, and between midnight and one o'clock in the morning on Saturday, he signed a five-year contract for himself, negotiated a three-year contract for each of his three assistants, and made an unprecedented request for a fourth assistant whom he stipulated would be of his own choosing.

At that moment, he became one of the youngest head coaches at a major university in the country. Whisked out of town early Saturday, he was taken to Winchester, Kentucky, to pose for press photographs under the name of "Mr. Lawrence," after which he was taken to the train station to make the return to Maryland. The University of Kentucky Board of Trustees was sworn to secrecy until such time that Bryant officially resigned from Maryland. More importantly, Bryant wanted to gather his players together to inform them of his plans and say goodbye.

For all of their boasting to colleagues and the excitement about the unparalleled talent of the three Alabama football stars who, under his leadership, would propel Maryland to the top, in the end, it all came crashing down in quick fashion. Despite being relieved that they now had a viable situation to move on to, they were all devastated at the bitter turn of events. Bryant privately shed many tears upon resigning. His hopes for a beautiful home for his family were shattered, a crushing personal blow and disappointing end to his first job as a head coach.

On Monday, January 14, Bryant and President Byrd met in the president's office where he announced the news that he had accepted the head coach position at Kentucky, and he would be taking his entire staff with him. Lexington, he told Byrd, was a place he felt was more suitable overall for his family. What resulted was a shouting match behind closed doors that lasted by some accounts almost two hours.

Frank wrote to Edy the night the bombshell news of their departure hit the papers. "I suppose Art Lewis [head coach at Washington and Lee] and Pooley were quite surprised to learn about that 'great' coaching staff moving to Kentucky. I would like to have seen them both when they read about it," Frank wrote.

Depending on which paper you read, it was reported as a resignation by Bryant or a firing by Byrd. After the news spread across campus, students gathered to protest Bryant's leaving and what they deemed to be an unfair bullying of their new coach who had brought winning back to their floundering football program. The unprecedented protests outside of the president's house, with angry students shouting slogans and carrying signs berating President Byrd, was an absolute embarrassment to all the coaches.

The coaches' departure was swift. In the early morning hours of Friday, January 18, the same day the university's newspaper reported Bryant's resignation and the student protests, Frank Moseley left College Park for good. Carney Laslie departed later that same day, locking the door to the little cubby of a room for the last time, closing the door for good on a chapter with a sorry ending to what they had hoped would be a long run together at Maryland showcasing their talent.

In contrast to their somber departure, when Bryant had arrived in Kentucky the day before, he was welcomed in a ceremony held outside the alumni gym surrounded by celebrating Kentucky football cheerleaders, fraternity brothers from chapters holding welcome placards, and the university band. They were joined by a swarm of students and faculty and a large contingent of reporters. The students presented the newly hired football coach with a token of good luck: a cardboard horseshoe which they draped around his neck. With the "hoss shoe around his neck," Bryant addressed the students specifically, referring to them as "his employers," and promised he would serve them faithfully and loyally. He further pledged to keep "horse collars" [a term for zeros] from following the University of Kentucky's name on scoreboards.

Fans and reporters were fascinated by their new coach, and the curiosity around his nickname, "Bear," prompted numerous questions as to its originations. Larry Shropshire interviewed the new coach privately for the *Lexington Herald-Leader* the day after it was announced that Bryant was Kentucky's new coach. After much pleading and acknowledging the new coach's reluctance to answer the question in public and that sharing it would put those questions to rest, he persuaded Bryant to tell his story. In order to preserve the narrative in its purest form, Shropshire made the noble attempt to capture the yarn just exactly how it was related, leaving the Arkansas drawl, with its Deep-South mellowness, to one's imagination:

> Ah was 12 yea's old when ah got it, still in jun-yah high school. One time ah went intuh town-ah was livin' in tha country near Fo'dyce, Ahkansah—and they was havin' some kinda little ole show at the movie house.

One of tha acts had a fella with a bea-ah, and they was offerin' a dollah a minute for anybody who'd wrestle with the bea-ah. Ah'd plowed a lot of times for 50 cents a day, and it sounded like big money. And then the otha kids kina egged me on, so ah went up on the stage.

It was a putty big bea-ah, but he had on a muzzle. He was standin' up on his hine laigs, so as soon as ah got up the-ah ah charged him. We went down on the floor and rolled over a time ah two and then he got up agin. Ah thought you got paid only if you wrestled him, so ah charged him again—ah was 'bout as big then as ah am now. We hit the flo-ah agin, putty haad, and rolled ovah some moah, but finally he got loose and stodd up agin.

Ah got up, too, and sta'ted to charge him agin, but ah felt omethin' kinda wa-am on the side of mah face. Ah rubbed mah hand ovah mah face, then looked at it , and it was covered with blood.

Then ah took a good look at the bea-ah, and that muzzle had pulled 'way round to the side, cle-ah off his snout. Right then ah took off from the-ah—(swishing sound)—just like that.

But better than the story itself, wrote Shropshire, is the sequel. It goes like this:

'Sa funn thing, and yah probably won't believe it, but yea's later, when ah was at Alabamuh, ah went ovah one day to a little town, Fayette, Alabamuh, with Don Hutson. That was the home town of Hutson's wife. They were havin' some kin uv a show the-ah—and theah was that same man—and that same bea-ah.

Ah wanted to go up to 'im—the man, not the bea-ah—and ask 'im for mah money. Yah know, ah left the-ah so fast that day ah never did collect a thing for wrestling with that bea-ah.

The publication of the humerous, down-home tale quickly endeared the new coach to the university community, kicking off a new chapter for both the ambitious coach and the Kentucky Wildcat football team.

PART IV

A DREAM TEAM OF COACHES

UNIVERSITY OF KENTUCKY "WILDCATS"
LEXINGTON, KENTUCKY
1946–1952

L-R Laslie, Bryant, Moseley, January 1946.

CHAPTER EIGHTEEN

Highways and Byways

"Carney should be on his way there by now. He was going from Orange, Virginia, then to Richmond and from there to Lexington, Virginia, that is, if he didn't change his mind after he got started, but he will come through there before leaving for Lexington, Kentucky."

—Frank Moseley to Edy Alphin Gilbert, January 19, 1946

UNIVERSITY OF KENTUCKY
LEXINGTON, KENTUCKY
1946–1948

THE PUBLICITY FROM STUDENT protests and Bryant's very public departure from Maryland was nothing short of humiliating to the three coaches. They had begun their careers at Maryland characterizing themselves as a "cracker-jack"[87] coaching trio, and they hadn't been quiet about it, boasting as much among their peers. Now they wondered what their friends and coaching colleagues would say when they read about the debacle in the press.

Reports of Bryant being fired and the angry student protests that followed reached the newspapers in Kentucky. The UK Board of Trustees rushed to shape a narrative to ward off any criticism of the university's decision to hire the young coach. Press releases went out quickly and were published alongside articles that gave Curley Byrd's version of Bryant's departure. One University of Kentucky trustee was quoted as saying in Kentucky's *Alumni* magazine, "They're coming in to go to work the last of this week January 12—but they're already at work, rounding up material. And they're already on the payroll!"[88] It was a done deal and the university leadership wanted everyone, including the coaches, to know it.

L-R Frank Moseley, Paul Bryant, January 23, 1946, Kentucky Hires Bear Bryant. © The Courier-Journal—USA TODAY NETWORK

They also wanted to highlight their great feat in snaring Bryant for the head coach position. Here was a coach, they argued, who was clearly going places. He was a coach who could produce results. He had turned Maryland around from its lone victory the previous season to an impressive 6–2–1 record the next.

Kentucky had long floundered as a member of the SEC. To boost Bryant's credibility, they pointed to rumors that swirled around Bryant being on Alabama's short list for the approaching vacancy when the Crimson Tide's own head coach, Frank Thomas, would retire. Historically, Alabama had a strong program and was a long-time rival of Kentucky. When Kentucky beat them to the hiring punch, it was billed as a victory over their opponent—a virtual coup of sorts. The university publicity machine publicized Bryant's legendary Rose Bowl appearance in '35 when it was said not even his broken leg kept him off the field. Not only that, they boasted, but Bryant was bringing with him two other former star Alabama players as his top assistants.

In his first public interview in Kentucky, Bryant was asked by Kentucky reporters if he thought the Wildcats could beat the Crimson Tide. Bryant declared without hesitation that it was part of his intent to bring Kentucky into the top tier of teams in five years, which meant, of course, beating his alma mater, Alabama. Later he regretted his five-year plan, saying he wished he had been more aggressive in his goals. But his cautious tone is understandable. The coaches were still licking their wounds after their departure from Maryland.

Moseley had meticulously plotted his route from College Park to Lexington, Kentucky. He planned to arrive in Ohio in a couple of days, and arrived at Beaver Falls, Pennsylvania, his first stop, at 8:30 p.m. that first night. The 285-mile drive had taken over twelve hours, which included four stops. It was to be a foreshadowing of what the next several months of recruiting would look like for the coaches as they began the difficult task of starting over. "I have never felt quite as low, lonesome and blue," Frank wrote Edy upon checking in at the General Brodhead Hotel in Beaver Falls.

The next morning, he drove straight to Youngstown, Ohio, where "No Occupancy" lights flashed on each hotel and motel he drove by. He was bone tired. Without a reservation made ahead of time, it looked more than bleak, adding to his overall sense of defeat. Finally, in what seemed to be a stroke of luck, he came upon a vacancy at a hotel, where there was only one room left. A room without a bath. He tried to make the best of it in his letter to Edy that night: "I suppose it won't hurt a body too much to go without 'washing' for one day, although this is Saturday," he wrote.

With heavy snowfall predicted and the distinct possibility of getting stranded, Frank decided to leave Youngstown earlier than planned, arriving in Lexington, Kentucky, a full day ahead of schedule. In his next letter to Edy, he bemoaned the fact that he was the first of the three to get there. He was exhausted, lonely, and lovesick. He checked in at The Kentuckian Hotel, stopping at the hotel bar for a couple of drinks before turning in at 11 p.m. Sitting at the small desk in his room, he pulled out the seven-by-ten souvenior note paper, the name of the hotel pre-printed at the top of the page. He carried out this routine throughout the next year, writing each night from his hotel room, the name and insignia on the paper indicating his location for that evening. "Please pardon this short letter but it's getting pretty late and too I think I am doing exceptionally well," he wrote, alluding to having had too much to drink. He ends the letter as he does most all of them: "I miss you very, very much and want to see you so badly, Love, 'Chesty.'"

Hard work for all three loomed. The race was on to beat out other scouts from more established football programs in search of promising talent from high schools for the next season. Carney Laslie's scouting itinerary while en route to Kentucky was to drive into the small towns of Washington and Orange in Virginia, and then on to Richmond before he finally turned toward the western part of the state, where all roads led through Lexington, Virginia, to see Alice and Mary Lou. "He may change his mind after he gets started," wrote Frank to Edy, alluding to the ever-changing schedule that plagued such trips, "but he will come through there before leaving for Lexington, Kentucky." Paul Bryant, too, was on the road trying to coordinate best they could. "If when Carney gets to Lexington, Virginia . . . he hasn't called Bryant, please tell him to do so as there are a couple of boys Carney is supposed to see in West Virginia on his way down," Frank wrote.

Housing worries continued, although the prospects were much brighter than in College Park, Maryland. Once the news became official that the Wildcats had hired Bryant, President Donovan set about to make sure there was a house for their new head football coach, an obvious stipulation of the contract. He got the word out to boosters and alumni alike and immediately had eighteen to twenty offers from various members of the community. When Bryant arrived at his new job a week after leaving Maryland, he not only had a home to rent but one that was furnished as well, provided by a Mrs. Lowry Dean of Jessamine County located on Hart Road in Lexington. It was not the "finest house" in Lexington as was promised by Curley Byrd at College Park, but as far as Paul Bryant was concerned, it might as well be. Instead of a home located on campus next to academic buildings, it was in a neighborhood perfect for a family with two children. The Bryants' daughter, Mae Martin, was then nine, and Paul, Jr., was one year old.

"I certainly hope that we can find Alice [Laslie] a house right away, then you can come down and help her move," Frank wrote Edy as soon as he heard the news.

The new coaches embarked immediately to recruit football players. The University of Kentucky was widely known for its basketball program, led by the legendary and colorful Adolph Rupp, which easily captured the state's top athletic talent. Boys from the state who wanted to play football chose to go to rival schools in neighboring states for the chance to play in well-regarded, winning programs like the ones at the state universities in Tennessee or West Virginia. But change was coming. They all—from the coaches to the board of trustees—began in earnest to build a football program that would find a slot beside the firmly entrenched basketball culture. They planned to turn the tide for the Kentucky Wildcats in just three years.

Like miners panning for gold in the mineral-rich streams and mountains of the pristine wilderness of the West, the coaches went in search of their own brand of Mother Lode: a young man with potential. Indiana had strong prospects, as did Virginia and Pennsylvania. Straddling the Mason-Dixon Line, West Virginia, the most northern of the Southern states and most southern of the Northern states, looked to be fertile ground for their efforts as well. Venturing into areas off back roads and byways into impoverished towns and communities, they sought to capitalize on an untapped pool of prospective high school players.

It wasn't long before Coach Laslie's reputation for luring top athletes to Kentucky preceded him. He made his mark notably in West Virginia, where he combed the hills of Appalacia and the Alleghany's for the finest talent in the state. One year he plucked nine prize prospects from the Mountain State, including future All-American Bob Gain.

Tony Constantine, columnist for the *Morgantown Post*, wrote of Laslie's recruiting prowess describing him as having a warm and amiable countenance that, combined with a "syrupy drawl born and sweetened in his native Alabama," likened him to a pied piper when talking to boys who had the desire to play football. When WVU coach Art Lewis took over in 1950, he staked off his state against what he characterized as the annual pillaging of talent from the South, a not-so-subtle allusion to Laslie's efforts there. Laslie confessed that the "hunting wasn't so good after that," though Constantine wrote that Laslie was reluctant to attribute it to the greater charm of the Mountaineer coach. Laslie, a born competitor, was not one to be outdone by the West Virginia coach, as was evidenced after one particularly stinging loss of a recruit suffered at the hands of Lewis.

Following the North-South game played in Charleston, West Virginia, Laslie went to have a conversation with a brilliant young player he thought was all set to go to Kentucky. When Laslie got to the boy's hotel room where the meeting was to be held, Lewis was already there doing the talking. Laslie vowed, "he would be back to whip Lewis right on his own doorstep."

True to his word, Laslie would go on to swoop in and recruit

Lewis's own son right out from under his father's nose to play football for him. The joke, however, was on the reporter who may or may not have known the long friendship that existed between Lewis and Laslie dating back to their days in Lexington, Virginia, where Lewis was the head coach at Washington and Lee. Who knows what kind of back door deal these two had made, one recruit for another? In all probability, "The Silver Fox", an affectionate nickname given to Laslie, had pulled the wool over this reporter's eyes.

The sophisticated interstate highway system we know today did not exist, and aggressive scouting meant coaches drove for days on end, abandoning main thoroughfares, traveling narrow two-lane roads that led to dirt roads that eventually ended in tiny mining towns. On one scouting trip Frank reported in his letters to Edy that to get to the high school athletic field in Uniontown, Pennsylvania, he had to leave his car on the shoulder of the highway and walk three miles down a road too muddy to drive on. On another trip, he drove 382 miles "in exactly nine and a half hours," equaling a slow pace of forty miles per hour. The coaches sought not only a talented athlete but one with heart and grit as well; the combination of those traits was deemed most likely to ensure success. Life in the coal camps of Appalachia was never easy and guaranteed they'd find boys who had "grit." Streets in those camp communities were most often unpaved with no sidewalks. In these towns, catching the eye of a college football coach recruiter was a young man's dream. For some, it was their only ticket out.

Years later, it was often Coach Laslie who shepherded freshman recruits personally through the process of orientation at Kentucky. He described how many of these coal mine camp boys showed up to their first day on campus barefooted, the athletic department's official athletic shoes issued to recruited players often the first pair of shoes they owned that fit. For some, it was the first pair of shoes they had ever been able to call their own.

The process of scouting players was tedious and lonely despite what at first glance passed as a fun-filled, socially exciting life. Coaches attended party after party while on the road. Away from their families and loved ones, scouts and coaches were many times recruiting on their own or with one of their colleagues. They attended high school game after high school game, spending time with booster club members, high school coaches, and other recruiting and scouting agents during days that seem to never end. Evenings were spent talking with boys, their coaches, representatives, and family members. Nights found them back at their hotel with a slew of other recruiting coaches, which meant, Frank wrote, that because they were "naturally all alike," they drank more than he knew Edy would be happy about.

In early March, Frank arrived back in Kentucky late at night after driving 600 miles home from Memphis in one day. He and Carney had spent most of their last few days of scouting/recruiting on the road at a hotel, which Frank described to Edy in his letter that night. The hotel's lounge, the Sky Room, he wrote, was the "finest affair" of good music and fine food that he had enjoyed in a good long while. But it was no cure for his loneliness, he told her. Even with such glamorous distraction, he felt there was not a "thing to do. . . . I have gotten to the point where I'm not very good company for anyone because all I do is think of you. That's the reason I like to be around Carney because I can not only think but talk which is a little help."

By the end of January, the three coaches realized there was little to no organizational structure that existed in the football and baseball programs at Kentucky, or at least not at the level they wanted. Moseley, charged with building the infrastructure during these early weeks, worked night and day. He met with administrators, athletic department officials, and community leaders. He met with players individually, coached, and then made guest appearances on radio broadcasts in the evenings to spotlight the progress made on rebuilding the football program. These and other concerted PR efforts were orchestrated to bring football back into the good graces of sports fans in a state that had always had a love affair with basketball.

Moseley, whose affinity for baseball was well known, also began work with the existing baseball coaching staff and players in between his football development responsibilities. The practice season was already underway when they arrived at Kentucky, the first game being scheduled at the end of April, which gave him a couple of months to try to recruit additional players to the team roster. He expressed how hopelessly inadequate he felt during this time in his letters to Edy, telling her, "There is not much in place here and I'm not sure how I will ever get it done."

In a rare candid photograph taken in 1946 (see below), Coaches Paul "Bear" Bryant and Coach Carney Laslie are standing, their eyes locked on some action taking place downfield. Both sport a white dress shirt, coat, and tie. Bryant's tie is tightened at the collar. Laslie's is loosened. It hints at some personality differences: Laslie was a bit more comfortable in his own skin; Bryant was disciplined, demanding, young in his role. Bryant was described then in some newspaper accounts as a thirty-two-year-old handsome hunk of man. Laslie, at thirty-five, had a thick head of silvery white hair, giving him an older, mature appearance. Offsetting the "inexperienced" label that Bryant carried by virtue of being the youngest head coach in college football, reporters described him as being "dynamic and bursting with energy," oozing both humility and egotism, a hard combination to embody but one that resulted in a charisma that was undeniable. As Coach Gene Stallings wrote in his foreword in *Building a Championship Football Team*, Bryant was a man who evoked strong emotions from both his detractors as well as fans, either unapologetically despised or unconditionally loved. Whichever side one landed on, he wrote, it couldn't be denied that he knew how to coach young men.

Like Bryant and Laslie, Moseley was prone to mumble, which, combined with their strong Southern accents, made them sometimes difficult to understand. One writer noted, "[I]f you did not know him [Moseley], you might well conclude he was a fractious, irritable individual with a poor opinion of the whole human race."[89] But those who knew him attested to his warm and generous spirit.

From left to right the coaches: seated Frank Moseley, Paul Bryant, and in far-right corner, Carney Laslie. © The Courier-Journal—USA TODAY NETWORK

They were on a mission, these three, to prove their mettle and to redeem themselves from the turn of events at Maryland. They were determined to succeed. Not only was their mission born of personal drive and ambition, but it was also what put food on the table. Families across the country had many challenges of re-acclimating to post-war life, as did the collegiate sports programs around the country. And football families had their own unique brand of challenges.

CHAPTER NINETEEN

Growing Pains

"Are you gonna marry this boy or not?" he asked. "Cause if you are, June's the only time anybody in football can get married."

—Paul Bryant to Edy Gilbert, March 1946

LEXINGTON, KENTUCKY
1946

FAMILIES TRIED DESPERATELY TO stay connected and normalize family life after the trauma and separation of World War II. It was a challenge to stay in touch with family and friends while on the road. Letter-writing continued to be the most popular and reliable mode of communication, and Frank wrote Edy daily. There were times, though, when a letter wouldn't do, when the voice of a loved one was the only balm for the lovesick or lonely. Telephone service during those years was unpredictable and always overcrowded the use of a shared phone line, known as a "party line."

A party line was a local telephone loop circuit shared by more than one subscriber. Anyone on the loop could pick up their telephone and listen in to whatever conversation might be in process at the time and no one would be the wiser that their privacy had been breached. This could serve more than just personal entertainment as evidenced when the University of Tennessee football coaches in 1942 discovered the inadvertent wiring of a telephone on the Ole Miss team bench went to their same party line used during the game. When nothing but a phone call would do, the coaches, like everyone else, had no choice but to endure the unreliability of the telephone system and with it the listening ear of the competition who would be none the wiser of the breach.

Some cities had better service than others. But not in Memphis where Frank Moseley and Paul Bryant routinely made a pit stop prior to their final destination to place a call to home. Frank complained bitterly to Edy in his letters how difficult it was to get a call through from there, sometimes waiting several hours before they were successful. Carney and Frank became used to making calls to Lexington, Virginia, from the Bryant home phone in Lexington, Kentucky. During one such call, Edy kept exhorting Frank to cut down on his drinking. One can imagine a sheepish-sounding Frank telling her it was an easy indulgence when the "womenfolk [weren't] around"[90] and the men were on their own. Later, when he finally got off the road and was back home in Kentucky for a couple weeks to host visiting boys who were checking out the football program, he was able to write to Edy that "this clean living is really great stuff. . . . I sure have felt good for the past couple weeks and have had only two or three little drinks."

The travel started to take its toll on Carney. In mid-March, two months into their new job, while Frank was in Tennessee, Paul in Alabama to scout talent, and Carney off to Louisville for the three-day state high school basketball meet, Frank wrote of Carney, "If that guy doesn't hurry and get back together with Alice and Mary Lou I really think he will go crazy." Later, back in Lexington, Kentucky, they planned for a time when the "girls" could come for a visit. With both temporarily living at Kentucky's Hotel Lexington, it wasn't the best arrangement. After the years spent overseas on a submarine and in cramped military housing, coupled with months of sharing a dorm room at Maryland, they were both anxious to find a place they could really call home. Housing inventory remained low, and often when a place came on the market, it was quickly snatched up. They remained hopeful, however.

By late March, with Paul still away scouting in the South, Carney was due to leave for Pennsylvania. Before he left town, however, he had heard about a duplex for sale. Not having had time to see it for himself, Carney asked Frank, who had stayed behind in Lexington, to take a look at the property. With a new quarter beginning in a week, it was a jam-packed time as Frank hosted boys coming and going—about forty in all—who had an interest in joining the Wildcats. But in between he found time to preview the building, which had two large apartments, one up and one down, each with a living room, dining room, two large and one small bedrooms, kitchen, and bath, both in fairly good condition. The idea was to go in on it together, the Laslie family in one apartment, Frank, still the bachelor, in the other. They agreed the two separate spaces were perfect. One was large enough for the Laslie family, while the other apartment provided just the right amount of space for Frank, who had an eye toward a future with Edy. They liked everything about it except for the price, though they concluded it was the best they could do.

"It's in an old but good section of town," Frank wrote to Edy. "I may be able to hold the man off until you and Alice get here next week." Even though Edy and Alice were due to arrive in a week, the seven days seemed to both Frank and Carney an unbearably long time to have to wait. Frank's enthusiasm for her to see the apartment caught Edy a bit off guard. She was surprised at her own excitement for the possibility of moving to Lexington to be with Frank but also thought it might be too soon after the death of her husband, a sentiment her family shared.

Her family had other concerns as well. Coaching was a dubious profession in their eyes. They constantly reminded Edy of her often-expressed disdain for such a life during her first years of friendship with the Laslies, back in the earlier days when she and George frequented the coaches' group that gathered around the Laslies' kitchen table. They reminded her of her adamant statement that she would never marry a football coach given what she had observed of the lifestyle— the men gone for long periods of time, a job that was not guaranteed from year to year, depending on a win-loss record that was largely out of their control. Despite this, the family's fondness for the Laslies was evident. Edy's sister, whose nickname was "Bill," knew Carney loved her homemade custard, making him special batches whenever he had the opportunity to come home to Lexington during this time of transition.

Other factors complicated the love affair. Edy's mother had passed away many years prior and her father was dependent on his two daughters. They were closer and protective of each other because of this. Also, it hadn't been too long ago that Bill's own recent love interest had been squelched, it was said, by the overall disapproval of their father. The family's overall concerns were deeply rooted in their hope for Edy's happiness, but they also wanted her to stay close to home.

Edy herself, admittedly smitten by the persistent and charming Frank Moseley, was surprised he had managed to catch her eye and emotion given her unfavorable view of his profession. Despite all, the romance had developed quickly, a not-so-unusual occurrence in post-war America. Life, they had all discovered, could be quickly and unexpectedly snatched away. The possibility of regret was not to be entertained going into the future.

Frank expressed his undying devotion to Edy a mere four weeks into their relationship, and Edy was not far behind. He had to make a case not only for himself, but also for Lexington, Kentucky, if he was to lure Edy away from the beauty of the town nestled between the Blue Ridge and Alleghany Mountains where she had lived her whole life. The brochure he sent along with one of his letters extolled the "beautiful scenic region noted for its many points of historic, romantic and traditional interest," noting too that it had horse farms that were, like those in Lexington, Virginia, world renowned.

During their very busy early weeks and months at Kentucky, Frank managed to fit in "fly-over" type stops in Lexington, Virginia, on his way to or from West Virginia or other scouting destinations. Sometimes he arrived too exhausted to do any more than collapse on the couch and apologize for not being any "ray of sunshine" while he was there. Despite all this, their commitment to each other grew. As he wrote in one letter, he hadn't been on a date, nor been interested in one, since they met in December. She was the one who had "rung the bell," he wrote.

Coach Paul Bryant was well aware he needed to get both of his top assistants out of the doldrums of loneliness and lovesickness. It was with some consolation that all the travel and work kept both men focused on football, their minds off missing their family and girlfriend. But work, movies, phone calls, letter-writing, and taking solace in each other's company were no cures for their ills. The weekend of Edy and Alice's visit in late March, Paul took matters into his own hands. He cornered Edy for a private conversation at the Laslies' apartment.

With Edy standing with her back against the kitchen counter-top, Paul Bryant made his move, positioning himself with one large hand on either side of her. He meant business, and he told her exactly what he thought of the whole situation between her and Frank before ending with a stipulation of his own: a timetable. "Are you gonna marry this boy or not?" he asked. "'Cause if you are, June's the only time anybody in football can get married."

By the end of the weekend, Edy and Frank were officially engaged. In his letter dated Tuesday, April 1, Frank expressed his hope that now that they were officially engaged, her family would be more supportive, writing he would do his "damn-ist" to make them most happy with her choice.

Shortly afterward, Carney went with Frank to purchase nylons and chocolates (scarce commodities in post–World War II America) to send to Edy. The romantic gesture said it all for the longtime, self-proclaimed bachelor. He was head over heels. Caught up in the moment, Carney jumped on the bandwagon, springing in for a splurge that, given his tendency to pinch pennies, was quite out of character. One can picture the two large, manly looking men trying not to blush in the women's lingerie department while they mumbled to the salesclerk that they needed *two* pairs of stockings.

May found Frank alone in Lexington as baseball started up while Carney and Paul continued their football recruiting efforts in various regions and states. As the weeks passed, tension increased between Frank and Edy, spilling over into Frank and Carney's friendship. Despite their decision to marry and officially announcing their engagement, word reached Frank that Edy's family was making it difficult for her. They were open about their unhappiness with the engagement, doubtful that a life as a football coach's wife would bring her happiness, and dubious at best of the fast pace of their relationship.

The strain of being apart started to take an even further toll on Frank. Suspicious that Carney hadn't been "all for them," they, too, began to argue, a very out-of-the-ordinary occurrence for the two men. In later correspondence, Frank wrote that their heated and open arguments only served in the end "to make their friendship stronger."

By early May, Frank was despondent. With two weeks until the wedding day, he told Edy she should just forget about him. He would not blame her, he wrote, if she simply walked away. He was thoroughly distressed at her situation, not wanting to be the cause of the unhappiness she told him she was experiencing from all the advice and pressure of well-meaning family and friends. Contradicting his insistence that she "just walk away" were his adamant declarations of his undying love and devotion to her.

Edy finally overcame the familial pressures. A stalwart, steady, and insightful woman, she had carefully considered the questions of family members and withstood the disapproval from Frank's friends and colleagues who worried about the emotional wringer she was putting him through while she did so. In the end, it was their devotion to each other that never wavered and stood the test.

They married in early June in Lexington, Virginia, at Edy's paternal family home. The ceremony was a small, modest one with Edy's father, her sister, Bill, and Carney and Alice Laslie standing in support nearby. It was a happy event, though ten-year-old Mary Lou Laslie couldn't hide her disappointment when she wasn't allowed to play the wedding march on the family piano, despite her hours and hours of practice in the weeks leading up to the event. Mrs. Gilbert, Edy's former mother-in-law, was also in attendance at the ceremony to wish her former daughter-in-law well. Edy, wearing a silk dress of pastel print, had no attendants, and a simple reception was held for the couple afterward. They arrived back in Lexington, Kentucky, with plenty of time for Frank and Edy to get situated in the duplex apartment above the Laslies before the football pre-season started on July 1.

Edy, Alice, and Mary Lou quickly settled into a routine, a natural extension of sorts from the days when the men were off at war. For years afterward, friends and family in Lexington, Virginia, jokingly remarked that the reason Edy married Frank was so as not to be away from Alice.

The Laslie-Moseley residence in Lexington, Kentucky bought in July, 1946.

CHAPTER TWENTY

The Coaches' Wives

"Scotland and England may sometimes be rivals, but by geography,
we are also neighbors. By history, allies. By economics, partners.
And by fate and fortune, comrades, friends, and family."

—Douglas Alexander

Coaches wives at the reunion dinner for Coach Wallace Wade in 1960.

From left to right: Seated, Mrs. Pooley Hubert, Mrs. Paul Bryant, Mrs. Newt Godfree, and unidentified woman. Standing, L-R: Mrs. Carney Laslie, Mrs. Frank Howard. The Birmingham News, *Tuesday, June 21, 1960. Staff Photo by Ernest Hardin, Catapult Sports.*

"You can be the moon and still be jealous of the stars."

—Gary Allan

TUSCALOOSA, ALABAMA
1933-1935
LEXINGTON, KENTUCKY
1946-1952

ALICE LASLIE WAS BORN in Piermont, New York. Her grandfather, Fred Backus of Glenn Falls, New York, was the founder of the International Paper Company, prominent in political and religious society in New York. Her uncle, Eugene Ashley, was the founder of Georgia Railway & Power Company. Alice's father, Lester Backus, attended Colgate University in Madison County, New York, before he too relocated to Georgia on an entrepreneurial venture to mine limestone in the mineral-rich soil of northwest Georgia sometime in 1916, settling with his young family in Atlanta.

Alice was said to never have met a stranger, her charm and distinctive personality winning over the most skeptical, described in her engagement announcement in the *Atlanta Journal-Constitution* as having a winning personality with many friends throughout the South. She was known as a "flapper", a term used in the 1920s to describe a fun-loving girl with an independent mind.

Not surprisingly, she lacked an interest in academics, though she enjoyed writing, and penned a humorous summary of the year for her freshman high school class which appeared in the yearbook. Sent to an exclusive all-girl high school boarding school in Atlanta for her last two years of high school, Alice then, we can assume unhappily so, attended two years at Sullins College for women in Virginia. Her parents then conceded to give their spirited daughter the opportunity to join her best friend Louise Grenell at the University of Alabama, where she began her junior year in 1932.

Carney was described by friends as being a "man's man," a term used to denote someone who enjoys the company of men, exudes masculinity, and whose skills in knowing how to shoot, hang, and dress his kills were enviable. Despite his overall quiet manner, he was known for entertaining his friends with humorous stories delivered with a heavy southern drawl and dry wit.

Carney and Alice's mutual friends may have had an inkling that Carney, who though mild mannered could also kick up his heels on the dance floor and belt out rousing renditions of his school fight songs, and the outgoing, unacademically inclined Alice, might well hit it off. With the football season behind them, players could now turn their thoughts toward love instead of only having a pigskin as the object of their affections. It was that February of 1933, at the annual Alabama Athletic Association's sponsored dance (the "A-Club") held on campus at the Supply Store, when the two, according to Alice's diary, met.

The day was filled with athletic stunts, feats and other attractions, including a varsity baseball game, and a "smoker", a so-called event where a menu of food and dessert, along with trays of cigarettes, were served. Entertainment at the smoker was highly anticipated, and could include a play, songs, and short sketches considered to be humorous and fun. The day was capped off by the dance.

It was hardly a surprise that when Alice spotted the just under six foot tall, handsome linebacker on the dance floor, she set about to find someone to introduce them. Carney himself had noticed the attractive, petite, five-foot-five, strawberry blond coed. It is unclear who actually introduced the two: Alice's friend, "the always smiling"[91] George Christian, or Jess Eberdt, Carney's former teammate and by this time an assistant coach at Alabama who was at the dance as well. Both would take credit for the introduction years later.

According to Alice's diary, the weekend after the dance, Alice and Louise Grenell accompanied the flamboyant George Chrisitan, who was known to cruise down University Avenue, "the pulsing artery of the Capstone, in almost every make of automobile," to swap out his car for a newer make and model at his father's car dealership in Atlanta.[92] It was to be a quick trip. Both girls had to be back on campus in time for dinner, a double-date planned, Alice's first with Carney, Louise paired with his best friend Frank "Chesty" Moseley.

It is no surprise that they fell in love. They were both quick-witted and fun-loving, Carney a tease and great practical joker and Alice who loved to laugh. Each, too, had experienced the trauma of losing their mother, Carney at sixteen and Alice at nine when her mother died at the age of thirty-eight from pneumonia in 1921, a casualty of the Spanish flu. Alice was also still mourning the loss of her beloved nineteen-year-old sister, Betty, who died from pneumonia on New Year's Eve in 1928, when Alice was seventeen. But it was Alice's generous spirit and fun-loving approach to life despite her hardships, that captured the young man's heart.

Romance was also on the mind of Paul Bryant. Mary Harmon Black, voted one of the most beautiful girls on campus, had attracted the attention of the charismatic, handsome, and confident football player. Bryant confessed in his autobiography that he felt Mary Harmon was "out of his league." She was the campus beauty queen and regularly dating law student Albert Lamar Rankin, Jr. Rankin left Alabama to start his law practice in West Palm Beach, Florida, at the end of the spring semester, which opened the door of opportunity for many a prospective suitor, including one "Buster" Bell who had long been enamored with Mary Harmon. Though Buster was perfectly fine playing second fiddle to Mary Harmon's line of suitors, Bryant was not. As Bryant tells it in his autobiography, when he approached Mary Harmon and asked her for a date, she demurred, saying she would have to check her calendar. It was not quite a rebuff but certainly taken as one by Bryant, who basically said, "Never mind." Later, Mary Harmon had a change of heart, letting him know she was available and would be happy to go out on a date with him.

Whether Mary Harmon Black or Alice Backus knew each other personally while they were both students at the University of Alabama is unknown, but the probability is they did not. They were, for one, members of different sororities, which defined their social circle. There is a high probability, however, that Alice knew of Mary Harmon as she had been voted one of the beauties on campus in 1933, her portrait displayed in Alabama's 1934 Yearbook, The Corolla of Progress.

Mary Harmon, serious minded, conservative and academically focused, and Alice the fun-loving party girl, did have one thing in common: their men were driven to win and were consumed by the game of football.

By April 1935, Alice Backus was engaged to Carney Laslie, who had finished his first season as a high school football coach in Blytheville, Arkansas, a little over a year after their first date. Their engagement was announced in the social pages of the *Atlanta Constitution*: "Social interest is centered throughout the east and south in the announcement by Mr. and Mrs. Lester Jay Backus of Cartersville, of the engagement of their beautiful daughter, Alice."[93] The extensive article highlighting a list of relatives assured the reader of her blue-blooded roots, reading like a list of "Who's Who" of high society in both New York and Atlanta.

They married on June 3, 1935, leaving immediately after the reception for the mountains of North Carolina where they had a reservation at a popular honeymoon resort. It was, however, a disappointment, as Alice described in her journal. Their "room was shabby" and the ambiance not up to her liking. They packed up the next morning and made a spontaneous decision to drive to Virginia Beach, where they were able to get a room at the luxurious Cavalier Hotel for a relaxing beach vacation. But calamity followed them when at a brief stop in Norfolk, just outside of Virginia Beach, Carney's suitcase was stolen. The newlyweds, already stretched financially, had to go out to shop for new clothes for Carney. It is hard to imagine that Alice, who loved everything about shopping and fashion, didn't delight in outfitting her new husband in style. It is also safe to say it was probably the first and last time the notoriously tight Coach Laslie indulged in anything resembling a shopping spree or, for that matter, gave his wife permission to do so.

Three weeks later, Mary Harmon Black and Paul Bryant were secretly wed, reportedly just days after Mary Harmon graduated from Alabama. With one more year of school left for Bryant and football practice starting that July, it was crucial the marriage be kept secret. The Laslies were one of the very few to know of their clandestine marriage.

To get married while a member of a football team was no small infraction. In 1934, word got out that the University of Pittsburgh, a powerhouse of a football program at that time, fielded a team in which a majority of the starters were married. The school was already known to pay its players high subsidies and with the additional infraction of a rule upheld by most all other schools gave both their football opponents and "anti-football" school administrators a reason to cry foul and curtail Pittsburgh's football program, the complaint framed in the argument that "Pitt now sported a reputation as a semiprofessional, 'married man's' team whose players received a worker's wage."[94]

Alabama's rule about being married and a member of the football team was strictly enforced given the current climate. Any excuse opponents might find to show a lax attitude under the NCAA rules could jeopardize the team's standing in the sport. They risked much if they turned a blind eye to such developments among their players. But Bryant was prepared to take the risk.

By July, Bryant was getting ready for his last season of play and Laslie was beginning his second year as head coach at Blytheville High School. And by August, both the Bryants and the Laslies discovered they were pregnant. Sometime between getting married and the start of the season it became clear to Bryant he couldn't hide his marital status from his coach. Pleading his case to Coach Thomas, Bryant was spared the ultimate penalty of being kicked off the team. Whether he also shared that he and Mary Harmon were expecting their first child is unknown. But at the conclusion of the football season, while packing up his room on campus to depart for what would have been the Christmas break, Bryant casually mentioned his marital status to his unsuspecting roommate and had to show the marriage license to prove it!

With Alice and Mary Harmon both due in March of 1936, the two men bet each other five dollars that they would have a boy. On Friday, March 13, 1936, Mary Louise Laslie was born. Carney dutifully sent off his $5 to Paul. Three days later, Mae Martin Bryant, the oldest of the Bryant's two children, was born. Their five-dollar bills crossed in the mail.

Alice and Mary Harmon were not close, but they were friends and had mutual friends between them. Their kind and generous natures overrode what were decidedly different opinions about a myriad of issues in addition to having distinctively different personalities. Alice, an extrovert, and not academically inclined, was in sharp contrast to the more introverted, modest, and studious Mary Harmon. In addition, Mary Harmon leaned toward being a teetotaler compared to Alice, creating life-long tensions between the two.

Jealousies, a natural occurrence but worth the mention, could not be denied. Mary Harmon, who had many friends, was often confounded by Alice's large, socially elite friends in Tuscaloosa that were apart from the football world they inhabited. As time went on, Alice was jealous of the financial rewards and overall recognition and credit for the team's success that went along with the head coach position. But she kept these thoughts to herself, only hinting at her opinions to her closest of friends, who most probably were sympathetic to what they would surmise was a difficult situation. Neither of these issues were ones their husbands concerned themselves with.

From the beginning of Alice and Carney's marriage, his sisters,

Florence and Fanny, had voiced their concerns about Alice's inability to live on a budget and how that would effect their brother's overall financial future. Since Alice never had the worries about money that the Laslies did growing up, they predicted Alice would have no idea of how to manage on the meager salary of a high school football coach. "She'll be his financial ruin," Florence predicted.

Carney took the job of acclimating his wife to a new financial reality to heart, giving Alice a strict cash amount for groceries at the beginning of every month. Not long into their first year in Blytheville, Carney bragged about how thrifty Alice had become, pointing to the fact that she had scrimped and saved enough from the grocery money to be able to buy a stylish pair of new shoes at the local Penney's store, a shoe sale advertised in the *Blytheville Courier* that boasted an assortment of the latest styles of suede, calf, and kid leather shoes discounted to prices of $1.88, $2.88, and $3.88. It was a sale Alice couldn't resist. Later, he discovered she had a workaround for staying within a budget, buying groceries on credit while using the grocery cash to buy what she considered "necessities." The debate of what constituted "necessities" lasted their entire marriage.

Although both head coaches and their assistants were paid meager salaries during these times, a savvy head coach could add to his salary with paid endorsements and investment opportunities that would naturally come his way. As Bryant cultivated those opportunities, the financial gap between the two families grew. Alice continued to struggle to stay within a budget, her spending habits affectionately described by friends and family alike as being "generous to a fault" to overlook her less than frugal ways. This continued to keep the Laslies in a perpetually precarious—or at the very least strained—state of financial affairs. Despite Alice's issues with her husband's renumeration, Alice and Mary Harmon maintained a genuine friendship, always gracious and polite to each other, their good humor a remedy for even the prickliest of situations. But as the financial gap between the two grew, so too did Alice's overall discontent.

Their daughters, Mary Lou and Mae Martin, were the same age, but the families lived in separate neighborhoods, and the girls went to different schools. Mary Lou remembers how she loved going to the Bryant home especially to admire Mae Martin's extensive collection of doll houses. She especially recalled Mrs. Bryant's kindness to her, but despite their mutual fondness for dolls, the two girls didn't have much else in common.

Mary Harmon took her role as the head coach's wife very seriously. She understood her husband's ambitions and supported his goals wholeheartedly. She did not demur from voicing her displeasure to reporters, however, when Bryant charged ahead with plans that involved the family without keeping her in the loop. Focusing on her husband's overall success and on her children, to whom she was loving and attentive, Mary Harmon worked to create a home environment that was calm and peaceful so her husband would not be distracted by family matters.

The Laslie household, though committed and understanding of the demands of a coaching career, differed significantly from the Bryants. This was never more apparent to Mary Lou than during the Cotton Bowl in 1952, when she and Mae Martin Bryant were sixteen. The two went on a double date together on the eve of the game. At 9 p.m., Mae Martin looked at her watch and surprised the group by fretfully stating she had to back to the hotel as she didn't want to "upset Poppa" before the game. This despite that they had all been given permission to stay out till 10 p.m. It was all very puzzling to Mary Lou. Why, she wondered, was Mae Martin so worried and distraught at the possibility of upsetting her father? It was obvious to everyone that Mae Martin was the apple of her father's eye. He adored her. For her own part, Mary Lou had never known her father to ever have been upset with her or that she would ever be the cause of his being in a bad mood.

The dynamic was a sharp contrast overall. Mary Lou and her mother lived their lives less tethered to the demands of the profession.

Their home life, as Mary Lou perceived it, revolved around what made Mary Lou happy and did not cater to the football season schedule. Of course, football did many times take precedence, such as when Mary Lou, pregnant and living with her parents while her husband was overseas with the military, successfully delivered her second child at Druid City Hospital in Tuscaloosa. Thrilled at the arrival of their first grandson, Alice visited the hospital early in the day on the Friday after his birth. Mary Lou was anticipating her departure from the hospital and going home. "Oh, no, honey, not today," her mother told her. "It's homecoming weekend!"

Mary Lou understood perfectly. She stayed at the hospital until Monday.

With their husbands well-ensconced into the rigors of coaching in Lexington, Kentucky, Alice and Edy now settled into a routine of their own while living in the same duplex. Years later, Edy's daughter, Alene, described her mother and Alice's friendship this way: "If it weren't for Alice, Edy would never have had any fun!" She characterized the two as a "Lucy and Ethel duo," Alice's reddish, strawberry-blond hair identifying her as the Lucille Ball character. They were inseparable. Edy was to Alice what Ethel was to Lucy: conservative and balancing out the spontaneous, fun-loving Alice. Likewise, Edy, known for her frugal ways, contrasted with Alice's sometimes flamboyant spending and generosity. In one instance, while visiting the Laslies with her parents, Alene Moseley remembered telling Alice how much she admired her stylish shoes. Alice promptly removed them and gave them to the young teenager. Later that same day, she commented that she loved Alice's sunglasses. "Here, darling! They're yours!" she declared, taking them off and handing them over to Alene. Edy's protests fell on deaf ears until the two, both soundly scolded, were warned that there would be no more of such nonsense!

After two seasons, despite the fun and convenience of sharing the duplex with the Laslies, Edy had grown tired of the football life away from her family in Lexington, Virginia. By 1948, the Moseleys had an infant and a toddler —both a welcomed surprise since it was their understanding that soldiers who spent long periods of time exposed to radar, as Frank had, suffered from male infertility. Frank's ongoing travel, a demanding schedule, had him away from home for weeks at a time, "Sweetie, why don't you put some old linens on the little bed in the front room and ask Gloria [the household help] if she will stay there with you at night while I'm away," Frank wrote, trying to offer some suggestions to ease the burden of caring for two small children.

Paul, Jr. had fonder memories of this time when the three coaches would arrive at the Bryant home directly after football practice. After eating a quick dinner together a lively wrestling match between the young boy and the men followed until Mary Harmon would announce, "Bath time!" and Paul, Jr. would be ushered off to get ready for bed never understanding why he was the only one who had to take a bath since they had all come directly from practice. Reluctantly he would shuffle off for his bath and bedtime routine while the men stayed on until the later hours of the evening strategizing about the upcoming season. It wasn't until many years later that he realized that the men had showered at the locker room before they came home.

Alice often expressed her disappointment that the three men didn't come to the Laslie or Moseley home directly after practice, though there were many occasions when a group of assistant coaches, along with Bryant, would meet there. However, despite it being the prerogative of the head coach, their evenings spent at the Bryant's home instead of their own homes with their own children, grew tiresome and fueled the discontent of the wives of Bryant's two senior assistants.

The football season didn't begin or end with the playing season. Summers had the coaches engaged in all manner of off-season football clinics and pre-season competitions held at various schools across the country. Alice and Mary Lou spent those months at St. Simons Island, Georgia, where they visited Alice's brother Billy and his wife, Ruth, who lived there year-round, as well as Alice's father, who summered on the island.

Edy, too, departed the university town during the summer, retreating to Lexington, Virginia, for the company and help of family. When Edy returned that September of 1948, not even being back with Alice to entertain and bolster her spirits helped. She was more homesick than ever.

With the dawn of 1950, Edy made it no secret that she longed to return to her beloved Lexington, Virginia, confiding to Alice regularly about her homesickness. She was burdened with two small children, and though she had household help, it was still difficult without the support of family nearby. Alice, on the other hand, had settled in more comfortably, established in social circles and a regular bridge club. Mary Lou, too, was happy, excelling at Henry Clay High School. Contract renewal, always a stressful time, was fast approaching for Laslie and Moseley.

During these years when the three men worked tirelessly to build the football program in Lexington, their families too, like many who had been separated by the war, sought to normalize life as best they could. Each family had their own set of unique demands and despite their differences strove to, above all, support each other in their common pursuit: a winning season.

CHAPTER TWENTY-ONE

Thick as Thieves

"When it came time to sign, Coach Bryant sent Carney Laslie to pick me up in a limousine. He told me we were going to Pittsburgh, to Forbes Field, to see the Pirates play. Coach Laslie then took me and another player, a player from Virginia, John Nestoskie, on a ride straight to Lexington. I don't know how long we were on the road, fifteen or sixteen hours maybe more. But while we were on the road, there was no chance of any other school getting to us. I think they called it kidnapping back then."

—Babe Parilli, recruited to Kentucky, 1948,
Allen Barra, *The Last Coach,* page 127

UNIVERSITY OF KENTUCKY
LEXINGTON, KENTUCKY
1946–1948

THE THREE WORLD WAR II–veteran coaches brought all the power of their military experience to their college coaching, a threesome of what one player described many years later as "tough hombres." The coaches were driven, hard at work to redeem themselves as the "cracker-jack coaching trio" they knew they could be. They were direct from their days of readying the troops where practices were mentally like skirmishes preparing for a major battle. Now they were preparing for *the* game, and the practices rivaled any the players had experienced before. The drills, which included endless running and additional conditioning done in the weight room outside of regular practice, assured the players were in top physical shape. The coaches, too, put in rigorous days stretching for fourteen hours and more.

It was a formative time in all three of their careers, but it was Laslie and Moseley's part of the coaching trifecta that kept the three in balance overall, dividing the work into the tasks they were strongest and most skilled in. Bryant respected both tremendously and trusted them uncategorically. Their mutual goal, a winning season, would carry them through clashes of opinion and translate into tolerance of each other's egos, unavoidable in the sport. They knew in the end it would make their collaboration strong as they pushed toward victory in all aspects of the game, the season, and their careers. Too, their bonds of wartime survival and shared experiences of Navy Pre-Flight were always with them.

Bryant's metamorphosis as a head coach can be seen during this time in how he dealt with both the press and the players, trying to find his footing, fine-tuning his interactions and reactions in the locker room with players, and during press conferences with reporters. Off the field and away from football, the Paul Bryant who arrived in Lexington in 1946 was known to be a charming and likable fellow in most respects, with a magnetic personality. That would change rather quickly, as he could not contain his surliness and contempt for the press and their armchair opinions. He began to be described by reporters as being belligerent and rude to outsiders, perhaps because he perceived sportswriters as unfriendly critics who never let up, seeming to always be after his scalp. But over time he adopted a more humorous and easy style when interviewed and was rewarded by less skeptical and bruising coverage.

But Bryant's detractors were ever-present. They characterized him as someone who would "sell his own grandmother to win a game,"[95] a cutthroat, ruthless competitor who would spare no one in his path to win. Bryant's ego was no secret. Fans, however, defended their new coach, explaining that his ferocious competitiveness and appetite for winning was tempered by his homespun humility.

The Kentucky head football coach enjoyed the spotlight, and he soon made it his mission to understand and use the press to his advantage. Laslie, too, knew the power of the press. When a reporter tried to attribute the team's success to Laslie's coaching skills, he was quick to reply, "Bryant is the first one at the field in the morning, and last one at night. I've never known anyone to work harder."[96]

With players, too, Bryant was fine-tuning how to motivate players both as a group and individually. In later years, Coach Laslie would point to Bryant's handling of Kentucky's star quarterback, Babe Parilli, as an example of how Bryant's insight into what motivated an individual player resulted in brilliant results. But it was Don "Dopey" Phelps, who in later years characterized Bryant as a "just plain mean individual"[97] who proved to be one of the more turbulent and challenging players Bryant would deal with during his time at Kentucky.

Phelps went by the nickname "Dopey," given to him by his friends due to his similar shy and bashful persona as the dwarf from the character in Disney's *Snow White and the Seven Dwarfs*, which had just been released. The name stuck. He entered the service for the duration of the war, and after it ended, he pursued his college degree. An All-State running back from Danville, Kentucky, when he graduated high school, he was considered Kentucky's top athletic recruit and was anticipated to be one of the Wildcats' star players. Many years later, Phelps recalled his first scrimmage at Kentucky in an interview in the *Louisville Courier Journal*:

The first time we ever met the man on the football field [when Bryant arrived in 1946] he had a two-hour-long scrimmage and he ran off forty-eight players. Can you imagine that? We had 116 players on that field. He made a list and he called out mostly all the veterans and lined 'em up against all the eighteen-year-olds because he was going to get rid of 'em. We made up the plays in the huddle . . . and we didn't want to hit those kids. Bryant said, "That's what's wrong with you SOBs. You can't beat your way out of a paper bag. I want you to start hitting people." Bryant was great to grab those big tackles and bust 'em in the nose with his forearm. They were carrying those eighteen-year-olds off something awful. The next day he ran some more off. That's the way he started off . . . I can see now that it took a coach of that type to get Kentucky back on its feet. For years they had relaxed and didn't train as well as they should've. And they didn't have any discipline. Bryant gave 'em that, but I think he went to extremes in some of it and ran a lot of good players off.[98]

Phelps, known to be a flamboyant player, had a standout performance that first year, his brilliant punt returns scoring four touchdowns to rack up a 34–14 win over Michigan State in front of a roaring crowd of 20,000. Phelps was the poster boy for Kentucky's football program, an example of why talented high school football players should choose UK over other schools. The star player joined Bryant and Moseley at a Booster Club dinner at his own Danville High School where he explained plays from films of Kentucky football games shown to the audience. Bryant, as the invited speaker, took the opportunity to emphasize to the crowd that "the best teachers, scientists and football players should remain in Kentucky rather than gallop off to a variety of other states. . . . We have a splendid group of colleges here in Kentucky, and all of us should work to keep them going in Kentucky."[99] It was an echo of Frank Moseley's pitch to players in Kentucky a decade before.

Phelps was dropped from the squad after he cut practice that spring. Bryant explained that the decision was made in fairness to the rest of the squad. "We can't make any exceptions," he declared. The decision was decried by many of the older squad members. They went to the coaches, pleading their teammate's case. Coupled with Phelps's own explanations, he was allowed back on the team two days later. The coaches were tough, no doubt. But also fair.

It was, however, a clear message sent to the team by their coach. There would be no favoritism shown for breaking any rule, even for a player the likes of Phelps. Not showing up for practice carried as much weight as what was seen as a more serious and blatant infraction: getting married. This was ironic given Bryant himself had secretly married the summer before his senior year at Alabama. Despite this, Bryant had singled out this rule in his first year of coaching at Kentucky, emphasizing that a player would lose their scholarship money if he married while playing football. They wanted boys who were first interested in completing school and obtaining their degree, countering the ongoing criticism that athletics was overemphasized at Kentucky. Playing football, Bryant stressed, should always be the second consideration. But there could be no close third. Marriage was not an option. They wanted the full focus of every player.

Unbeknownst to anyone, Phelps married a month before the '47 football season opened. He informed the coaches and his teammates in December and was spared being cut from the team. It can be presumed Bryant was sympathetic in this regard given his own marriage when it was strictly prohibited during his playing years at Alabama.

In '48, however, Bryant continued to have difficulty with Phelps. After losing their first three games of '48, the coaches didn't think the boys were trying their hardest. They decided to leave the entire starting backfield behind for an away game between Kentucky and Marquette to give them time to think about it and get their heads back into the game. The response from the Kentucky fans was harsh, their booing from the stands when the team entered the field leaving no doubt of their opinion on the matter. When they returned from the game, Bryant learned Phelps, along with his teammates, had not practiced with the freshman players while the team was away as the coaches had directed. They were immediately suspended. But when Phelps also did not come to practice the next day, he was cut a second time from the team. And though Phelps' had an excuse that evoked much sympathy among all who were privy to his situation, Phelps himself understood his coach's postion:

> My child was only two months old and almost died a couple of times. I lost a lot of weight, and my wife had a nervous breakdown. I was trying to play football and take care of all those bills, all those hospital bills. We lost three games in '48 right off the bat. Naturally Bryant was interested in football, and I was interested in my family. Bryant cut me and some of the others off the team. He said we had too many outside interests.[100]

Bryant made clear that this time it was permanent. Phelps himself accepted his suspension without complaint and denied the rumors, which were rampant, that he was looking to transfer. His plan was to win over Bryant with his repentant attitude, hard work, and skill.

The decision to suspend Phelps seemed harsh given Phelps's reasons for his lack of focus and absenteeism, but Phelps himself understood his coach's stance, conceding, "He was a great coach." By the start of the '49 season, Phelps had won over the coach and was reinstated on the team, although he would be disappointed in the amount of actual play time he had that fall.

It was a rocky start, but despite this, the brass ring of a major bowl game loomed in sight for the season of '49, the roster of players by then the strongest since the three coaches' arrival. The optimism for the upcoming season, however, was juxtaposed against national economic and political concerns due to a new era of scientific advancement that followed the end of the war.

Russia's development of an atomic bomb two years ahead of Western scientists' projections combined with the West's development of a homing rocket device that could destroy missiles in midair ramped up world tensions. And in an aggressive move, Russia established a two-state Germany, declaring Russia's position of opposition and poising communism as a threat against a democratic, free Western Europe. A potential international conflict was once again in the forefront of the news.

Families were naturally anxious, but so were the leaders of football programs across the country. Tennessee reported it could lose its entire team, as did Alabama, if an escalation occurred and the National Reservists and National Guard units were mobilized. On the other hand, Kentucky could have a football team and not a coaching staff as its head coaches, Bryant, and assistants Laslie and Moseley, were all Naval Reservists. War was again on everyone's mind.

The unexpected loss of a coach or coaches to another program also undermined the stability of teams. Schools recruited behind the scenes all year long if looking for a new head coach in the hopes for a better season than their last or if they were seeking out a good replacement for a retiring, beloved coach.

VMI approached Laslie during his first year at Kentucky, seeing him as a natural replacement for resigning head coach Pooley Hubert in December 1946. The two coaches had remained close friends since Laslie left VMI at the outbreak of the war. VMI and Hubert had been wooing Laslie back to VMI ever since. Laslie definitively turned down the $6,400 a year job in January of '47.

It was most likely not the salary that discouraged him. He had no desire to take on a head coach position for several reasons. Known as a "players' coach" he was gaining a reputation for being a "coach's coach" as well, committed to the coaching partnership with Bryant and Moseley and a big-time football program. He had experienced the challenges of coaching at a military academy, and knew the handicaps of working within such a system. Practice periods were shorter due to the cadets' scholastic and military training schedules. During these first postwar years, VMI was further disadvantaged by potential players reluctant to enter military schools, a nightmare for recruiting players to military colleges.

In January of 1949, it was publicly reported that the Washington Redskins had offered Bryant an attractive salary to move to the pros. Laslie, it is known, was also offered a position with the Redskins. Much was made of the offer to Bryant in the press with its significant boost of salary. The two, however, had always known they had no interest in ever coaching in the pro leagues. It was also construed, by one reporter (who happened to be Frank's brother, Max Moseley, of the Montgomery Advertiser), that the two other coaches would not join the pro's on account of Moseley, who had helped gain recognition for them in the coaching world. Bryant, it was surmised, felt that with seven years left on his contract he had an obligation to his coaches; an obligation he was not inclined to break, knowing that a new head coach at Kentucky would replace the entire existing staff. Bryant's loyalty to his staff was lauded, and he was portrayed in the press as a man of the highest principles to whom money wasn't the most important thing in life.

It played well in the press. But the main reason they didn't leave Kentucky to coach in the pros was because they always been convinced that young men would be motivated to play harder for their school and teammates than they would be by playing for money in the pros. They loved college football overall, and at this time in history, pro football had nowhere near the following that college football did.

Frank, too, had opportunities to coach in the pros as well, approached by the Chicago Bears who knew Frank from his time there recruiting high school athletes. He, too, never gave it serious consideration. He was all too familiar with the cold winters in

Chicago, writing in one letter during a visit to Edy that it was the coldest he had ever been.

Alabama as well approached all three, Bryant and Laslie and Moseley during this time. But they were each friends with the incumbent Coach "Red" Drew, and they were not inclined to displace him.

But there was another reason, perhaps, which had greater potential to upend their hoped-for tenure at Kentucky. By the summer of 1949, the tension was now at an all-time high between Kentucky's basketball program, headed by Coach Adolf Rupp and the football program, headed by Coach Paul Bryant. It was exacerbated by a basketball scandal that drew national attention and that by association spilled over into the football program. Bryant was in the headlines once again, the use of summer work programs for athletes coming under scrutiny.

Laslie and Moseley had no illusions about Bryant and football displacing the widely popular Rupp and the sport that kept Kentucky in the national limelight. They both hoped that Bryant would come to the same conclusion: they would either have to coexist with Rupp and accept his being more influential and having greater status there than Bryant, or there would be no future for the three at Kentucky. But Bryant was confident winning would change minds and hearts of fans and football would rise and displace basketball's, and Rupp's, dominance.

The Laslie's had their share of doubts about whether Frank and Edy would make Lexington, Kentucky their permanent home. For Alice, though she was happy with her own social life and approved of Mary Lou's close group of friends, she continued to struggle with her overall unhappiness at not having her husband's paycheck keep pace with her spending habits, a sore subject overall. The Bryant family was settled and content in Lexington, hopeful the repercussions of the basketball scandal would be short-lived.

CHAPTER TWENTY-TWO

Bowl Games and Football Rivalries

"Spectacle and controversy."

—John Sayle Watterson, *The History of College Football*

Mary Lou Laslie and Alice Laslie at a Wildcat's Homecoming Game in Lexington, Virginia. © The Courier-Journal—USA TODAY NETWORK

LEXINGTON, KENTUCKY
1947–1949

IN BIG-TIME FOOTBALL, teams winning major bowl games reigned as kings of the sport, while their schools gained prominence as well, often ensuring increased applications for student enrollment. Thus, the reward for a stellar season was an invitation to one of the prestigious Big Four—the Rose Bowl, Orange Bowl, Sugar Bowl, and Cotton Bowl. It meant a share of the nearly $3,000,000 that would result from play in the championship contests. Each team profited with the financial lift of a bowl check. It meant the ability to build bigger and better football programs and the prestige that came along with it to attract talented athletes.

Rivalries too provided increased gate receipts and fan interest. With Kentucky and Alabama set to clash in 1947, the Southeastern Conference matchup between the two was spotlighted as a highlight of the season.

To best prepare for the game, Kentucky sent Coach Moseley, whose scouting of Georgia and Vanderbilt had strengthened Kentucky's game plans going into those two contests, contributing to Kentucky's shut-out wins—respectively 26–0 and 14–0—over those two schools. Returning from Alabama's shut-out win over Tennessee, Moseley reported Alabama had played the best game an Alabama team had played since 1945.

But Alabama wasn't about to be lulled into over-confidence. In one interview, Alabama's Coach Harold "Red" Drew declared that if Kentucky's 26–0 win over Georgia and its 14–0 decision over Vanderbilt meant anything, it was that Kentucky was a tough team and could be one of their toughest games of the season, noting Bryant had what was probably the best Kentucky squad an Alabama team had ever played.

A thirty-year-old rivalry, when they the two teams met at the end of the season, Alabama dominated. Out-runnning, out-blocking, and out-kicking their opponent, Alabama handed the Wildcats its second loss of the season and first shut-out in a 13–0 victory. But although they were out-played, the Wilcats never lost heart. There was, however, one Kentucky player Alabama couldn't hold back: Don "Dopey" Phelps. The one bright spot in an otherwise disappointing defeat, Phelps led in gained yardage, an impressive seven yards per run, picking up sixty-three yards in nine runs.

Their overall record that year justified Kentucky's first bowl game appearance, which occurred on a bitterly raw day in December 1947 at the Great Lakes Bowl in Cleveland, "great" only in name, being a minor bowl game that attracted few fans and held little financial gain for the two schools. It follows that the only people there to witness Kentucky's defeat of Villanova, 24–14, were the players, the peanut vendors, and sports writers.

The following season of '48 proved to be a disappointment overall. With three big losses early in the season, as they approached their game against Tennessee (the forty-fourth meeting between the two), a win would provide needed balm for their bruised and battered egos. With a rivalry dating back to 1893, the game against the Tennessee Volunteers was much anticipated, described as one that was "traditionally glutted with color and drama, suspense and legend."[101]

Kentucky was optimistic. Both teams had racked up four wins, three losses, and one tie for the current season. In recent weeks, Kentucky's quarterback, George Blanda, ranked sixteenth in the nation, had been coming on strong, the last game showcasing his sensational passing talent which led the Wildcats to a jubilant 35–15 win over the University of Florida.

Celebrated Tennessee head coach General Robert Neyland ranked high on the Kentucky trio's list of coaches to beat. All three had the highest regard for Coach Neyland, an icon of the sport, and none more than Laslie, who had turned down the general's overtures to come to Tennessee when he was a star high school tackle. Now the three ex-Alabama players were facing the legendary coach not as players but as a new generation of coaches ready to prove themselves.

The Vols, favored by thirteen points, had the hometown advantage, the game being played in Knoxville. General Neyland was prepared to whip Kentucky. He was sorely disappointed. The game ended in a scoreless tie, the first of such in their annual match-up since 1928. Kentucky fans were just short of jubilant upon leaving the game, the Kentucky defense holding the Vols time and again, despite coming close to scoring numerous times. Despite a Wildcat touchdown that was called back, a call that was debated "all night long," and the Cats' field goal in the final minutes, which missed by inches, General Neyland still had bragging rights. His record stood as never having been whipped by a Kentucky team.

There would be no bowl invitation for Kentucky that season. In fact, no SEC team had a bid to play in the major bowl games of the '48 season. The Dixie Bowl, played at Birmingham, and in its second and last year of existence, seemed to be where friends of Paul Bryant believed to the last that his popularity in Alabama would outweigh the losses suffered by the Wildcats that year. Instead, the post-season invitations went to Wake Forest and Baylor.

The passing brilliance of sophomore Vito "Babe" Parilli as quarterback and eleven straight wins put Kentucky on top in its next season. Speedster "Dopey" Phelps, permanently suspended from from play in '48, was reinstated after pleading with Bryant to put him back in the lineup In November, they seemed unstoppable, and as the game neared with archenemy Tennessee, sportscasters, college football pundits, and statisticians predicted the game would be dominated by the Wildcats, who were favored by thirteen to twenty-one points. Ever since "the General" had arrived at Tennessee in 1926, he had boasted of never having had to "bow before Kentucky."[102] The expectation of a Kentucky win had the Wildcats salivating at the prospect of bringing General Neyland's twenty-three years of dominance to an end.

There was another element of this game that added to its contentiousness. Twice Kentucky had successfully nudged Tennessee out of top bowl bids with ties: once in 1929 and again in 1931. Both of those seasons Tennessee was riding high in its prospects for a bowl game appearance. But their dreams were dashed by Kentucky when both games ended in a tie. With the season of '49, in an ironic twist of of fate that lent added interest and drama to the game, it was Tennessee's turn to deal the same type of blow to Kentucky and their fans. Tennessee was already out of the running for a bowl game invite, but should Tennessee defeat Kentucky, the Wildcats would be knocked out of any opportunity to play in the Sugar Bowl. And the Volunteers, without question, relished the possibility.

A. B. Nichols, a leading member of the Sugar Bowl Committee and scouting staff, arrived in Louisville at 5:30 p.m. on game day, driving straight to Lexington to watch the age-old rivalry.

A record Kentucky home crowd of 38,000 came to cheer on the highly anticipated contest against their longstanding foe. But instead of jubilation in the stands, there was anguished silence, Kentucky's hopes for a bowl game lowered when they failed to overcome Tennessee's first-quarter lead. It was agonizing for fans to watch, the performance by All-American tackle Bob Gain and several goal line stands giving them their only thrills.

On the sidelines, the large, confident General Neyland appeared totally satisfied, clearly amused that the sports pundits had doubted him, acknowledging to reporters immediately after the game that Tennessee had been given the psychological advantage when the point spread was announced, one that also caused the other side to be overconfident. Standing erect like the Army general he was, he maintained calm even when Kentucky, a touchdown from victory, drove deep into Tennessee territory, threatening to score with only a few minutes left on the clock. He exhibited the sportsmanlike attitude he was known for, chewing his gum as he smiled, yelling words of encouragement while he watched the last minutes play out

"Across the field, Bryant was attempting every effort in his power to lead a comeback. He was drawn and tense. He tried everything, it seemed, but all of the offensive strategy failed."[103] It came down to the final minutes of play, and Tennessee prevailed, 6–0. Meeting Neyland on the field after the game, they shook hands, Bryant extending his congratulations before disappearing into the crowd. The Tennessee players picked up their coach and carried him off the field.

In the Kentucky locker room, it was quiet, but not so much in defeat as in disgust. The players didn't look at each other or speak. They dressed in silence. The Tennessee locker room, too, was quiet, not loud with victory as one might have expected. The players quickly dressed, anxious to get on the team busses, board the train, and get back to Knoxville. They agreed it "was a rough one,"[104] and were glad it was over with.

The opening of hunting season for quail, one of Laslie's great hobbies, was announced the next day in Sunday's newspaper. It's hard to imagine Laslie didn't make the most of it by taking his father's prized 20-gauge shotgun and blasting away at his quarry, bagging a different kind of prize, using a hunter's skills of focus and patience to give him some measure of comfort after the hugely disappointing loss.

Laslie may have snagged some quail while out hunting that next week, but it wouldn't compare to bagging the prize they had all been gunning for the following weekend. Taking a knee surrounded by players and coaches, Bryant posed for the camera to read aloud the official invitation on November 26, 1949. Despite their loss to Tennessee, the Wildcats had been selected to play Santa Clara in Miami at the Orange Bowl on January 2, 1950. Standing amongst the players encircling Bryant was Laslie, his fist raised in victory as the photographer caught his and Bryant's locked eyes, Bryant's eyebrows raised, an expression of pure joy on his face combined with a slight smile as if to say "Can you believe it?" Laslie's expression conveyed pure satisfaction, an "I told you so!" expression, their non-verbal overall "We did it!" passing between them. The boys' jubilance was evidenced by their giddy faces, fists raised, jumping in exhilaration.

The all-star Orange Bowl–bound team of '49 included sophomore quarterback "Babe" Parilli, the SEC's top passer. When commenting on the team and its players in later years, Coach Laslie would point to Bryant's impressive handling of Parilli as one that impressed him, crediting Bryant for handling him perfectly to get out the best performance of the young man possible. Bob Gain, a junior lineman, narrowly missed being selected as an All-American, though he had the distinction of making the Players' All-American first squad. He was also voted "Best Lineman in the SEC" that year by both the influential Atlanta Touchdown Club and the Birmingham Quarterback Club.

Parilli and Gain were both known as "team men," as most distinguished All-Americans are, and reporters wrote of their being impressed with their humbleness, commenting in one article that they had "not allowed their press clippings to increase the size of their hat bands."

Bob Gain accepting his award from Coach Laslie to Look *magazine's All-America Football Team.*

Shortly after announcing the bowl teams, the National Collegiate Bureau also confirmed that the number one defensive team in the nation was Kentucky. It was the first time in the school's history it had reached such a record of distinction. All of Kentucky celebrated the achievements of the team, players, and coaches. The recognition also solidified Coach Laslie's reputation as the best line coach in the country.

The week before Christmas, the official Orange Bowl warm-up drills at Cocoa Beach opened, and the Wildcats used the time to try to acclimate to the seventy-five-degree average temperature they would face in Miami, a notable forty-five-degree difference from their usual climate of play in Lexington. On December 28, three days before the big game, the team was sent through one of its most grueling workouts, the athletes perspiring profusely under the hot, bright sun. Injuries, too, were racking up as scrimmages were played full force. For their rivals from California, though, the warm temperatures weren't an obstacle. They did, however, still use the time to keep up their rigorous conditioning schedule.

The Sixteenth Annual Orange Bowl had expanded its fan capacity to 80,000, which included viewing from outside the stadium, a monumental increase from the 8,000 fans that watched its inaugural game in 1935. Described as the most colorful of the bowl games, the pre-game week was filled with coronations of every type, from parades and crownings, to various sports events including not only the football game but sailing regattas and tennis, golf, and basketball tournaments, all used to hype up fans, players, and commentators alike. And, as the organizers were also quick to point out, to keep tourists coming and staying.

The Bryant and Moseley families arrived on Saturday, Christmas Eve, with children in tow: Mae Martin Bryant, a freshman in high school, five-year-old Paul, Jr., three-year-old Ruffy Moseley, and Alene Moseley, age one. Coach Laslie arrived early to be with the team as well, while Alice stayed behind with Mary Lou who didn't want to miss the annual Christmas parties in Lexington. The two planned to join the group after Christmas Day. The Kentucky contingent stayed at the Flamingo Hotel where it's hard to imagine that Bryant and Laslie, avid golfers, didn't take advantage of the adjoining golf course, and the party ambiance of the hotel, which boasted in their brochures "open air dancing under coconut palms," adding to the almost giddy mood of Kentucky fans. A confident but understated Bryant remarked to the press prior to the game that in his estimation, despite the heat, the Wildcats had looked good during training.

The game was played before the largest crowd in Wildcat history. The fashions made headlines, and dignitaries and socialites were listed among the 65,000 fans in the stands.

In what was reported as one of the most thrilling Orange Bowls played to date, the Santa Clara Broncos, who surged in the second half, won 21–13. Santa Clara's head coach declared post-game that his team's superior conditioning proved to be the winning factor. It played into what Bryant acknowledged as well: his pre-game conditioning demands may have been too much given the time needed to fully recover in time for game day.

The players flew back to Lexington post-game, stopping in Louisville due to weather before boarding a bus for the remainder of the trip back home. Immediately upon disembarking the plane, the team swarmed the airport grill, ordering fifty-five hamburgers. A reporter on hand mentioned to Coach Laslie that the players looked a little "green around the gills" when they got off the plane, wondering if they were air sick. "I think it was something they ate," replied the ever-pithy Coach Laslie. Indeed. His allusion was to their having eaten the proverbial crow and it had made them all sick to their stomachs. The humiliation of their loss, being proven wrong after being so publicly confident, was as hard to swallow as the repulsive meat of a cawing black bird.

Don "Dopey" Phelps, the running star phenom who arguably felt he was demoted to a secondary role on the team by Bryant during the regular season of '49, had been on display in full force at the bowl, his magnificent play setting running yardage records for the Orange Bowl. At the sports banquet in January of 1950, Phelps was awarded a varsity football letter. Bryant, in his address at the annual sports banquet later that month, called the team of '49 "the finest group of young men I've ever been connected with since I've been in athletics. I'm proud of them and their record is evidence that they did an outstanding job."[105]

CHAPTER TWENTY-THREE

Band of Brothers

"Help your brother's boat across and your own will get to shore."

—Hindu Proverb

LEXINGTON, KENTUCKY
1949–1952

THE COMPETITIVENESS BETWEEN THE basketball and football programs and their respective coaches Adolf Rupp, known as "the Baron of the Bluegrass," and Paul "Bear" Bryant grew more and more intense with each passing year. This was especially true after Kentucky basketball won back-to-back National Championships in 1948 and 1949. The two men were comparable in their stern, disciplined approach toward coaching, and both were mumblers. But where Rupp rarely spoke to his players off the court, holding firm to the opinion that it was better not to have any type of interaction other than strict and business-like dealings involving the game only, Bryant chose a different style. Though Rupp's players respected him, they were never close to him, and he only gained their admiration many years after they had graduated. Many of Bryant's players, in contrast, reported Bryant always displayed a genuine affection toward them when they happened to have an encounter with him, always remembering details about them that surprised them.

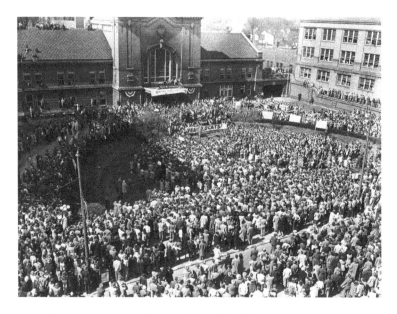

Fans welcome University of Kentucky basketball team, April 2, 1948, outside Lexington's Union Station on Main Street. Photo by the Lexington-Herald Leader.

On April 2, outside of Lexington's Union Staion on Main Street, 15,000 cheering fans greeted the University of Kentucky basketball team after they won the 1948, NCAA national championship. It was the school's first NCAA title, and when the team stepped off the train they were met by politicians and three bands. Also amongst the crowd to welcome the triumphant basketball team back home was Coach Paul "Bear" Bryant. One day he hoped, the football team would be the cause for celebration. But on this day, it was Coach Adolph Rupp and members of the basketball squad who assembled on a platform in front of the door of the station for a brief ceremony. The crowd overflowed all standing room on the ground level around the station, covered building roofs, and filled windows furnishing vantage points. Center

Alex Groza, the NCAA Tournament's Most Outstanding Player, was met with a roar of approval after he told the vast crowd, "We said we'd bring home the bacon and we just hope we brought enough." After the bands played "On, On, U of K," the team climbed aboard a fire truck for a ride through a decorated downtown Lexington to campus before at least 5,000 more fans. Groza, would find himself in the headlines a year later, but for far less than noble reasons.

The two programs vied for athletic talent above all, with 80 percent of Rupp's basketball players recruited from the hills of Kentucky, turning them into local heroes at the expense of football, which was secondary in the minds of in-state athletes. Bryant, however, was determined to win the hearts and souls of fans, alumni, students, and the university board of trustees by producing winning football teams. One day in the not-too-distant future, he hoped football would be less of a stepchild sport and he would become more a "king" than a "prince" to Rupp. Sooner or later, he believed, Rupp would ride off into the sunset, and he already had the full support of his program from President Donovan. Bryant's senior assistants, though, weren't as easily convinced. But the prospect of success seemed too enticing to give up on just yet.

In 1949, when it came to light the NCAA was investigating a national betting scandal in basketball that occurred during the 1948 season, Rupp adamantly declared that his boys were beyond reproach and that nothing could be further from the truth to imply they would be involved in a scandal the likes of which were being reported. But there were strong rumors within the Kentucky athletic department to indicate otherwise. Moseley and Laslie, seeing the proverbial writing on the wall for their future at Kentucky, began actively strategizing their next move. They warned Bryant of the revered Rupp's ability to undermine their goals for the football program, convinced early on they would be forever hampered and overshadowed by Rupp, sabotaged by his wily ways, never exchanging his power or influence in the athletic department for anything more than a polite, collegial coexistence.

The controversy, which at its fringes reached into the football program to involve a star player, resulted in what many saw as an overreach to penalize the entire athletic department and the school for years of skating on the edge of, but not rising to, flagrant violations of NCAA regulations. The resulting penalty, a suspension of conference play for the basketball team and the permanent suspension of two players from the football team, served as a red flag. As long as Rupp was around, his success was a lightning rod for both programs for those who were interested in seeing his dynasty fall. Kentucky's basketball program, it seemed, would always cast its shadow over football.

Despite his frustrations, Bryant was comfortable at Kentucky, his television and radio programs supplemented his salary, and he continued to cultivate a network of lucrative business opportunities through his contacts there. His family was happy in Lexington, and he was achieving a level of status that he had always wanted.

Kentucky's traditional, much-anticipated Blue-White intrasquad game, which began the tradition of offering a peek into Kentucky's upcoming season, was played in April every year. The 1949 game between the Blues and the Whites, coached respectively by Laslie and Moseley, showcased freshman tackle Gene Donaldson. Hailed as one of the finest guards ever to enroll at Kentucky up to that time, the 202-pound, five-foot-nine-inch-tall player from Indiana was an All-State performer three times while in high school. It was said of Laslie that he could take a mediocre tackle and turn him into a good tackle. A good tackle, it was added, he could turn into an All-American. Donaldson was no exception, highly regarded as having Kentucky's best potential to be an All-American lineman, and all but assured of reaching that goal by his senior year of play in 1952. Donaldson was described by the press as "a burly, talented prospect" for the line, said by Bryant to be a player who "will be great one of these days."[106] The scandal involving Rupp's basketball players in 1949 would drown Donaldson in its wake, his arguable suspension by the NCAA proving to be the last straw for Bryant's assistants.

While football teams around the country prepared for the football season of 1950, the country was steeped in a healthcare crisis. By July of 1950, polio was spreading through the state, responsible for five deaths, with reportable cases numbering eighty-one. Kentucky hospitals began to prepare for the worst, and health and government officials tried to frame their messages of caution so as not to cause panic. As the deadly virus spread and the number of outbreaks rose, so did the level of anxiety experienced by parents, as children and teens were most prone to contract the virus.

War, too, continued to loom as a threat: a quiet, "warm" war being waged against Korea by politicians and military strategists concerned about the spreading of communism. In August, just prior to the start of the season, football programs across the country were put on notice as President Harry Truman's plan to boost the nation's fighting forces to three million or more got support from lawmakers in Washington.

Amid this tense background, signs of a crack in the usually close liaison between the coaches began to surface. Four years after their arrival, a reporter witnessed a communication foible between Laslie and Bryant during their first game of the season against North Texas in September of 1950. Bryant was having trouble injecting a Kentucky substitute into the game. The sub made several attempts to enter the contest but each time circled and came back to the bench. Finally in desperation, Bryant yelled, "Damn it, Laslie, call time out." Laslie tipped his hat in elaborate fashion, a non-verbal "your wish is my command," and immediately the Kentucky captain called time.[107] Although the two had a close friendship that included good natured kidding and teasing, this exchange and mocking of the Bryant "command" was unusual.

By this time, the program had matured into, if not a well-oiled machine, at least one that appeared to be working extremely well. Bryant had morphed Moseley's early radio PR campaign into a regular Sunday morning radio talk show debating college football and the weekend play, and football seemed to be rising to a place of prominence as they continued to vie for the hearts of sports fans in Kentucky. Bryant remained confident, if not expectant, that if he delivered a nationally recognized, bowl-contending team, Coach Adolf Rupp's power and influence would diminish or at least be shared equally with football. He had been assured Rupp's retirement was nearing, his expectation being that the mantle of power would be passed to his shoulders. Laslie and Moseley, doubtful of Rupp's fading into the background any time soon, again tried to convince him otherwise.

Although the Wildcats of '49 had been described as the "surprise team of the South,"[108] it was no surprise that the team of 1950 was a force to contend with. From the beginning, Kentucky was considered a front runner for a bowl game invitation. Babe Parilli, a now seasoned junior quarterback, was all that a coach could hope for. His passing abilities made him a unanimous choice for the pre-season all-SEC backfield, and he had all the offensive strengths of a T-quarterback. With a cornerstone defense led by Bob Gain, sports editors' unanimous choice for outstanding lineman in the conference, and help from a young sophomore guard, Gene Donaldson, also named to a sports editors' all-SEC's team, it was hard imagine they wouldn't be a sure bet for a major bowl appearance.

It had been a remarkable climb since Bryant in 1946 took over what was described as "a ragamuffin Wildcat eleven."[109] Kentucky had played forty-five games. In fifteen of them the opposing team never crossed the goal line. And these included some of the strongest teams in the SEC: Tennessee, Georgia (twice), Louisiana (twice), Vanderbilt, and Ole Miss. According to one admiring sportswriter, "The man who was said to be the most responsible for this record was the silver-haired, handsome, and amiable assistant coach, Carney Laslie."[110]

As predicted, by the time the Tennessee-Kentucky game was played in November, the Tennessee Volunteers had already snagged and accepted an invitation to play in the Cotton Bowl. There was little doubt Kentucky would get an invitation to play at the Sugar Bowl the day after the game, barring a one-sided defeat.

Game day, to be played in Knoxville, was preceded by six inches of snow, the icy roads hampering travel to the game, with temperatures predicted to be freezing. As usual, it was slated to be an emotionally charged game. This time, however, a win for Kentucky meant reaching the pinnacle of accomplishment in several categories. Winning would mean, in addition to breaking the streak of losses since 1926 against a General Neyland–coached Tennessee, that the Wildcats would be the first undefeated, untied team in the history of the school since 1898. A win in Knoxville would also fairly ensure the election of Bryant as Coach of the Year and establish the Wildcats as a bonafide football power in the SEC. The pressure could not have been greater. But not only would they be playing against each other, but also against the elements, in below-zero temperatures, a matchup to prove who could perform best in snow-covered, icy conditions that numbed the hands and burned the lungs.

Kentucky governor-elect Lawrence Wetherby traveled with the team, stayed with them till game time, and flew back with them on their return home. "They are relaxed and determined," he stated pregame. "I think they will play their best game today." Upon leaving the press box after the game, he summed up the result this way: "All of them played their hearts out. I think they lost for the same reason many other great Kentucky teams have lost in the past. They wanted that win a little too much."[111] The game ended with a score of 7–0.

Despite having suffered once again a heartbreaking loss against their nemesis Tennessee, an invitation to the Sugar Bowl was extended to the Wildcats the next day.

It was the opportunity of a lifetime when Virginia Polytechnic, or as it was known then Virginia Polytechnical Institute or VPI, located in Blacksburg, Virginia, came knocking on Coach Laslie's door sometime in October that year and offered him the head coach and athletic director position. VPI's coach, Bob McNeish, had resigned in mid-season, the school's young, freshman-squad coach taking over until a replacement could be found. Laslie had no intention of accepting the offer. Not only was he still strongly aligned with and committed to a Bryant partnership, VPI didn't meet his standard of a big-time football program. But Laslie did have other designs in mind.

Laslie knew Moseley had become disillusioned with Kentucky's overall continued reliance on out-of-state athletes. A longtime proponent of focusing their efforts on in-state recruiting, Moseley had worked hard to elevate Kentucky's football and baseball programs in the minds of the state's high school athletes starting in the '30s, prior to World War II. Moseley's opinion was well known to both of his colleagues, who both agreed in theory. But basketball's rise in prominence during the same time as the Kentucky football program was beginning to gain momentum meant that by 1949, Bryant saw the necessity to continue their out-of-state work to attract top talent.

As Moseley's impatience with their reliance on athletes coming into their program from other states grew, so had his and Edy's family, which now included two young children. His travel responsibilities seemed to have grown as well during this time, as he was regularly visiting Indiana and Illinois. It would appear from the letters he wrote to Edy during this time that he loathed the cold almost as much as he disliked being away from his family; every letter to Edy is filled with complaints about the weather.

"I sure hope that it didn't turn as cold there as it is here—must be just about zero. I have been in the hotel here about fifteen minutes and am still cold," he wrote from Kentland, Indiana, in November 1947. From the Palmer House in Chicago in January of '48, he lamented the frigid temperatures while missing hearth and home, writing, "Here we are 'way up here in the big city and it's so cold that you almost freeze every time you get outside. Right now, its two o'clock in the afternoon and the temperature is one degree above zero—last night it was four below and will probably be the same again tonight. So far, we haven't gotten into any snow, but the papers say that there's plenty on the way. I sure miss my two 'chillun' [that short] stay at home sure did spoil me." And in May 1948, when vestiges of spring and warmer weather were expected, "It seems that every time I come up this way they have snow, rain or hail and this time is no exception. Yesterday was as pretty as could be but today is just about thirty-five degrees and it is really cold."

But it wasn't only the travel, which kept Frank on the road up to six months a year, that was causing his discontent. Frank was miserable knowing Edy was more unhappy and homesick than ever and there was nothing he could do about it.

Though he wasn't interested in the coaching job at VPI in Blacksburg, Virginia, he realized it was a perfect opportunity for Frank Moseley. Laslie knew, however, that if he lost Moseley to Virginia Tech, it meant their coaching partnership would end. Moseley would plant himself in Blacksburg, with Edy close to family, and nothing would lure him back. Weighing all of this together, Laslie turned down the offer from VPI. "I'm not your man," Laslie told them. "Frank Moseley's your man."

Frank accepted the position, and VPI officially announced in December 1950 that he was Virginia bound, his departure for Blacksburg slated to occur in January, a day or two after the Sugar Bowl. For VPI's part, the leaders were "optimistic with such an experienced coach in charge . . . with a fine personality and who was smart."[112] Frank never did know that Laslie had been offered the position first. The offer, however, had come at an opportune time, a high and a low for all three of the close friends who had shared so much of their lives and coaching journey over the years.

The Sugar Bowl of '51 between Kentucky and Oklahoma still stands as one of the most exciting ever played. Bryant and Laslie routinely shared a hotel room during away games, a tradition that continued until the latter days of their career together when Laslie's snoring made it impossible. That New Year's Eve, as Bryant recounted in his autobiography, in the Governor's Suite at their hotel in Baton Rouge, the night before the game, Bryant paced agitatedly while smoking one unfiltered Chesterfield after another, at a loss as to what to do about the weaknesses he saw in their game plan, the players, the strength of their opponent, and worried at the prospect of losing, seeing doom and gloom ahead. Laslie listened dispassionately from his chair, involved in his own usual superstitious routines performed every evening before a game: snapping the newspaper at each turn of the page while he pretended to read, his lips pursed around a cigar, a shot glass of whiskey nearby, listening to Bryant's non-stop talk and analysis. Finally, at the end of his wits, Bryant turned to face the dispassionate coach relaxing in the chair nearby. "Damnit, Carney, we've screwed up again. We've spent ourselves."

"I don't think so," Laslie said cryptically from behind the newspaper.

Not to say that Laslie didn't experience anxiety and worry. Like Bryant, he threw up before every game.

Prior to game day, Oklahoma was named the National Champions. It was an unprecedented move, but Kentucky, with its loss to Tennessee, had dropped to no. 7 in the polls. Both teams had much to prove on game day. In one of the sport's most thrilling games, Kentucky prevailed, 14–13, the coaches' "four-tackle defense" said to surprise Oklahoma just "a little."[113] To this day, both schools lay claim to the title—but Oklahoma only legitimately so.

Three days after the bowl victory, Laslie and Bryant went duck hunting with their former teammate and good friend, Don Hutson. Enthusiastic hunters, they commemorated the historic win by enjoying the camaraderie that hunting had always provided for them, the success celebrated in the company of good friends with a shared football experience.

Following the victory, Frank and Edy packed up their belongings and loaded themselves and their two children into their car to make the six-hour drive from Lexington, Kentucky, to Blacksburg, Virginia. Frank had chosen the love of his life over his love of what an ambitious pairing of coaching talent with his friends might have been able to achieve. Edy, though relieved at moving closer to family, could not be consoled as they drove to Lexington, Virginia. She knew that Paul, Carney and Frank had had such plans. And she was heartbroken about being separated from her best friend, Alice Laslie. Although she and Alice still enjoyed many years of friendship, they would never enjoy the closeness that came from not only enduring so much together but living together for so many years. "She cried her eyes out for the entire six-hour journey," daughter Alene said.

Upon Coach Moseley's departure from Kentucky, Coach Paul Dietzel, in between assistant coaching positions, his wife, Anne, and his mother-in-law, moved into the vacated duplex apartment above the Laslies. Dietzel would go on to make his own mark as a head coach and administrator for the next forty years, most notably at Louisiana State University and the University of South Carolina.

For Frank, the departure was a relief. He could now call the shots. Alene speculated years later that there had been a rift between her father and Bryant that had caused Frank to leave. Mary Lou, however, was emphatic that was not the case. It can be said though, that it was highly likely they had clashed on a number of issues over the years. But in the end, it was an opportunity that had presented itself at just the right time that made the decision to leave an easy one for Frank.

CHAPTER TWENTY-FOUR

Scandals

"... every team in the conference could be wrecked overnight if the SEC meant business, which of course, it emphatically does not."

—Sports reporter Ed Danforth, *Louisville Courier News*

LEXINGTON, KENTUCKY
1951–1952

THE GROWTH OF FREELY TELEVISED football games began to emerge as a lucrative arm of the industry creating more controversy when it began to eat into the gate receipts at games. The NCAA, in an attempt to ban live broadcasts altogether, found itself "edging perilously close to ringing an alarm in the antitrust division of the Justice Department."[114]

All of this spilled into the season of '51 at Kentucky, when Kentucky cried foul after the NCAA refused to televise the sold-out Kentucky-Tennessee game, which was to be played in Knoxville. Kentucky's governor Lawrence Wetherby protested the action, sending a telegram to the attorney general of the United States charging conspiracy, noting the NCAA's television policy had, at the last minute, been reversed so as to televise the popular Notre Dame–Michigan matchup after pressure from Michigan football alumni and then Michigan congressman Gerald Ford. Weatherby's failed to change the decision. The local Kentucky TV station planned to defy the NCAA's ruling at the last minute, but the University of Kentucky refused to go along. And with good reason. The NCAA was contemplating drastic action against the scandal involving Kentucky's championship basketball team, which had been under investigation for over a year. Kentucky thought it wiser to refrain from irritating the powerful association.

Laslie's disdain for the Fighting Irish of Notre Dame solidified during the ensuing years, as politics and money began to have an increasing influence on the sport. Gate receipts mattered, and he was no fool in that regard, saying, "He who has the gold makes the rules." This was not lost on his aspirations for any university he would serve in the future. Now media contracts, too, added greater weight to the ability of a school to make money from its sports teams. Winning figured prominently in a school's ability to attract media, and thereby future students.

After Kentucky's spectacular upset of Oklahoma in the Sugar Bowl, the team suffered the loss of its seniors to graduation, upending the championship defensive line going into the fall. Offensively, however, Vito "Babe" Parilli returned with his passing prowess, which promised to provide a dazzling display of football that fall.

On the day of the Wildcats' opening football game against Villanova in 1951, the basketball point-shaving scandal dominated headlines. Rumors had swirled over the past year with allegations investigated vigorously by the NCAA. The timing of the findings couldn't have been worse, coinciding with the opening of the fall football season. Kentucky basketball players Alex Groza, center, and guard Ralph Beard from the team's so-called "Fab-Five" and another teammate, Dale Barnstable, all admitted to conspiring to shave points in exchange for bribes from gamblers. They were arrested in a sting operation that netted a total of nearly forty players and several gamblers. It was a nationwide roundup of those accused, and the ramifications were severe, as they all faced possible jail sentences.

But even more shocking was the implication of Kentucky's football program, with two of its players accused of receiving illegal payments. One of those was All-American hopeful Gene Donaldson. Many saw this inclusion of the football players, who were accused of taking payment for work not actually done in university-sponsored summer jobs, as an overreach by the NCAA. Others saw it as the association's way to make an example out of Kentucky by exhibiting a zero-tolerance policy for any workaround that schools may have in place to help athletes financially, no matter how meager the amount.

The accusation against Donaldson consisted of receiving a dollar-an-hour job at a local architect firm for dubious work. It totaled a paltry amount. The other implicated football player, Chet Ludowski, was charged with accepting a hundred dollars to purchase clothing. Many athletic programs, specifically football, at universities across the country were doing the same: a nod and a wink toward the NCAA's policy as they sought to support their athletes who struggled financially.

When the case went to trial in New York, it became the face of what all considered was wrong in big-time sports in general. Judge Samuel S. Streit, who oversaw the case, expressed "disgust at the reckless disregard of the coaches, alumni, townspeople and their most flagrant abuse of 'athletic scholarships.'"[115] He went on to criticize the basketball and football squads at Kentucky as the epitome of a school focused on commercialism and overemphasis of sports over academics even though the scandal of point-shaving that he was addressing had taken place only on the basketball court. Streit assailed what he saw as an athletic scholarship racket that threatened to undermine the amateur code. It was those athletes who attended schools in New

York whose involvement was considered criminal, the only ones given prison sentences.

When the closed-door hearings with the NCAA finally concluded, the decision regarding the football program was announced. Football players Donaldson and Lukowski were permanently suspended from football. UK President Donovan, however, agreed to Bryant's request to appeal the decision on behalf of Donaldson, whose allegations were more likely to be challenged, and whose All-American title was hanging in the balance. At the release of the ruling, Ed Danforth, sportswriter for the *Atlanta Constitution*, tellingly wrote, "If Donaldson's rewards were done for work done out of line, then every team in the conference could be wrecked overnight if the SEC meant business, which of course, it emphatically does not."

Donaldson's fate hung in the balance until the fall of '52, his senior year, when the appeal process was to be finalized. Hounded by reporters for months prior to the ruling, he found refuge at the Bryant's home where he was shielded from the unwanted publicity, sometimes joining Mrs. Bryant at the University of Kentucky horse stables where the quiet and peace of a wooded horse trail was a welcomed retreat.

CHAPTER TWENTY-FIVE

The Day the Music Died

"I've had a lot of applications for this job. You were not one.
But I want you to take it if you will."

—Col. Earl "Red" Blaik, head coach, West Point, 1941 to 1958

LEXINGTON, KENTUCKY
1951

IN A REVERSAL OF fortune reminiscent of the previous year's pre-game Cotton Bowl selection, officials surprised Kentucky with an invitation to the 1952 Cotton Bowl prior to the annual Tennessee-Kentucky game. It was nothing short of stunning. The 'Cats, with three losses that season, had assumed they needed a victory over Tennessee to ensure their place in the bowl lineup on New Year's Day 1952. Now, a third straight major bowl game appearance for Kentucky in three years was assured.

The coaches and players were jubilant, accepting the honor

without hesitation, matched up with a soon-to-be-determined Southwest Conference champion after a game played in two weeks. The pressure associated with the game against Tennessee was clearly relieved. A little. There was still that little matter of defeating Coach General Neyland, and Bryant and Laslie wanted nothing less.

But the accomplishment was quickly overshadowed, the news that Kentucky was Cotton-Bowl bound reported on the same day it was announced that Jack West, one of the accused "Fixers" in the basketball point-shaving scandal, was sentenced to two to three years in prison. Details about the prison sentences of five of the accused basketball players, three from Long Island, and two from City College New York, who were involved in the scandal, were included in the report as well. The three Kentucky players, Ralph Beard, Alex Groza, and Dale Barnstable, who had confessed to taking bribes from gamblers to affect the outcome of Kentucky games, were reportedly given suspended prison sentences and barred from all sports for three years. In addition, players from two other New York schools implicated in the scandal – Manhattan College and New York University – were given suspended sentences, along with four players from Toledo University, and three from Bradley University in Peoria, Illinois.

In his published statements from New York City where the trial took place, Judge Streit chose once again to summarily chastise coaches and their role in what he considered a pervasive exploitation of athletes in the amateur college ranks. The scandal, described as a network of athletes at various schools running an illegal gambling racket, exposed what he warned were the dark realities colleges and universities faced with the increasing profitability of the sport and the ongoing tension between athletics and education.

In his lengthy comments against collegiate basketball, which was a tirade against college athletics in general, Streit pointed to an overemphasis on recruiting athletes and singled out programs he felt to be especially egregious: Kentucky, Oklahoma, Texas, Texas A&M,

Southern Methodist, Pennsylvania, Tennessee, and Maryland. Of those schools listed, only Kentucky had been directly implicated in the basketball scandal. Directly adjacent to an article on the sports page where Judge Streit's scathing indictment of collegiate sports appeared, was a column in which Coach Bryant extolled the hard work done by the players that year which had earned them an early invitation to play in the coveted Cotton Bowl game of 1952.

Four days later, on November 28, 1951, Kentucky played Tennessee in their annual contest, the game ending in a tie. Although the Wildcats were disappointed not to have won the game, they were also relieved not to have lost, acknowledging a game well played by both teams. The playoff for the other spot in the Cotton Bowl was as much anticipated as the Bowl game itself, Baylor predicted to prevail over Texas Christian University, giving what many believed would be the most thrilling match-up against Kentucky. But it was Texas Christian that prevailed, disappointing sports pundits and, of course, Baylor fans alike.

Kentucky went on to decisively beat TCU, capping a three-year streak of back-to-back bowl wins. At the first post-game press conference, Bryant stunned the college football world with his announcement that he would stop all recruiting of players outside the state of Kentucky. They would offer only "five grants-in-aid" or scholarships, and these would most likely go to brothers or sons of former UK players. It was a bombshell.

The years from 1946 to 1951 are now remembered as the golden era of Kentucky football. It had been built on aggressive recruiting efforts spearheaded by Bryant, Laslie, and Moseley as they took the Wildcats from a struggling and inconsistently talented field of players to one that was consistently able to deliver. Star players from Kentucky who had topped national polling lists of the best in the sport were all out-of-state recruits. These included players like quarterback Babe Parilli, from Rochester, Pennsylvania; tackle Bob Gain, from Akron, Ohio; and Walt Yowarsky, the MVP of UK's epic 1951 Sugar Bowl upset of number one Oklahoma, who was from Cleveland. Gene

Donaldson came from East Chicago, Indiana, and All-American end Steve Meilinger from Bethlehem, Pennsylvania. The out-of-state recruiting ban was a controversial move, but Bryant, who had already lost one crucial senior aide in Frank Moseley, didn't want to lose his "wing-man," Carney Laslie, as the rigors of travel were taking a toll on his family as well.

Alice was more unhappy than ever now that Edy and Frank had left, though Paul Dietzel and his wife, Anne, had become friends while living in the other half of the duplex. The decision to stop out-of-state recruiting played out as if to appease university officials after the point-shaving scandal and reflected what many presumed to be Bryant's bowing to the pressure of the trustees and President Donovan to change the "win at all costs" narrative.

Rival programs jumped with glee, and others raised eyebrows in skepticism, wondering what had truly prompted the turnabout. But as Bryant stated in his autobiography when the decision was announced, he wasn't worried about the success or failure of the new program. He had been "discussing the move with intimate friends for several years," stating what he hoped would be the result: having fun overall. He was ready to settle in and enjoy the fruits of their labor having arrived at a place that they had worked so hard to achieve.

President Donovan made his own statement. He rewarded Bryant immediately after the victory by extending his contract another ten years. Rupp was given a Cadillac. Later, at a luncheon in Oklahoma City, Bryant's address to the Quarterback Club included a humorous illustration of how he felt he and the football program were valued as compared to Coach Rupp and the basketball program. Coach Rupp was given a Cadillac at the end of the season, Bryant told the crowd, and I got something like a "little old cigarette lighter."[116] Though it was not a literal fact (though Rupp did receive a Cadillac) the narrative spanned for decades, and is a case of "when fiction becomes fact, print the fiction."

Sharing the headlines with Kentucky's basketball debacle in August

of '51 was the fallout of a cheating scandal of historic proportions that
had occurred at West Point. Although it happened over 740 miles away,
the scandal would come to impact the University of Kentucky, landing
right at the doorstep of its own football program.

It was early in the month when the United States' premiere military
academy at West Point announced that almost its entire varsity football
team had been accused of violating the school's hallowed honor code.
Among the players accused was the son of the school's revered coach,
Coach Red Blaik. The shock of the failure of these young men, an
elite group whose mere attendance at the academy identified them
as some of the nation's most honorable, rocked the foundations of
the institution, from the highest-ranking officers in the whole of the
military to the plebes, or freshmen, newly arrived on campus.

The Black Knights of the Hudson had fielded some of the country's
best football teams from 1943 right after WWII through 1946, and
had captured the imagination of the nation. This despite the criticism
leveled against Coach Blaik accusing him "of cutting corners to get big-
time talent."[117] The school was now in a different and unwelcome type
of spotlight with even President Harry Truman weighing in, voicing
his disappointment and concern about the incident and its future
repercussions if it wasn't handled expeditiously. After all, this was
no ordinary school, but was where the nation's top army officers and
leaders were trained.

Ninety players were implicated, and swift action followed. The
varsity squad was decimated just as the season of '51 was about to
get underway. The prestigious program had gone undefeated five
seasons in the previous ten years. It was a bitter turn of events for the
powerhouse team that had great expectations for the upcoming fall
season of '51.

Calls for speedy hearings abounded, forty-five out of the ninety cases already processed a mere week after the scandal broke. Col. Blaik strongly recommended honorable discharges for the players but recognized the backlash it would cause from both the cadet corps and the public. The final result of the disciplinary action left only two members of the previous year's varsity team to start in September.

While Kentucky football basked in its achievements at the end of the season, West Point suffered their first losing season in twenty years. Thus began The Point's search for the most exemplary coaches in the nation to rebuild its demoralized team for the '52 season. One of the first coaches consulted by the search team was General Neyland, Tennessee's famed coach, a West Pointer himself. Though he conceded his recommendation was a Navy man, Neyland endorsed the top defensive coach in the country: Carney Laslie.

March of '52, Kentucky basketball was in the headlines once again. In what seemed to be a redemption of sorts from the betting scandal the year before, Kentucky narrowly won the NCAA's Southeastern Basketball Conference in Louisville, Kentucky. The celebration quickly faded however, when, the day after their win, the university announced that Kentucky All-American center, Bill Spivey, a key player on the NCAA championship team of 1950, was barred from further play at Kentucky. It was an ominous predicator of what many warned would occur as a result of the ongoing investigation, the implications for the entire Kentucky athletic program hanging in the balance. It didn't take long.

The day after that announcement, the phone at the Laslie home rang. "New York calling," said the operator when Carney answered. Carney was trying to recall who he knew in New York when he heard, "This is Earl Blaik calling. I've heard a lot of good things about you and your coaching. We are interested in men of your caliber at West Point. Would you be good enough to come up and have a talk with us?"[118]

Laslie dropped his cigarette on the living room rug. Alice rushed in, stepping on it lightly to put it out as Carney replied, "I'm very happy here. I have a good job. I like Kentucky—but I'll be glad to come talk."

The next weekend, the Laslies traveled to West Point visiting with Colonel and Mrs. Blaik, touring the campus and the community of Highland Falls. As they readied to leave and travel back to Lexington, Col. Blaik posed the offer. "I've had a lot of applications for this job. You were not one. But I want you to take it if you will."

Alice was delighted for a number of reasons, not the least of which was a raise in pay for her husband. Added to that was a choice between four homes, all different types. A thrilling prospect. She was also happy to be moving closer to "home."

Born in upper state New York, Alice's parents, Harriet Louise Hitchcock and Lester Jay Backus, were both from the Empire State. When the two met, Louise was teaching at a school outside of West Point, and Lester was tutoring the two young sons of the Carnegie-Mellon family in New York City. Although Carney and Alice knew Mary Lou would be hard to convince the move was "good news", the opportunity for Alice, who had lost her mother at the age of nine, to follow in Louise's footsteps seemed a bit full circle to Alice. She remembered a story from her childhood, chronicled in her grandfather's journal, about an infamous trip her then twelve year old uncle, Louise's younger brother, made by train to visit his sister. Looking forward to spending the weekend with his older sister and in particular seeing some of the historic sites, he was heartbroken when he arrived on Friday and learned that Louise had accepted a last minute invitation from a cadet to attend a football game being played at West Point the next day. Not be be deterred in his own plans, he walked several miles to the home of Revolutionary War traitor Benedict Arnold and back. Hopeful as the Laslies were that Mary Lou, too, might be as enthusiastic as her great-uncle was about moving to a place with such historic significance, they were not surprised when that was not the case. Instead, they promised their daughter the larger bedroom in their new home complete with the private bath, and threw in the use of the family car.

On March 13, Mary Lou's sixteenth birthday, Carney accepted the position. He would be the top assistant at West Point, becoming the highest paid number two man on a coaching staff in the country, with an impressive $11,000 annual salary plus a house on campus and the privilege of buying groceries at Army prices. Travel, too, would be minimal.

Years later, Bryant revealed that General Neyland contacted him and informed him he would be recommending Bryant's top assistant for a position at West Point. Bryant, however, admitted later that he never thought Laslie would accept. When the news leaked, reporters clamored to reach Bryant at his home. "We'd like to speak to Coach Bryant to get his reaction to the news that Coach Laslie will be leaving," one caller asked.

"He can't come to the phone right now," replied Mary Harmon. "He's in the bedroom crying his eyes out," one sportswriter reported in his weekly column for the *Lexington Courier*.

Sports pundits speculated that the addition of Laslie to the West Point coaching staff paved the way for Coach Blaik's eminent departure given the scope of the scandal, assuming Laslie would take over the head coach position. But Col. Blaik had no such intentions. He was committed to rebuilding from the ground up. And he would stay on to see it through.

Others, including friends, were puzzled by Laslie's move. One hastily written note from a fellow coach and friend from his Pre-Flight Navy days was found in Laslie's papers. Now at the University of Arkansas, he wrote of his surprise at learning of Carney's departure from Kentucky. "You must have your reasons," he wrote, "but I was surprised you were separating from Bryant." One reason may have been a pragmatic one related to Kentucky's basketball scandal, as many believed big time college basketball was nearly destroyed by the scandal of '51. With the appeal of Kentucky's Gene Donaldson's player status hanging in the balance and not to be decided until mid-year of '52, Laslie may have weighed what he would have considered to be continued problems with Rupp in the picture, hampering his own reputation overall. It was a situation he didn't see changing. As it turned out, basketball survived its near-fatal blow, but Bryant's tenure there did not.

Many attributed the decision to end out-of-state recruiting at Kentucky as the reason for the football program's eventual decline, 1951 being its last season of sporting triumphs. To this day, the late '40s and early '50s remain the greatest years of success in UK sports history. But it can also be said that on March 20, 1952, when Coach Carney Laslie announced he would depart and move to West Point, also marked the end of Kentucky's run as a football powerhouse program. And even though Laslie would later lament over never having beaten Tennessee while he was at Kentucky, Bryant would finally deliver the blow without his top assistant the following year.

Bryant stayed on for two more seasons with rumors continuing to swirl during that time. Rumors, however, continued to swirl during this time. Many wondered if Bryant would leave Lexington after the '52 season, which he consistently denied. Friends asserted he would return to Alabama, a program that had diminished significantly over the years, "a shadow of its former self when he played there." It was strongly rumored, though, that Coach Rupp would soon retire. It was a hope that Bryant had always held out for, the university board asserting as much behind closed doors as well. It would, Bryant believed, pave the way for football to become Lexington's toast of the town over the next seven years remaining on his contract. But in August of 1953, Rupp laughed off the rumors of his retirement, telling reporters he had no such intention. That would be Bryant's last season coaching the Wildcats.

On Thursday, February 4, of 1954, Bryant announced, to the utter consternation of the Kentucky alumnus, his intention to quit the coaching post at UK and go to Texas to coach at Texas A&M. On the front page of February 7th's edition of Lexington's Sunday morning Herald- Leader, a prominent, unidentified alumnus, blasted Bryant's announcement: "Our Athletics Association, fortunately, is composed of men of courage, men who realize that Fair-Play Boulevard is not a one-way street: men who know that others' obligations to those they represent will not allow them to cancel a contract which results in such deep hurt and great damage to people, who, in good faith, relied upon." President Donovan followed suit, announcing that he would not recommend to the UK Athletic Association that Bryant's resignation be accepted—at least not until a satisfactory replacement was found. The stern criticism aimed towards Bryant could just as well have been uttered by Bryant himself about what he had understood the University's obligations to him were. His only response to the outrage, however, was to reiterate his decision to quit Kentucky and become the new head coach and athletic director at Texas A&M.

The news of Kentucky's unwillingness to release Bryant from his contract travelled fast and Texas A&M quietly rescinded their verbal offer. Bryant, however, made the decision to leave Kentucky, even without the assurance of a signed contract at A&M. Alone at the train station in Lexington on his way to Texas, when asked of his plans he confessed that at the moment he didn't have a job. It was a bold move.

A&M was back on board with Bryant soon enough. He knew the Aggies, who had had lagged in performance for thirteen years in the Southwest Conference, needed someone like him to shape-up their program and make them winners. Bryant, true to his word, embarked on his own brand of shaking-up the program, leaving both criticism and accolades in his wake, and a scandal which evolved almost immediately upon his arrival. The players who survived his tough tactics used to weed out players that summer and fall came to be known as "The Junction Boys."

PART V

COACH CARNEY LASLIE
WEST POINT, 1952–1957

CHAPTER TWENTY-SIX

Moving On

"Coaching at the Point could produce ulcers. The responsibilities toward the Cadets, toward the Pentagon, toward the great American football public, are greater than those besetting a coach in any other institution in the college field."[119]

—Dan Daniel, American Sportswriter, Chairman of the
Football Writers' Association

WEST POINT, NEW YORK
1952–1954

THE THREE-STAR GENERAL played only one year of freshman football at West Point almost sixty-five years ago, but he still remembers Coach Laslie's booming voice as he paced between the rows of cadets prone on the field doing push-ups. "Assholes and elbows! All I want to see are assholes and elbows!"

"I wasn't exactly sure what that meant," said General Thomas Griffin III, chuckling bashfully. "But I got the gist of it." Head down, butt up, and keep up the pace. Every player on the field knew they were out there to push themselves past their own perceived physical limits each time they reported to the athletic practice field. "At West Point, they didn't churn out All-Americans by being soft," General Griffin stated. "The coaches demanded 110 percent. And they got results."

Coach Laslie described his new boss, Coach Earl "Red" Blaik (always referred to as Col. Blaik by players and coaches alike), as part General Neyland, Tennessee's illustrious coach, part Coach John Bain "Jock" Sutherland of University of Pittsburgh fame and part Coach Wallace Wade of Alabama. "They're the same type, though Col. Blaik might not have been as rough as the rest," he admitted in an interview years later.[120]

He knew Col. Blaik to be a good disciplinarian but suspected he didn't have the disciplinary problems of most college coaches, given the strict rules governing life as a cadet. Most of all, it was his ability as an organizer that Laslie saw as his greatest talent, a necessary skill since at Army practice was allotted an hour and a half a day, with only one meeting a week with the squad on Sunday after chapel for the scouting report on the upcoming week's game. It took organization to make the most of every moment. For instance, photos were taken during practice, developed on site, so they could be studied the same day after supper.

When Coach Laslie arrived at West Point, he was perhaps facing his greatest challenge. Col. Blaik focused all of his coaching on offenses, his strategies, according to Laslie, among the best he'd seen. Credited for the Wildcat's tough defensive line, which had placed Kentucky first in the nation in total defense in 1949 and second in the same category the following year, Laslie was known for his ability to build a rugged line. He had exhibited both aggressive and clean play on the defense and remarkable smoothness on the offense at Kentucky. West Point looked to the acclaimed coach to repeat much of the same with the now non-existent Army varsity line at the start of Army's season of '52.

The pressure that existed at West Point, however, had always had its own level of responsibility, as pointed out by Dan Daniel in an article published in the *New York World Telegram* and *The Sun*: "Coaching at the Point could produce ulcers. The responsibilities toward the Cadets, toward the Pentagon, toward the great American football public, are greater than those besetting a coach in any other institution in the college field." But there were other reasons why coaching at the famed military academy might produce ulcers for the new line coach.

A football coach at an all-male institution with a sixteen-year-old daughter was also a newsworthy event. Curiosity about what dating looked like under the auspices of being the "coach's daughter" abounded. Local newspapers clamored for an interview with the attractive, brunette Mary Lou Laslie. As Mary Lou revealed in one published interview, dating a member of the cadet corps had its drawbacks. The boys shunned any appearance of breaking rules that could possibly incur the wrath of the coach and were known to "run a block"[121]—that is, run interference—to protect the coach's daughter from any they believed were not exhibiting the manners of an officer and a gentleman. It was perhaps a disadvantage from a coach's daughter's point of view. But there were advantages from a parent's point of view when the football team of cadets had a collective protective eye watching out for the winsome teenager with the soft Southern drawl. "You always know where your daughter is and what time she will be home," Alice was fond of saying.[122]

Mary Lou Laslie was not amused at all the attention, thinking it silly and embarrassing. From the beginning she admitted feeling conspicuously unsophisticated among the group of other coaches' daughters. One of her earliest acquaintances was Linda Draper, daughter of the athletic director. Linda's aunt and Alice Laslie were longtime friends, having attended the same exclusive boarding school in Atlanta. Linda impressed the conservative Mary Lou right away, dressed in her Bermuda shorts cut scandalously above the knee, countering Mary Lou's mother's strict advice: "Girls at the Point never wear shorts or blue jeans even on a picnic." But it was Linda's down-to-earth personality coupled with her air of sophistication borne out of traveling the world that contributed to their lifelong friendship.

Three years older than Mary Lou, Linda made it her mission to indoctrinate Mary Lou into all things "West Point." Never say dance, instructed Linda, it's a "hop." A date is a "drag." And girls are always "femmes."

Mary Lou also learned about and joined in with those gathering to observe the football team running drills and training exercises. Among those regular spectators were the Reeder sisters, Dodie and Anne, daughters of Colonel "Red" Reeder, one of the Point's baseball coaches.

Colonel Reeder, considered by Coach Vince Lombardi, then a young assistant offensive line coach at West Point, to be among "the greatest leader of men I've ever been around,"[123] was often seen "rushing around from athletic building to one practice field or another, always sporting his signature Army baseball cap. Colonel Reeder had played football and baseball at West Point as a young man, then turned down an offer to play pro with the NY Giants at triple the salary," opting instead for a career in the military. He lost a leg in World War II, but despite this enjoyed nothing more than a good round of golf with his fellow coaches, often including Coach Laslie.

His love for the military life spilled into a love of writing after taking a correspondence writing course in 1954. Rising at dawn, he sat diligently at his desk, banging away at the typewriter keys for hours before having to report for duty at 0800 hours. This led to penning thirty-five books over the next twenty-five years, including one that would inspire the movie *The Long Gray Line* about the legacy of West Point and its contributions to the growth of a nation. His series of young adult novels, most notably *West Point Plebe*, were influential in moving a generation of boys to choose the Army life."

Dodie and Anne Reeder, two years Mary Lou's junior and two years her senior, respectively, had become close friends with her almost immediately after the Laslies' arrival. The sisters also imparted sound advice to the newest member of the Junior Army Daughters Club. "Never, never hold hands on the street with a cadet or the boy will have to walk the area." This is a form of discipline for all cadets. The only exception is Flirtation Walk, they told her, where the cadets take their "drags." In Mary Lou's opinion, all these girls were much more grown up and worldly-wise than she was.

One afternoon at the practice field, the mostly female spectators lining the chain-link fence at the edge of the field quickly drew the ire of Coach Laslie. The "fans" routinely created an unwelcome and unappreciated distraction for the cadets. Being ordered to take two laps around the field at the conclusion of practice by the eagle-eyed Coach Laslie if he as much caught a glance toward the fence, a grueling punishment for a player who managed a momentary glance, was not enough of a deterrent. It didn't take long for Coach Laslie to come up with a solution. Soon there appeared a large black curtain on wheels placed strategically in front of the observation area, successfully blocking any spectators, female or otherwise, to prevent spectators from seeing the field and players from seeing the spectators. Needless to say, there were disappointed fans. But for Coach Laslie it was a creative solution to a serious mental distraction for his players. Touchdown.

Coach Laslie's future son-in-law, Cadet James R. Henry,
West Point, Class of '54.

CHAPTER TWENTY-SEVEN

The Nation is Watching

"A cadet shall not lie, cheat,
or steal or tolerate anyone who does."

—West Point Honor Code

WEST POINT, NEW YORK
1952

WHEN WEST POINT SUPERINTENDENT Major General Frederick Irving's letter to retired Brigadier General Chauncey Fenton, president of the school's Association of Graduates was made public it would ignite both support and outrage among cadets and alumni alike. In the letter, he accused the ninety West Point cadets dismissed in 1951 as belonging to an "organized cheating ring". The result was that they all were immediately and summarily dismissed. Irving also addressed the overall clamor of criticism of football by a vocal group of alumni who accused the academy of misplaced priorities with too much emphasis on winning. "This situation has nothing to do with itself," he wrote at the conclusion of his letter.[124]

Coach Laslie arrived in 1952, in the midst of this scandal and controversy, joining the existing staff, (including a young Vince Lombardi) to coach the line. They were all given a clear objective by West Point's already legendary head coach Blaik: to rebuild a team gutted by the dismissal of most all of the varsity players and to recapture the pride and honor of the cadet corps. Just five years prior, Col. Blaik had been chosen Coach of the year by his peers, the Football Coaching Association of America. Now his reputation was sullied, the breaking of the cadet honor code—"a cadet shall not lie, cheat or steal or tolerate anyone who does"—occurring during his watch. The humiliation included his own son, the quarterback on the team, implicated in the scandal and subsequently kicked out of West Point. There was much at stake with the upcoming season of '52, not the least of which was restoring the confidence of the nation in the academy's ability to train future officers leading the military.

Approximately eighteen months prior to the cheating ring bust at West Point, a star football and track athlete at Erasmus High School in Brooklyn, New York, named Pete Manus, was being aggressively recruited by universities around the country including West Point and it's head coach, Col. "Red" Blaik. Not only did Pete respect Blaik, who was a pillar of the coaching world, but like most, he was in awe of him.

Savvy for his age and possessing enough bravado to act as his own "free agent," Pete made what would be a bold move by any standard.

During a private meeting with Col. Blaik, the high school senior offered Blaik a two-for-one deal: Pete would accept West Point's offer with the condition that Blaik guarantee his brother George, then a high school sophomore and also an excellent football player, be accepted to West Point in two years, fulfilling a dream the brothers had of one day playing at West Point together. Pete promised Col. Blaik he would keep the deal to himself, telling no one, not even his brother, assuring

Blaik he would get two excellent players in the deal. It was agreed, and they shook hands, the mutual understanding of one's word of honor sealing the deal passing between them. Neither Pete nor Col. Blaik could foresee the disastrous events that would befall the football program in the ensuing months. It would change everything.

When Col. Blaik released his new roster of players for '51 in the wake of the scandal, it was a team that had been stripped of all but two players, reduced to a squad thirty-one men instead of the normal number of forty-five. Nineteen on the new varsity squad were from the freshman team of the previous year, including Pete Manus. The rest of recruits came from the "B"-team, Including a 152-pound player by the name of Bill Haff, who was described by the coaches as a "very fine runner who will make us a good offensive man despite his lack of weight."[125] The coaches, desperate to field a team, had to justify their reasoning for assigning Haff to the fullback position, since fulllbacks are generally bigger in size, stronger and more physical than the half-backs they are assigned to protect.

The football schedule of the season of '51 was a grueling one. There was no bravado as the coaches looked at the lineup of games. They were lucky to be able to field a team at all, let alone win one game against any of the schools they would be playing, even those teams they had always easily beaten.

Pete found himself on the Black Knights varsity squad as a sophomore defensive back-fielder, all the rising seniors and most of the rising juniors having been kicked off. In one of the first games played by the reduced squad early in the season, Pete suffered an injury, benching him for several games until October 27, 1951, in a game against Columbia University. Scouts at the game noted that although the cadets were faster than many of their opponents their inexperience showed; sixteen fumbles already in the season up to the Columbia game. Every game day had the potential for serious injury, their opponents being bigger, stronger and more experienced. Despite being bruised and battered, taking a beating every game, they suited up week after week knowing they would be facing a bigger, stronger, more experienced foe on the field. Looking back, Pete wondered how they made it through without more severe injuries. They finished the season, forfeiting none, with their worst game record ever, losing seven of nine games played. Army's first losing season since 1947.

Soon after the season's end, Pete learned his brother, George, would not be accepted into West Point. Despite his just objections, the decision was final, the cheating scandal negating any agreement made by Col. Blaik between anyone outside of the appropriate channels. Instead, George who never knew of his brother's private arrangement with Blaik, was none the wiser, and would go on to be an outstanding cadet at VMI. However for Pete, his disapointment in the revered coach lasted a lifetime.

On a hot day at the end of August, fifty players showed up for the first official practice of the '52 season and despite the heat donned full gear. Greeting the cadets was West Point's new line coach Carney Laslie. The 1952 squad consisted of forty-four players. Nineteen were members of the previous year's freshman squad and ten were from the "B" team whose primary purpose had been to give the varsity a workout. Despite the clear challenges they were still battling, up against teams composed of mostly juniors and seniors with more experience who were that much bigger and stronger, they were not spared from a tough, seemingly impossible game schedule. Each school they faced was a leader in its region. It was immediately described as the most difficult schedule in West Point history. Among the schools they were slated to play was an undefeated Georgia, and the number one ranked team in the east, Pennsylvania. The twenty-two players from the season before who had gained experience were counted on more than ever to provide the leadership the team so desperately needed for the daunting task that lay before them.

The cheating incident had also left lingering, never-publicized effects on Army football players in the seasons that followed, effects witnessed and painfully felt by the young, inexperienced B and C teams. In several cases, the players became subjects of totally unwarranted suspicions and stinging criticisms simply because they were Army football players, creating disunity between the overall Corps of Cadets, who were angered by the damage done to their own reputations, and the players themselves. The surviving players, too, were left disillusioned. The varsity squad, which they had looked up to not only as models of athletic accomplishment but also of character, had failed them all.

CHAPTER TWENTY-EIGHT

Army vs Duke

"When Bob Mischak, who was posthumously enshrined in the Army/West Point Sports Hall of Fame in 2017, made that unlikely play, what Blaik called 'a marvelous display of heart and pursuit,' the Army football team regained its soul."

—David Maraniss, *When Pride Still Mattered*

THE POLO GROUNDS STADIUM,
UPPER MANHATTAN, NEW YORK CITY
1953

WHAT HAD BEEN KNOWN as a one-platoon system, also known as iron-man football, where players played on both offense and defense, was changed to a two-platoon system, and remains an integral part of the modern game today. Teams scrambled to compete under the more complicated substitution rules. Col. Blaik, with an already pared-down roster because of the cheating scandal, didn't have the ability to add players to the team like non-military universities, which had a variety of ways to quickly bolster their number of players needed for the new rule change.

The NCAA rule changes impacted other areas that weren't visible to cadets and Army sports fans but were quite clear to team members, and that was the pursuit of varsity status and the Major A award. This coveted award was given annually to the cadet(s) who displayed the "most valuable service to intercollegiate athletics during a career as a cadet."[126] Those 1953 team members who at the end of the 1952 season believed they had almost secured a starting offensive or defensive platoon position suddenly found themselves being retested and moved from one position to another to determine who could play both offense and defense and had the conditioning, strength, and stamina to play both ways. Some had their standing for an award jeopardized due to the reorganization. Their extraordinary individual responses, chronicled by teammates and classmates alike in the nomination of the team for the Army's Hall of Fame, were inspirational, highlighting individual willingness to sacrifice for the team.

After the disastrous events of '51 and posting their first losing season in five years, the focus of all the West Point coaches in '52 was on rebuilding the team and restoring morale. They clawed their way up, posting a four-win, four-loss, and one tie season: a monumental accomplishment for players and coaches alike. Coach Lombardi, looking to move to the NFL, left to become the offensive coordinator for the New York Giants before taking the head coach position for the Green Bay Packers in 1959. Lombardi would later name Blaik as the man he admired most, the most influential, and the "greatest grid-iron teacher" of his career. The remaining coaches looked to the fall of '53 and the season of '54, where they knew a seemingly impossible season lay ahead.

In a game Col. Blaik himself called "The Game never to be forgotten," Army made it's comeback. The game took place at the Polo Grounds Stadium in Upper Manhattan in 1953. Duke, ranked number seven in the nation, was undefeated and had won the first four games of the season. The Blue Devils were favored by ten for the game to be played that Saturday, October 18. Duke was a "big team of musclemen [who] outweighed the cadets by fifteen pounds per man on the line."[127] But it was a 225-pound, All-American from Duke, Ed "Country" Meadows, that had Army staff the most worried. Even Col. Blaik, who rarely gave accolades to players on his own team let alone an opposing team, singled him out while giving an interview for the local paper, saying, "He has wonderful pursuit. He's big, tough and very aggressive." The only way Army could prevail would be a passing game that went over Meadows's head. Or so they thought. It would instead be the Black Knights' defense that stopped the Blue Devils in their tracks.

The corps' preparation for the game was more than unusual. The cheerleaders imposed a silence in place of the traditional pre-game sendoff, not to be broken until they reached the stadium. After Coach Blaik finished a stirring address to the entire Corps of Cadets during the noon meal, the cadets maintained a steely silence. One can imagine the clenching of teeth as they remained so until the designated time when the "result [was] likened to a cork in the bottle," an explosion of emotion let loose after more than two years of pent-up frustration.

Duke fans, in anticipation of a Blue Devil victory, dominated the stands. They watched quietly as the cadets' entered into the stadium, the traditional pre-game march strangely silent. When "the last man double-timed onto the first step of the stands the men in gray exploded. They shook that old stadium almost non-stop in the sunshine and shadows of that Indian summer afternoon. The chanting—'Go! Go! Go!'—is remembered to this day by the players. 'It was continuous, just deafening.'"[128]

Mary Lou Laslie heard the roar from outside the stadium. She had lost her ticket to the game, delayed at the ticket gate trying without much success to convince them to let her in. Her father was an Army coach, she kept asserting. She needed to get into the stadium to watch the game. When the stadium rocked with the roaring of cheers that didn't let up, those at the gate were so overtaken by the commotion they finally conceded. She ran to find her place among the cheering Army fans just in time for the kick-off.

Back and forth the scoring went with Army putting the first seven points on the scoreboard in the first quarter. Duke tied it up in the second quarter and the score stayed tied until the final two minutes of the second quarter when Army scored again, the scoreboard showing Army 14, Duke 7 at the half. The Army stands had not let up, their cheers deafening. During halftime, a drum major for the Duke band found an Army cadet, saying, "I had to come over and tell someone. That's the most beautiful noise I've ever heard. I don't see how you could lose."

The second half was a thrilling back and forth with Duke fumbling, Army recovering, then Army fumbling again, only to recover and then fumble again, losing possession on the twenty-nine-yard line. It took Duke five plays to make it to the goal line when Duke's quarterback, Worth Lutz (known as Worth "A Million" Lutz), ran eighteen yards down the sideline before being stopped at the four. Lutz again took it from the four in for the touchdown but fumbled at the goal line, the ball bobbling in the air wildly before he was able to grab it and fall into the endzone. The kick that would have tied the score went wide. The score at the beginning of the fourth quarter stood at Army 14, Duke 13.

As the game clock wound down, the possessions went back and forth, each team fighting for field position and the possibility to widen their lead with either a field goal or a touchdown. The unabated cheers of the cadets in the stand kept up the fervor and excitement. Duke got possession of the ball on the nineteen-yard line and on third down executed a double reverse, the ball tossed from quarterback Lutz to first one teammate, who then tossed it to another, reversed direction, and broke loose from the pack of Army defenders. He ran seventy-three yards before Army's Bob Mischak tackled him from behind at the seven-yard line. At one point in the radio broadcast of the game, an announcer was heard to say, "These boys have gotten me so excited I can't even finish the broadcast! Take over, Walter!"[129]

On Army's seven-yard line, it was first and goal, Duke poised to score. Three attempts by Duke failed. Now fourth down, the linemen remembered what Blaik had told the team: when the Blue Devils get inside an opponent's ten-yard line, they run the ball between their own tackles on 95 percent of plays, and when they get close to the goal line, they run quarterback sneaks.

Prior to the fourth down play, a Duke assistant threw a kicking tee onto the field, indicating a field goal attempt. Lutz picked up the tee and threw it back, disdaining the field goal. As Duke huddled for Lutz to call the fourth down play, the Army defensive guards were ready. "Remember, he's going to try to sneak," they reminded each other. Lutz did just that, but he was met by a wall of white jerseys. The Black Knights had held the line, with forty seconds left to play. Army took over, inches from the goal line, while the Corps of Cadets shouted their frenzied approval. Throughout the final two minutes of play, especially during Duke's four thrusts at the Army goal, it was almost impossible to hear or think because of the roar from the crowd. Cadets streamed out of the stands, pressed around the Army bench and close to the sidelines, imploring their defense to hold."

Army, on orders from Col. Blaik, punted from deep in their endzone. Duke had thirty more seconds and four more plays from the Army thirty-seven-yard line—all passes—all knocked away. Peter Vann, Army's second-string quarterback, batted away the last pass in the end zone, a pass thrown by Duke's second-string quarterback, Gerry Barger, to their starting quarterback, Worth Lutz. The final score: Army 14, Duke 13.

In the locker room, Col. Blaik, with tears in his eyes, uttered those simple but powerful and memorable words, "Don't ever give up." He then handed the game ball to Bob Mischak, who made the game-saving tackle.

This newspaper photo of Col. Blaik leaving the field victorious after the Duke—
Army Game is hanging in Room 405 of the historic Thayer Hotel at
West Point, dedicated to the 1953 Army football team.

The Miracle of '53

"After the Navy Game—he ordered the door secured and as he turned to speak his eyes were misty. 'I have never coached a team that gave me more than you did. I never have coached a team that has given me as much satisfaction. Considering all the conditions since 1951, you have done more for football at West Point than any other team in the history of the Academy.'"

—Coach "Red" Blaik, West Point, 1953

MUNICIPAL STADIUM
PHILADELPHIA, PENNSYLVANIA, 1953

THE 1953 ARMY/NAVY game was just weeks away. At each day's football practice, the sidelines and stands on the practice field were packed with both cadets and officers. It was a rivalry that spanned over 150 years, inaugurated in 1890. Through 1952 the record stood at Army 27, Navy 21, and four ties. Their next meeting, traditionally played in Philadelphia's Municipal Stadium (renamed John F. Kennedy stadium in 1964), would be their fifty-fourth.

The passion with which this game was played surpassed even those played when a victory over higher-ranked opponents was needed to guarantee, say, a bowl invitation. At West Point, all roads led to the ultimate game of every season: the Army-Navy game.

The cadets and midshipmen entered this contest with the full realization that the success or failure of an entire season rode on the outcome of the game, the most colorful spectacle on the American sports scene. It was a game that conjured up for reporter Oscar Fraley of the United Press Corps a fighting spirit he associated with well-known fierce Army battles fought from the Revolutionary War to the Korean War, or from crucial and brutal naval conflicts conducted in foreign seas aboard aircraft carriers with names such as the USS *Coral Sea* or the USS *Bon Homme Richard*, during the Korean War.

As far as Army was concerned, nothing counted all season except a win over Navy. A quarterback could be a dismal failure all season, such as in the season of '55, but with the win against Navy, his college career was considered a total success by the end of that game day afternoon.

The coaches, who regularly worked fourteen-hour days, broke only at noon for lunch and 8:30 p.m. for dinner, working the team from 4:30 p.m. each day till six, planning continuously for the upcoming matchup. Sundays were considered their "day off"—six hours of watching game movies to fine-tune their strategy for the game. One weekend night at dusk in the fall of '52, Coach Paul Amen drove Coach Lombardi home from practice. They were so consumed with their own thoughts about the game that when Amen pulled up in front of the Lombardi house, Lombardi turned towards Amen and absentmindedly kissed him on the cheek. Startled, Amen blurted out his surprise asking what in the world Lombardi was doing? The embarrassed, bleary-eyed and now red-faced Coach Lombardi hastily offered his apology to the still dumbfounded Amen. Excuse me, but I thought you were my wife, he explained.

In 1951, Army went 2–7, defeating only Columbia and the Citadel, and was trounced by Navy. The 1952 season was better, 4–4–1, but again the team lost to Navy. But the win-loss stat was only half the story.

Army was top in the nation in scoring defense, fourth in total defense, ninth in passing defense, and tenth in rushing offense. The team featured an All-American at end who finished eighth in the Heisman Trophy balloting, and two tackles who received votes for first team All-American. After the cheating scandal of 1951, General Douglas MacArthur gave his opinion that it would take a decade or more for Army to recover its previous status in football.

Though they weren't expecting miracles for the season of '53, the Corps of Cadets did look for better things than the previous heartbreak of the '51 and '52 seasons with the two consecutive losses to Navy. *The Pointer*, West Point's alumni publication, published the day before game day, carried this column highlighting the importance of the game:

> Tomorrow afternoon, radio sets will be tuned to Philadelphia all the way from Berlin to Panmunjom. Graduates will be listening for news of an Army victory. But they'll be listening for something more—something none of them talk about. They'll be listening for evidence that the Corps is on its way back. They want to know that the values which they stand for are still alive in the Corps.[130]

These were the values that had always been, and are still, the backbone of the academy's mission: a mission to educate, train, and inspire the Corps of Cadets so that each graduate is a commissioned leader of character committed to the values of "Duty, Honor, Country" and prepared for a career of professional excellence and service to the nation as an officer in the United States Army.

On November 28, 1953, nearly half of all Americans in the US would watch or tune in to the 54th meeting of these two teams on TV and radio.

The weather bureau was predicting a snowstorm, an alert not

removed until 11 p.m. Friday before the game. By Saturday afternoon, any threat of precipitation had moved on, and the game was played under cloudy skies with cold northwesterly winds.

Millions thrilled to the sight of students from the Navy and Army academies when they marched into the stadium, the annual game eclipsing any other dramatization of American ideals. As the two teams came onto the field, the fans in the sold-out, mammoth stadium would erupt into cheers, waiting for the game to start the two teams tearing into each other as if their lives depended on it.

These same players who opposed each other on the field in past years had later stood side by side, and fought for our lives when war came. "It is a picture of democracy that plays out on the football field every year when these two teams meet in Philadelphia," wrote George Munger, retiring University of Pennsylvania coach, the moving display of pageantry and patriotism chronicled in an article written for the *Philadelphia Inquirer*. [131]

"First came the cadets and midshipmen, then came the color guards, bearing American flags and their respective banners. Following that was perfection in the etiquette of respect for the National Emblem. All over the stadium men in service saluted and civilians removed their hats and stood at attention," Munger continued, confessing that even before Penn's most tense games against either of the two, Army or Navy, he used to slip out of the Franklin Field dressing room to watch the parades-on-field of the service teams.

Navy was outplayed all day by what was described as a magnificent Army line, Navy getting past the 50-yard line only three times, finally scoring with 45 seconds left in the game. It was a surprisingly easy victory over Navy that left Army's Coach Blaik prouder of the win and the team than any before. After the game, Col. Blaik ordered the locker room door secured, and as he turned to speak to his players, his eyes were misty. "I have never coached a team that gave me more than you did. I never have coached a team that has given me as much satisfaction. Considering all the conditions since 1951, you have done more for football at West Point than any other team in the history of the Academy." Army had won. The score: 20–7. It was the football miracle of '53.

The inspirational teamwork and stunning achievements that epitomized the season of '53 would wash away the effects of the scandal of '51. Blaik wrote years later in baring his bitterness and frustration over the cheating incident, "For two years these boys had seen the roughest action. They had lived with the coaching lash, dirt, blood, and defeat."

Four and a half years later, on Tuesday morning, January 13, 1959, Mary Lou Laslie Henry arrived at La Guardia airport to pick up her husband, Lt. James R. Henry, who had arrived back in the States direct from Lebanon where he was stationed. Mary Lou had promised her parents that while in the area they would pay a visit to the Blaiks, and she had dutifully called them from the airport. Col. Blaik sounded upbeat, expressed his eagerness to see them both, and encouraged them to come right over. They took the fifty-four-mile scenic drive on the Palisades Parkway up to West Point, the day cold and cloudy, and arrived just after 1 p.m.

Greeting them at the door, Col. Blaik led them to his library, eager to show them his collection: stacks of scrapbooks, one kept for every cadet involved in the cheating scandal who had been kicked off the team, expelled, or discharged from West Point, and including the one cadet who had lost his life in Korea after being deployed immediately to the battlefield after the scandal. They spent the afternoon poring over each book, with Col. Blaik providing commentary, well versed in each player's successes and disappointments, civilian or otherwise related with fondness and pride.

The afternoon passed quickly, and before long, with dusk setting in and not much time to spare, the young couple, after bidding the Blaiks a fond farewell, set out towards the Amens' home, where they were to have dinner with Coach Amen and his wife. When asked how they had spent the afternoon, Mary Lou replied they had spent their day with Col. Blaik. The Amens froze, disbelief on their faces at the announcement. "Did you not hear the news?" they asked.

"What news?" the couple asked in unison.

"Col. Blaik never said anything?" they asked.

Confused, Mary Lou and Jim shook their heads no.

"Col. Blaik turned in his resignation this morning! No one had any idea. Everyone's talking about it."

Later it was reported that West Point's newest superintendent, Major General Garrison H. Davidson, himself an Army coach from 1933 to 1937, who had arrived in 1956, made the request that Blaik hand over his license plate that read "No 1." In the new superintendent's opinion, the tag gave the impression the football coach was the "Top Dog" at the Point, not the academy's superintendent, and Davidson felt it undermined his position.

For Col. "Red" Blaik, the request was the proverbial last straw, showing the superintendent's lack of understanding about football and the sacrifices made by the players who had given so much to reclaim the standing of the Point on a field of combat in their own backyard.

Time to take his bat, or in this case his football, and find a different field to play on.

CHAPTER THIRTY

Coach Hank

"It's time to make your move."

—Coach Hank Crisp to Coach Carney Laslie

WEST POINT, NEW YORK
1955–1956

BY 1954, THE BLACK Knights were back on track, by all accounts a team to be reckoned with as their morale and performance roared back to its former status.

While Mary Lou Laslie finished up her first semester of college, the football season of '54 ended. But another chapter was about to start, and it wasn't one the Laslies were quite ready for. Arriving home after the traditional Winter Dance at West Point, Mary Lou excitedly entered her parents' bedroom to share her news, her father in his pajamas sitting in bed reading the newspaper. She flashed her engagement ring in front of her beloved father. "Daddy! Look! I'm engaged!" He glanced briefly at the ring before turning his attention back to the paper. "Humph," he snorted.

"Aren't you happy for me?" Mary Lou asked.

"I don't know what I've got to be so happy about," he mumbled in reply.

Mary Lou married West Pointer Lt. James Henry, a cadet his classmates described as being "movie-star handsome," that next July of 1955 in the chapel at West Point.

Mary Lou Laslie and West Pointer James R. Henry, Ring Dance, 1953.

At the end of the '55 football season, Alabama's Hank Crisp and his wife paid an unprecedented and memorable visit to speak personally with Coach Laslie. The timing of the unexpected December visit was recalled by Mary Lou who was home for the holidays and making preparations for her move overseas with her husband, Lt. James R. Henry, recently stationed at a US Army base in Germany.

Coach Hank Crisp, a longtime influential figure in Laslie's, Bryant's, and Moseley's careers, was admired for what he exemplified to the men: a man who had overcome extreme odds, worked hard, and achieved a success beyond anyone's wildest dreams. This despite his losing his left hand at the age of thirteen in a farming accident. A native of Crisp,

North Carolina, Hank Crisp went on to become a standout student-athlete at Hampton-Sydney College in Virginia before following his track coach, Charles Bernier, to VPI (now Virginia Tech), where he lettered in basketball and baseball. Crisp arrived in Alabama in 1921 after Bernier, recruited to coach at Alabama, hired him out of the West Virginia coal fields. His life was a testament to his toughness and self-discipline and an example to the generations of athletes he would go on to coach.

Crisp brothers at the Crisp tobacco farm Falkland, Pitt County, North Carolina, ca. 1920. L-R: George, Louis, Henry ("Coach Hank"), Sellers, Richard.

When Bernier went to Alabama to become athletic director, he hired Crisp as the track coach. Although Crisp was never Alabama's head football coach, he did serve as head coach of their basketball and track teams and, until 1957, served as the school's athletic director. He was a strict taskmaster but also a father figure to many young men under his tutelage and a stalwart supporter and career builder for those with the desire to coach.

In the 1934 Alabama university yearbook, *The Corolla*, student editors devoted a two-page spread dedicated to Henry Gorham

Crisp, on one side a pen and ink portrait of Coach Hank, on the opposite side a full-page dedication, which reads,

> To Henry Gorham Crisp: Whose capable supervision of athletics has placed our University in the galaxy of leaders in college sports and whose thirteen years with the Crimson Tide have been made bright by the production of stars in every sport; whose sterling qualities of manhood have made him loved and respected by the Student Body and Faculty; and to whom, we feel is due the continued support of all loyal lovers of Alabama, this Forty-Second Volume of the *Corolla* is dedicated.

Immediately following is another two-page spread, dedicated to President Franklin Delano Roosevelt, extolled as a man who had "carved a place in the hearts of Americans which time cannot erase," described as being "[s]incere in purpose, tactful in method, fearless in action." One cannot read the Roosevelt tribute without noting the comparison to Crisp they may have been making. He was that influential.

Crisp had a unique view of the football program, by virtue of his being one of its longest-serving staff members, and as such was a highly respected voice of influence and power, which he wielded for well over two decades. Coach Hank's extraordinary visit to West Point indicates he thought it was high time to have a face-to-face conversation with his protégé, friend, and colleague Carney Laslie.

The years 1954 to 1957 at Alabama had been rough ones since the glory days of Frank Thomas. The program had struggled to regain its prominence over the years. In 1954, as Alabama looked to replace another head coach, the fourth in just ten years, Frank Moseley was offered the position. Frank was happy in his job at Virginia Tech, and Edy was settled near her family. Moseley, however, did make a recommendation.

J. B. "Ears" Whitworth was an assistant on the Alabama coaching staff when Moseley was a junior and was also well known to Bryant, an assistant coach for the famed 1934 team that Bryant played on that went on to win the Rose Bowl of '35. Whitworth and Laslie also had a long history together, teammates on the famed 1931 Rose Bowl team, assistants together for the season of '33, along with vying for the job of head coach at Whitworth's alma mater high school in Blytheville, going head-to-head against his friend for the job those many years ago. Despite Laslie beating him out for the job, they had remained close. Whitworth had never been quiet about his aspiration to one day garner the head coach position at Alabama. Moseley, Bryant, and Laslie felt sure Whitworth would take the job no matter what conditions Coach Hank might place on a new head coach which included not bringing any of his own staff, and keeping all of the existing coaches, including himself as line coach.

Whitworth was confident of his ability to return a foundation of academic excellence to the football program, a fundamental philosophy held by his coach Wallace Wade, from his own Alabama days. Many were dubious, including his coaching colleagues Bryant, Laslie, and Moseley. Winning, they would argue, was what kept a football coach in business. It was two sides of the coin in college athletics that were distinctly at odds with each other, always striving for balance: academics versus athletics. Winning would always carry more weight, not only with the fans, but with the university. Whitworth, however, was convinced he could change the culture. Bryant, Laslie, and Moseley loved Whitworth like a brother, but they strongly doubted his approach would succeed and were also dubious of his prospects given what they knew were the conditions of his accepting the position. Despite this, they were all supportive of the university's (and Coach Hank's) choice of Whitworth as head coach in 1954.

"A coach dreams of returning to the school where he once played.

I would have returned to accept a janitor's job," Whitworth remarked not long after accepting the job. He had inherited a difficult situation, the scope of which he had underestimated, the organization riddled with "organizational, administrative and personnel problems that one man, even a man of his stature, could not cope with."[132]

The years leading up to Whit's tenure came to be known as the "modern lean years of the Crimson Tide," despite Alabama's Harold "Red" Drew producing three bowl appearances and an SEC championship in 1953. But the worst was yet to come.

Assistant coach Hank Crisp knew Whitworth well from his years as a player at Alabama and also when he was an assistant coach under head coach Frank Thomas. Crisp was now both athletic director and line coach, and officially hired Whitworth, introducing him as the new Alabama head coach on December 1, 1954. The job, however, came with some conditions: Whitworth was required to keep all of the existing assistants with no new additions of his own to the staff, and Coach Hank was to remain both athletic director and line coach.

Whether by design or not, it was no secret Crisp tried his best to influence players, coaches, and administration during Whitworth's tenure, often with the result of everyone being at odds with head coach Whitworth. During these years, many of the players recruited as student athletes chose to transfer. Morale declined and the team continued to lose. Some suggested these studen transfers were the result of Crisp's behind-the-scenes meddling. Whitworth also had to contend with avid alumni, sports reporters and members of Alabama's Board of Trustees, who would often attend practice, offering their own brand of sage advice, pressing the coach on all phases of strategy. By the end of the '56 season, with two losing seasons to his credit, critics clamored for Whitworth's resignation. Fans booed, and in one tasteless display, the kind, gentlemanly Coach Whitworth was burned in effigy.

When Coach Hank and his wife paid a visit to the Laslies' home at West Point in December of 1955, it was without precedent. He had never visited the Laslies' home, and this visit was done unofficially, off the books. He wanted to have a face-to-face with his former player now colleague to set things straight. Crisp had always been doubtful of Coach Whitworth's approach and abilities, as evidenced by what many considered his meddling. He only saw things worsening, so he had come with an offer in hand and to plead for Laslie and Bryant to return to Alabama.

Laslie was emphatic. Neither he nor Bryant would provide an impetus to push their friend out of Alabama. They would not displace him. Coach Hank would have to stave off those who clamored for his resignation or out-and-out firing of Whitworth. Crisp would see to it that the three-year contract would expire instead. He also agreed to step aside as athletic director upon the twos arrival. There would be no meddling on his part in the future, he promised, just his unwavering support. The time was coming, he told Laslie, when Alabama would come calling and they should be ready.

The timetable was set. But by August 1956, with a new superintendent at West Point and changes being made, Colonel Blaik would be leaving soon enough. Daughter Mary Lou and her husband were now living overseas in Germany. With the Laslie's first grandchild due in March of '57, Alice was set to depart in February for a lengthy stay to help with the new baby. The timetable had changed. Laslie was ready to leave West Point sooner than later, joining Bryant in Texas a year earlier than planned. Besides, the reasoning went, it probably would be better if he was in College Station with Bryant when the call from Alabama came. They would have that much more time to strategize their departure. Laslie placed the call to Bryant.

The laundry bin was piled high with sweaty jerseys and damp towels in the locker room at West Point, and the cadet, the last to leave at the end of a long day of practice, tossed one more onto the heap on his way out the door. He heard a muffled but distinctively deep voice and strong Southern drawl echo in the deserted locker room, causing him to stop in his tracks. He walked back toward the coaches' windowed, private office, careful to stay out of view. The door to their office was wide open, and Coach Laslie's voice was unrestrained. The cadet strained to decipher the one-sided conversation, picking up a few words here and there before hearing an emphatically clear, "Paul, you gotta get me outta here." The cadet, who was one of Coach Laslie's favorites, having come from Kentucky, hurried out, not wanting to be seen eavesdropping or potentially embarrass the revered coach. "When the news was reported in the paper months later," he told Mary Lou Laslie Henry some fifty years later, "I knew then who Coach Laslie had been talking to. I've never told a soul until now," he told her.

While Coach Hank had been pivotal in the timing of the reunion of Laslie and Bryant, Paul, Jr., recalled he also had been instrumental in having something to do with his Uncle Carney's return. With the departure of several members of the Aggie coaching staff in in '56, he sensed his father's quandary. The then eleven-year-year old Paul chimed in with his opinion. "What about Uncle Carney?" he suggested to his father. The now elderly son of college football's iconic coach chuckled at the memory. "I like to think I had something to do with Coach Laslie and Poppa getting back together."

The Bryant-Laslie partnership worked for a number of reasons. For one, Laslie was never interested in Bryant's job. This was important, as the more successful their teams became, the more his staff was joined by coaches interested in proving themselves under the Bryant brand. Bryant's list of assistants who went on to become a head coach, in both college and pro leagues, is impressive. With Laslie as his right-hand man, Bryant never had to worry about an ambitious coach undercutting him on their way up. Bryant knew he could trust Laslie to always tell him the truth. He would also need someone on his staff whose knowledge and skill he held in highest regard, who wouldn't be intimated by him if he disagreed, but who would respect his final decision if they came to a different opinion. He had no doubts about Laslie's loyalty. Their friendship spoke to that. They had established their roles and respect for each other long ago, with Laslie playing the self-deprecating assistant in public. Nor did Bryant ever question Laslie's skill. By this time, he was described as "one of the top defensive masterminds in the business" by his boss, the famed Coach "Red" Blaik.

In late January of 1957, the Laslies, along with their adored spaniel, Bobo, posed for a family photo at West Point, which was published in the *Fort Worth Star-Telegram* announcing their impending move. It was now official. The family would be moving to College Station, and as of February 15, Carney Laslie would become the assistant head coach of the Texas A&M Aggies.

The path was now set for the return to Laslie's beloved SEC. Though he had loved his years working with the young men who made up the West Point Corps of Cadets, it had never been his intention to stay but rather to someday rejoin Paul Bryant. Their friendship and professional respect for each other had never wavered since their earliest days together.

Though for a time, each had landed at universities that, for the only five years the two were apart in their post–WWII coaching careers, had been both challenging and fraught with controversy.

During their five years apart post-war each had endured challenging circumstances fraught with controversy. For Laslie, it was rebuilding a program embroiled in a scandal brought about by the players. For Bryant, it was his use of the infamous practice fields at Junction, Texas, where a grueling spring training regimen he implemented drew harsh criticism. Those who 'survived' being cut from the team came to be known as "the Junction Boys". Coach Gene Stallings, one of the original 'Junction Boy" players, who joined the

A&M coaching staff after he graduated, later an assisant and then head coach at Alabama, commented that had Coach "Laslie been on the coaching staff at the time," the incident that later became a lightening rod for Bryant critics "would have never happened."[133]

Also occuring prior to Laslie's arrival was an NCAA violation brought about by over-zealous alumni gifts to players (which Bryant later admitted he could have curtailed) that cost the A&M football team an appearance in the Cotton Bowl. But Bryant's record spoke for itself. At the end of the season of '56, A&M had a winning team and Bryant had a ten-year contract.

With Laslie's arrival in College Station, Texas, however, the wheels were set in motion. The promised land of Tuscaloosa was in sight.

Texas A&M Welcomes Laslie.

PART VI

THE BEAR AND THE SILVER FOX 1957–1961

Bryant (foreground) and Laslie (background) on sidelines at the Alabama vs Auburn game in 1958.

CHAPTER THIRTY-ONE

Lighting the Match

"I mean this affectionately,
but you're a nosy so-and-so, aren't you?"

—Paul Bryant at a press conference, College Station, Texas

COLLEGE STATION, TEXAS
TEXAS A&M
1957–1958

THE ANNOUNCED APPOINTMENT OF Carney Laslie as the
assistant head coach at A&M in January of 1957 caused a not-so-
subtle raising of the eyebrows by sportswriters. For one, Bryant had
always been insistent on using the generic "assistant" title to all his
staff, noting that they were each of equal status. Not so with the
appointment of Laslie, making it clear to both insiders and outsiders
that he was putting Laslie as second-in-command, in direct contrast
to the way Bryant started out in Aggieland. Many noted Laslie's role
was not dissimilar to his position at West Point under Coach Blaik.
In hindsight, they were putting in place a structure that would follow
them into their next move where there would be an abundance of

titles to go around, helping to establish an overall chain of command.

In another atypical move, his new hires went against the current trend at that time. Head coaches were not hiring young assistants, opting instead for, on average, men five years older than the men they had replaced. They ranged from Laslie, who arrived at the ripe old age of forty-five, to the other replacements, whose ages were forty, thirty-eight, thirty-three, and twenty-eight. Those that remained from Bryant's staff were Phil Cutchin, quarterback coach; Elmer Smith, Pat James, and Sam Bailey, line coaches; and Willie Zapalac, defensive backfield coach.

It was also no secret that Alabama's Coach Whitworth was struggling to stay afloat. Speculation abounded. Some pundits projected Bryant lining up either his own move into the athletic director position at A&M and leaving Laslie as the head coach while others predicted Bryant was lining up a transition out of A&M altogether, returning to his alma mater at Alabama and leaving Laslie as his hand-picked choice for head coach. Bryant would continue to emphatically state that the rumors were just that: rumors. He had seven years left on his contract from its ten-year extension after the 1955 season.

Laslie's arrival sparked unprecedented interest among Aggie football watchers as crowds of players as well fans and the press came to observe the defensive line drills conducted by A&M's new coach. This was unusual as offensive drills with its passing and quarterback hand-off plays were usually the more interesting to watch. But Laslie's reputation as one of the top line coaches in the country preceded him, and many were eager to see what new techniques from his time at West Point he would be bringing to strengthen the A&M line.

Although all eyes were on the new defensive coach, sports pundits also exhibited an interest in the overall shuffling of the coaching staff. Many left for other positions. Jerry Claiborne, a former player under Bryant and Laslie at Kentucky who had followed Bryant to A&M, left to assume an assistant role under Coach Frank Broyles at University of Missouri. Two other assistants left at the same time: Jim Owens, moving to the University of Washington as head coach, and Tom Tipps, who followed him as an aide there. Reunions among the former coaching staff at Kentucky occurred as well. Trainer Charles E. "Smokey" Harper from their days with Bryant greeted Laslie upon his arrival to Aggie-land, his welcoming handshake captured by a local newspaper photographer, smiles all around. Also on the coaching staff from Laslie's days in Kentucky was Pat James, a former Kentucky player who had joined Bryant at A&M direct from Kentucky. Along with Sam Bailey, an assistant who joined Bryant at A&M in '54, the slate of coaches seemed well equipped to tackle the upcoming '57 season.

While Carney Laslie was expected to arrive in College Station in February, Alice Laslie was excited about their first grandchild, expected in March. After arranging the move from West Point to Texas, she then had an extended visit overseas to be with Mary Lou, who had moved to Germany with her husband, who was stationed there with the Army, so as to be there when the baby was born. In early June, she departed to visit family in Cartersville, Georgia, before heading as usual, to her beloved St. Simons Island where she always spent her summers. Although it was a vagabond existence for a time, the prospect of landing back in Tuscaloosa among old friends at the end of her travels made it tolerable.

For Laslie, being away from his family had its own difficulties. His fondness for Paul Bryant, Jr., who was just entering junior high school, grew during this time. With his older sister gone from home, Paul (or "Pablo," as Laslie had nicknamed him) was lonely, too. He had contracted hepatitis, requiring him to stay out of school for a whole year. "Uncle Carney" provided company and fun for the noticeably frail, young boy, nicknamed "Chalk Bones" by classmates, due to his being tall, lanky, and extremely pale after his illness.

Paul, Jr., laughingly recalled a time in 1958, when his parents were out for the evening, he played a rambunctious game of cowboys and Indians with his two "sitters," his "Uncle Carney" and Coach Frank

Moseley, who happened to be in town visiting the Laslies. It was a game they regularly played, and Laslie, it seems, always ended up tied in a chair. Paul, Jr., chuckled in remembrance, "We whooped and hollered all over the house and around him until finally, Uncle Carney would say in a hoarse, kind of raspy voice, his hands scratching his neck like he was parched for thirst—he'd say, 'Boy, I need me some good 'ole Injun' water.'"

When Laslie arrived in College Station, it was on the heels of the football program being banned from postseason bowl games. A&M had been sanctioned by the NCAA on charges of violations of rules on recruiting and financial aid to football players. In later years, Bryant would admit he should have been clearer to alumni supporters and the booster club members that incentives offered to players could not and would not be tolerated. The university leaders took it in stride, however, still enthusiastic about their coach and their future as a winning program with Bryant on board.

With the arrival of Laslie, there was a reorganization and overall shuffling of coaches at A&M. It was seen as a way to better prepare them for the upcoming season and the expected lifting of the NCAA's probation period. Prior to 1956, most sports writers didn't give A&M much of a hope for a conference championship. But by 1955, the Aggies surprised everyone by coming in second behind Texas Christian University in the Southwest. Despite losing an opportunity to place in a bowl game in '56, nothing could dampen the Aggie spirit. The squad was unbeaten, winning its first conference championship since 1941

Despite the fallout from the NCAA penalty, fans were also staunchly behind their coach. At the awards ceremony for the team held in late February that year, there was no mention of their ineligible status to play in the Cotton Bowl. Instead, after receiving a standing ovation, Bryant was presented a new Cadillac by Aggie fans in appreciation for his success, a not-so-subtle show of how Texans knew how to appreciate a winner even if Kentucky didn't.

By May, the anticipated announcement of A&M's rights being fully restored was made. Immediately, university president Dr. David W. Williams was asked if that meant the Aggies would be playing in the Cotton Bowl come January 1. Laughing, he said, "All we've got to do is win the conference. But," he added, "that's a big assignment, isn't it?"[134]

Bryant was his usual understated self with the press when making predictions for the upcoming season's chances for success, listing his greatest weakness as "depth at every position" and his greatest problem as "down the middle strength." It was no secret that the ten seniors who graduated and led the team to their unbeaten season of the previous year were considered "the heart of the squad."[135]

That spring practice, the coaches were particularly demanding. They saw weakness, inconsistency, and lack of speed as areas that needed intense focus in order to build the physical muscle and endurance to go up against a tough fall lineup. The trainers had their work cut out for them, and the coaches expected—demanded—complete dedication.

There was plenty of speculation to go around that Bryant would be leaving after the upcoming season. Reporters were relentless in their questioning, but Bryant continued to keep them at bay, consistently denying the rumors that Laslie had joined the coaching staff in order to take over the head coach position while he moved into the athletic director role, or that he would be leaving altogether. At one notable press conference, one reporter once again asked Bryant for a comment on all the speculation. Peering at the so-called inquisitor for a few seconds, he broke into a slow grin before replying: "I mean this affectionately, but you're a nosy so-and-so, aren't you?"

CHAPTER THIRTY-TWO

One in a Million

"Parting is such sweet sorrow."

—William Shakespeare

TEXAS TO ALABAMA
1957

IT WAS WELL PUBLICIZED that Whitworth's contract as head coach at Alabama was ending on December 1, 1957. An official public announcement was expected any day of who his successor would be. It only added to the excitement and heightened the revelry in the state as Alabama prepared for the Auburn vs Alabama game scheduled for Saturday, December 2.

Both schools went to great lengths to make it an extravagant, never-to-be-forgotten meeting of the two powerhouse programs at Legion Field in Birmingham with Auburn celebrating their Coach, Ralph "Shug" Jordan, being voted Coach of the Year, and for many in Tuscaloosa, the celebration of the departure of Whitworth. The Auburn Tigers, also known as the War Eagles, brought with them their caged mascot Rajah, a Bengal tiger, transported from his home at the Birmingham Zoo. He was joined by Alabama's mascot, an elephant, brought in from a Memphis zoo. The two were paraded around the field during the "forty minutes of festivities that preceded the kickoff," a day that boasted a bitter temperature of thirty-eight degrees "laced with 20-mile-an-hour" winds.[136]

Auburn demolished the Crimson Tide, a blowout of 40–0. Spectators, despite both the frigid temperatures and the easy rout, came early and stayed to the bitter end. Huddled under blankets with "necks wrapped in heavy scarves and their feet enclosed in anything available (a rare sight in the sunny South), their teeth clacked and clattered between cheers that seemed to never let up."[137] Auburn fans were out for revenge for the humiliating loss—55–0—handed to them by Alabama in 1948.

After the game, Alabama's Million-Dollar Marching Band faced the Auburn stands and saluted the fans in honor of Auburn's being ranked number one in the nation and their coach being voted Coach of the Year, the performance drawing thunderous applause from the stadium. They then turned to face the Crimson Tide bench to honor their own, a man who was one-in-a-million, much admired for his honesty and abilities, despite the criticism leveled against him. They played the popular tune of the day "Can't Help Lovin' That Man" by Jerome Kern and Oscar Hammerstein, an appropriate swan song for their beleaguered but beloved coach. A warm send-off delivered on a blistering cold day.

As Benny Marshall, longtime sportswriter for the *Birmingham News*, wrote, "How do you write them off and watch them go? There's a sadness to endings, even with the gladness."[138] To this day, Whitworth goes unrecognized or acknowledged, as the most likely innovator of the spread offense, modern-day football's most potent offensive schemes, his contributions overshadowed by an extremely unfortunate set of circumstances.

Earlier that morning, the team presented their coach with a diamond-studded sapphire tie-clip as a token of appreciation. At the end of the game, one by one the players had lined up and with voices shaking with emotion, some with tears in their eyes, expressed their regret at failing him and their appreciation for his contribution to their growth as players and people. For Coach Whitworth, who had wanted nothing more than to coach his alma mater's team into another era of glory, it was a time to formally acknowledge and exhort his team with words he knew they would never forget:

> Men, I'm proud of the way you got up off the ground and fought that second half. You were beaten by a fine football team today. I don't think any of you have any reason to go around with head tucked down . . . The football season is over now, and my jurisdiction over you is ended. Remember, if you travel with the best, you'll come out best. Keep your feet on the ground, study hard, work hard, and give the new coach as much effort as you have given me, and a year from now I'll be mighty proud of you. I wish I could have given you better coaching . . . but I tried. Thanks.[139]

For obvious reasons, Paul Bryant and university officials were reluctant to announce his move from A&M publicly until after December 1, so as not to distract from Whitworth's last game at Alabama. The speculation was intense; reporters were hounding sources, anxious to be the first to break the news. Despite all efforts to keep it out of the papers, the official announcement came on December 1, when the Bryants' daughter, Mae Martin Bryant, then a twenty-one-year-old schoolteacher in Birmingham, returned home after visiting her parents in Texas. Calling a family friend, sports editor Bob Phillips of the *Birmingham Post-Herald*, she disclosed that her mother would begin house-hunting in Tuscaloosa around December 19. It was as close as they could get to confirming that Bryant had accepted the position of head coach and athletic director, and the news hit the Alabama papers.

Not long afterwards that, Bryant got what was called his first look at Alabama on a trip back to Texas from New York, holding a press conference in Birmingham on December 8 before heading to Tuscaloosa to meet those players who would be on his 1958 team. By December 10, with Laslie's teammate from the Rose Bowl, Fred Sington, a member of the coach selection committee, and with Coach Hank Crisp looking on, Bryant signed a ten-year contract as head coach and athletic director. After signing, Bryant said he'd announce the first member of his staff that evening. It was a toss-up as to whether he would be announcing Laslie or his previous assistant at A&M, Jerry Claiborne.

Some Aggie fans speculated that Laslie would stay on as head coach at A&M. Others predicted it would be Coach Laslie who would be sent ahead of Bryant to Alabama to head up a skeleton crew to organize recruiting. Head coach Frank Broyles at the University of Missouri, where Claiborne had been for the past year coaching defense, gave Claiborne his support, stating to reporters that he felt the twenty-nine-year-old was a capable and talented coach. Bryant announced his first staff appointment: Claiborne, who was to depart immediately for Tuscaloosa, giving him the assistant head coach title. Laslie was named assistant athletic director. He was needed in College Station where the Aggies had one more game to play, preparing to go up against Tennessee. It was a team he and Bryant sorely wanted to beat.

While "Ears" Whitworth was saluting his players, his tenure at Alabama officially over, there was even more scrutiny as to where "Bear" Bryant was that particular weekend. Tuscaloosa? Birmingham? At Legion Field? Reports had him everywhere but where he had told them he would be: deer hunting.

On the Thursday night before the Auburn-Alabama game, he, Carney, and H. L. Heep of the Texas A&M Board of Trustees were off to Faifurus, Texas, where Mr. Heep owned a hunting preserve. Bryant bagged a deer, as did Laslie, as well as some turkeys. Saturday the hunting party returned to Houston where Bryant, without any indication he was anything but Texas A&M's athletic director and head coach, announced that his team would play in the Gator Bowl, December 28.

The circumstances around this game were unusual to say the least. The A&M players were well aware of their coach's departure, which caused some observers to give a psychological advantage to Tennessee. Many, however, gave the Aggies the edge over the Volunteers, believing their players were pumped and primed to win their last game for their departing coach. Added to their overall mindset going into the game was Heisman Trophy winner John David Crow, who won for his skills both as a running back and a defensive player.

The former Kentucky coaches were eager to beat Tennessee as a coaching duo. This was especially true for Laslie, who had frequently expressed that one of his deepest regrets upon leaving Kentucky, was not beating the Volunteers while coaching in Lexington. Now that he and Bryant were back together, and a Heisman Trophy winner to their credit (the only Heisman winner in Bryan'ts career) this was looking to be his year.

That the players from both teams were well trained and in top physical condition went without question. But the Vols had a game plan they had the utmost confidence in—even with the knowledge it would be one of their toughest games played that season. They had won the SEC Championship the previous year, finishing second in the AP Poll. This time, the season of '57, was a different story. Tennessee had racked up three losses early in the season. But they had recovered by the second half of the season, earning a berth at the Gator Bowl against the no. 9 team in the nation, Texas A&M. They had momentum going for them.

The game was billed as a defensive contest from the outset, as A&M had allowed opponents only 4.7 points per game while Tennessee had held their opponents to 7.5 points per game. Former sportswriter and Tennessee football historian Tom Mattingly noted it was to be a "defensive struggle that has probably never been equaled in either team's history."[140]

Game day brought a record crowd. Over 40,000 flocked to the stadium dressed in their "Sunday Best to watch a game that was anything but angelic." The weather, too, was epic. Rain pouring in a deluge, monsoon-like, further relegated plays to a running and not a passing game.

Players on the field that day still recall the emotion and excitement sixty years later in what would be hailed as one of the classic games of Tennessee football.

"The game went nip and tuck for the whole time," said Jim Smelcher, a senior left tackle for Tennessee, who had gotten a scholarship to play there. "They wanted me because I liked to fight," he said laughingly in an interview.[141] And fight he did.

After three quarters, it was still zero to zero. Everyone could feel it. Something, sooner or later, was going to happen. And it did. In the fourth quarter.

With the ball on the Texas A&M nineteen-yard line, the offensive line created a "wide-open hole right through the gut of the defense"[142] and Tennessee tailback Bobby Gordon "sprinted ten yards untouched."[143] But meeting him on the eight-yard line was none other than the A&M Heisman winner himself, John David Crow. When the two collided, Crow was knocked out. Gordon stumbled and swayed making his way back to the huddle before falling to his knees. He remained in the game, however, carrying the ball three more times, putting Tennessee fourth and goal from the one-yard line.

Sammy Burklow, a kicker for the Vols, was tapped for the field goal attempt. It would be his only field goal of the '57 season. Not only that, but it would be his only field goal for his entire football career at Tennessee.

The game ended with the Vols victorious. The score was 3–0. "Tennessee finished the season 8–3. There was no SEC championship, no first place in the AP Poll. But the 1957 Gator Bowl will always have its place in history and in the hearts of the players on the field."[144] It was "one for the history books" but a heartbreaking loss for Texas A&M and a thrilling victory for Tennessee. Sixty-five years later, there would be no love loss between Bryant and Alabama and Texas A&M, the years never dulling the disappointment and disdain the Aggies felt for their old coach and their rival team.

For Coach Laslie, the former assistant head coach at West Point who was ready to start winning bowl games as the Bryant/Laslie dynamic duo, it was a defeat that was especially personally bruising. Even having a Heisman winner to his credit after a single year of coaching at College Station didn't lessen the sting of the loss.

CHAPTER THIRTY-THREE

The Return

"As I recall, that first year at Alabama, they wanted Bryant's hide and were ready to fire him."

—Jimmy Dellinger, Alice Laslie's step-nephew

TUSCALOOSA, ALABAMA
1958

L-R: Alice Laslie, Alene Moseley Danby, Mary Lou Laslie Henry, Carney Laslie, and Ruffy Moseley (who Laslie affectionately nicknamed "Marble-Eyes") in 1958 at the Laslies' new home in Tuscaloosa.

AT THE END OF A&M's season in '57, Mary Harmon Bryant and Paul, Jr., packed up the car and picked up Alice Laslie at the Laslie home to make the 630-mile drive to Tuscaloosa. It was the only time, Paul, Jr., remarked, that he ever saw his mother get more than frustrated with Alice. Along with Alice not being ready when they arrived to pick her up, there were requests along the way to stop and say hello to a friend here and there, a carefully planned itinerary in ruins. It was typical Alice. Stubborn and persuasive, her mantra that everything should be made into a fun and social event applied even to the serious business of moving. It was also typical of the gracious Mary Harmon conceding to her traveling companions wishes despite being more than a little inconvenienced.

Spring training at Alabama that year was like no other for the players left from the Whitworth years. With some on athletic scholarships for the upcoming year, the players were put through a brutal regimen seen by many to be aimed at separating the wheat from the chaff. Others saw it as sending players to a proverbial slaughter. An unnecessarily brutal culling of players who the coaches had already deemed as inferior — whether by lack of physical ability, lack of heart, or inability to stay in good academic standing.

It was more likely that the approach Bryant and Laslie took hearkened straight from their days at Pre-Flight where each new group of cadets were welcomed with the same speech. "We're here to prepare you to be naval officers [football players]. You'll be taught things in ground school that we think an officer [football player] should know and you'll learn the discipline of a close-order drill. But most of all, we'll be seeing if you can take it. If you can't take it now's the time to find out, not when you're Out There [in the game] with lives [winning or losing] depending on you."

Tom Stoddard described the methods in his account of that first season in his book *Turn Around*. By all accounts, including that of Alabama assistant coach Gene Stallings, himself a former "Junction Boys" player at A&M, they were reminiscent of the practice sessions he had endured. But they were still a far cry from the conditions the players suffered back at A&M, notably on the practice field where, according to Coach Stallings, the conditions would never have passed muster if Coach Laslie had been on board at A&M at the time.

An influential group in Tuscaloosa, namely alumni and ex-players who also had sons cut from team, were outraged at what they saw as a brutal elimination of players from the team. They called upon reporters to question the tactics used and it wasn't long before enthusiasm for Bryant and his methods began to wane. To combat the public criticism, Laslie contacted his former boss at VMI, Pooley Hubert, known as "the General," former Alabama quarterback who led his team to a never-to-be-forgotten Rose Bowl victory in the '20s, a legend among alumni and fans. Hubert, retired and living in Waynesboro, Georgia, was more than happy to lend his assistance. He wasn't finding retirement to his liking, as Bryant, Jr., recalled, and both Laslie and Bryant felt not only would it help them it would do the out of commission coach some good, too. Like many players before him, Hubert's coaching ambition had always been to return one day to coach at his alma mater. Hubert was put to work, this time in a popular coffee shop hangout in town where he would begin an informal campaign of persuasion.

He became a fixture there, his persona well known among the patrons—chief among them alumni, ex-players, and board members of the university. They were more than happy to talk football, and as they expressed their dislike of Bryant's methods, Hubert would voice his support of them. This did much to quell their criticism, and it wasn't long before the tide changed and Bryant had their support. Still, the controversy did give publicity to the criticism of the tough play Alabama was advocating, a scrutiny that would set Bryant up for one of the biggest controversies of his career.

Hubert's successful campaign garnered an invitation from Bryant to be a part-time, paid member of the staff as a clinical observer of off-season practice the following year.

Bryant and Laslie had other changes to make in their new roles at Alabama that didn't have anything to do with football. Both avid golfers, they determined the university's golf course was in need of expansion. Roadblock after roadblock was encountered until Bryant was overheard shouting out to Laslie while in the athletic department one day. "Carney," he yelled down the hallway, "why don't you call whoever you know up there in Washington and ask them about getting us the rest of that golf course?"

Although Coach Laslie would never say when asked, the "whoever you know" happened to be Senator Lister Hill, a forty-five-year veteran member of Congress who served on health-related committees in the Senate. Though Coach Laslie's beloved uncle Carney had passed away in 1953, Laslie had remained close to Uncle Carney's second wife, Amelie Hill Laslie, Senator Hill's twin sister.

Senator Hill had written legislation that resulted in the Hill-Burton Act of 1947 and in subsequent years had been responsible for providing federal funds for construction and renovation of over 9,000 medical facilities, particularly in lower income areas. He was a powerful and influential member of Congress whose legacy also included designating land use on Veterans Administration property in the state.

The university had submitted a proposal to the US Department of Health, Education and Welfare in 1956, two years prior to Bryant's arrival, to absorb 136 acres of federal land that was then part of the VA hospital campus located in Tuscaloosa. The proposal included twenty-seven acres for a nine-hole golf course as well as the biology department's request for acreage to house an arboretum, an ecological study center, and a lake. The proposal was then amended over protest to include a standard eighteen-hole golf course, which the biology department vehemently opposed, issuing an official rebuttal to the change: "We feel the statements in the 1956 application were made in good faith and that they should be kept," read the rebuttal submitted by the biology department. For two years, it had languished in committee, and by February 1958, the tug of war between the two for the additional acres needed for the expansion of the golf course had stalled the project completely.

It wasn't long after Bryant and Laslie arrived in 1958, that construction began on the arboretum, the roads for full access to the property completed by December 1959, and the golf course area expanded to create the standard eighteen-hole course shortly after. Many attributed the university's acquisition of the additional acreage to Laslie's behind-the-scenes influence. "I'm not sure who Carney knew up in Washington," said Dr. E. C. Brock, team physician, he and his wife, Hannah, close friends of both the Laslies and the Bryants. "He never would say."

Dr. Brock's role as the team physician from 1959 to 1982 gave him a unique place from which to view the two coaches up close and personal. Recalling an occasion where the three drove together to an event, Dr. Brock commented: "I'll tell you the difference between Carney and Coach Bryant," he began. "I don't smoke, and of course, both Carney and Coach Bryant were chain smokers. I would sit in the back, behind Carney, who always drove. Coach Bryant sat up front. Well," he chuckled, "the two immediately lit up. For the entire two sometimes three-hour drive, it was one cigarette after another. Carney cracked his window open a little bit, blowing the smoke out when he exhaled, and flicked his cigarette ashes and cigarette butt out the small vent window they used to have in cars back then. Coach Bryant, well," he said, chuckling again, "he blew smoke all in the car, not giving a mind to how full of smoke the car was. He was enjoying the conversation. By the time we arrived at whereever we were going the ashtray was overflowing with ashes, the cigarette butts covering the floor on his side. He'd open the door and they would spill out onto the ground."

The pressure of expectations for Coach Bryant and the football program could not have been higher. Here was a head coach that the press had all but ordained the savior of the football program. He had played a game for Alabama with a broken leg, an indication of his win-whatever-the-cost ways. He would demand no less of his players. The board had been clear: restore the university's reputation as a powerhouse collegiate team. In many respects there was nowhere to go but up given the dismal record of the Whitworth years. But it wasn't just an SEC Championship many clamored for, but a National Championship. And none wanted it more than Bryant and Laslie.

In *Turn Around*, Stoddard's book on Bryant's first year based on numerous interviews with players, there are hints at the concern that was brewing among the coaches. Players perceived that his assistants were afraid of Bryant. They noted that the coaches seemed to become agitated whenever Bryant's whereabouts was unknown, talking among themselves in a worried fashion. Stoddard also described Bryant's unpredictable and violent clashes with the players, often swooping down to the field from the observation tower in order to chastise them for what was perceived as lack of effort or a failed attempt altogether of some sort of training exercise. From Stoddard's view (and the players) this was a purposeful tactic to terrify them, and it appeared to work. What the players observed among the coaches, however, wasn't fear but rather Coach Laslie's concern. It was this which prompted the long and loyal service of Billy Varner.

A relaxing game of golf was one of Laslie's and Bryant's favorite pastimes whenever the demands of their coaching allowed. It was at Tuscaloosa's Indian Hills Golf and Country Club that they met Billy Varner. A bouncer/waiter at the club, Billy impressed Coach Laslie as a gentleman who could be trusted, a kind person who could be discreet and whose skills in security would be useful. Laslie took him into his confidence when he hired him to be Bryant's driver and bodyguard, first part time, then full time, a role which he faithfully performed till Bryant's death in 1983. The official records show Varner started working for the university police in February 1976. But he had been performing his duties long before then.

Linda Knowles, Bryant's longtime secretary, spoke candidly to Wright Thompson of ESPN.com about Varner's many years of being Bryant's personal chauffer and bodyguard. Riding in the back of Varner's crimson Buick LeSabre Varner was privy to Bryant's life as no other, she told Wright. Although Varner was offered a lot of money to write a book or help make a movie, he would have none of it, Knowles added. Varner's wife of fifty-seven years, Susie Varner, spoke with only a hint of bitterness of how Billy gave up his life, like Bryant did, and how he didn't get to enjoy retirement, also like Bryant. The only thing, she said, he had to show for over two decades of service were his memories. And by the end of his life, these, too, would be just out of his reach.

On March 8, 1982, a reception was held to honor Coach Bryant, commemorating his 315th win in Washington, DC, at the Sheraton Washington Hotel. Celebrities, including personal friend and evangelist Billy Graham, politicians, family and close friends gathered in the hotel's "Virginia Suites" balllroom to celebrate the coach's record-breaking accomplishments. When Mary Lou Laslie Henry spotted Billy Varner in the crowd, she purposefully made her way over to him. "Hello, Billy. I'm Carney Laslie's daughter." Billy grasped her hands firmly, his eyes filling with tears. "Coach Laslie was my best friend," he said. "I have missed him every day since the day he died."

Photo taken at the Sheraton Washington Hotel, March 8, 1982, honoring Bryant becoming the winningest college football coach with his 315th win. L-R: Edy Moseley, Paul Bryant, Mary Lou Laslie Henry

CHAPTER THIRTY-FOUR

The Boys are Back in Town

"I'll tell you how I felt about Carney Laslie.
I should have called him 'Coach.'"

—Paul Bryant, 1974, from his autobiography

TUSCALOOSA, ALABAMA
1958–1960

THE PRESS, ALUMNI, AND fans alike hovered in the background like a pack of wolves hoping for a turnaround of fortune for their team but ready to pounce if the scoreboard indicated otherwise. Bryant kept them at bay by producing their first winning season in three years with no embarrassing one-sided defeats.

With only a dozen conference-caliber players, the coaches emphasized strong defense and mistake-free play. Laslie, well aware of the pressures on Bryant, continued to be the friend Bryant needed as well as a colleague whose perspective of the game and drive to win mirrored his own. They were a team, and Bryant also knew Laslie was the one person he could trust. For one, he knew Laslie wasn't after his job. For another, Laslie's knowledge of the game, his experience, and coaching skills were unparalleled, as he had been mentored by and coached alongside some of the greatest coaches in the game: Alabama's own Wallace Wade and Frank Thomas and Col. Red Blaik at West Point. Laslie also wasn't out to promote himself, and took a self-deprecating stance toward his boss, as well as with the press. But it was also clear they considered themselves to be equals. A partnership born out of a long history of friendship, war experience, respect for one another's talents and true affection for one another. Bryant himself alluded to Laslie's unique role in his autobiography, explaining that Coach Laslie never did directly address him as "Coach Bryant" but always "Paul." Nor did Laslie ever call him or refer to him as "Bear", as others did. Neither did Bryant directly address him as "Coach Laslie" but rather "Carney," even in the presence of other coaches and players. This was a show of respect for their equal bearing with each other.

All of the Alabama assistant coaches knew what role Laslie played in the hierarchy of the coaching staff. "If you had an idea or something you wanted to pitch to Coach Bryant, or anything you wanted him to know, you had to go through Coach Laslie. Bryant wouldn't listen to anyone else," assistant coach Gene Stallings remembered. Officially starting off with the title of assistant athletic director, Laslie's role expanded to include assistant head coach when Jerry Claiborne left for the head coach job at Virginia Tech, joining Frank Moseley there in 1960.

The call to Jerry Claiborne to join Frank Moseley at Virginia Tech is but one example of how the three—Bryant, Laslie, and Moseley—valued loyalty and extended their help to those who had worked with them who they saw as talented, hardworking, and like-minded. Clairborne embodied the values and character that they wanted to promote among young players as well. Jerry Claiborne, known to be a man of integrity with his morals and goals set in stone, was but one example of such a coach. Claiborne, like Bryant, had always been clear: his goal was to be a head coach. The move from Missouri to Alabama with an eye toward a head coach position fit perfectly with all of their timelines. Assigning him the assistant head coach title would give him the stepping stone he needed to move into a head coach position. It would also lend to a seamless transition from A&M to Alabama with their coaching staff overall, layered with the experience they needed.

From the outset, starting at that first season at Alabama, Claiborne continued to be open about being on the lookout for a head coach position. Finally, the call came, from none other than his old coach from Kentucky, Coach Moseley at Virginia Tech. Claiborne left at the end of the '60 season and joined Moseley in Blacksburg in time to coach the Hokies for their '61 season. Claiborne and Moseley worked together for another ten years before Claiborne moved on to Maryland. He would be inducted into the College Football Hall of Fame in 1999.[145]

Bryant pushed hard for his dual role as head coach and athletic director and stubbornly clung to both job titles despite the obvious inefficiencies. Some suggested he wanted the two salaries, though there was a policy of keeping Bryant's salary under the university president's (one year the president's was $100,000 to Bryant's $99,999). Others felt he did not want an athletic director overseeing him. It was probably both reasons. He could appoint his own top assistant who he trusted implicitly. Though Laslie had the title of "assistant" athletic director, as Paul Bryant, Jr., pointed out, Laslie handled most of the load. Laslie, Bryant, Jr., noted, had skills in administration that his father did not. Bryant, however, held the title long after most major universities had split the two roles and continued to hold the athletic director title after he retired from coaching in December 1982.

Laslie and Bryant often adopted a "good cop, bad cop" strategy to deal with both players and support staff and switched roles depending on the situation. They had had many years together to perfect their so-called shtick, depending on their audience. In one instance, an athletic gear supplier pitching his wares somehow had been able to get an audience with the, by that time, famed coach. Bryant pointed him in the direction of the man who he himself described as being "tight as a tick," Coach Laslie, "keeper of Alabama's athletic exchequer,"[146] because, he added, "I'm a spending SOB." One salesman joked that Carney Laslie could eliminate the national debt in three years if given the chance.

Tom Stoddard, in his account of that first year at Alabama, described an incident that occurred at the very first meeting with the squad when they arrived in January 1958.

> Notified to assemble for a meeting at 1:15 p.m., most of the players arrived in plenty of time. When Bryant after consulting his watch began the meeting, he started by calling out a name: "Gilmer? Where's Gilmer? . . . Is Jerry Gilmer in this room?" Somebody said, "Coach, I don't believe he's here."
>
> Bryant turned to Laslie. "Dammit, Carney," he said, "go upstairs and pack his things. He's off scholarship."

Many players speculated the action was set up to send a message and that Bryant had known the player had decided not to return for the next season. But the message was heard loud and clear. There would be no tolerance for poor attitudes and no excuses for careless behavior. Being late for any reason was enough to get you kicked off the team.

On the field, Laslie routinely aligned himself with the trainers, conferring regularly with Jim Goostree, head trainer, to monitor player injuries. Bryant was known to push players who had suffered an injury, especially if it was perceived as a minor one, citing his own experience of playing in a game with a broken leg. Bud Moore, a player that first year, related his recollection about a two-year letterman at tackle named Sid Neighbors who had sustained a significant head injury. Sitting out in the breezeway with some players one afternoon, they were dressed out with pads on and waiting for practice to start, "dreading like the devil to go out to practice."

"We were just playing around," Moore recalls, "when Coach Bryant walked out. He went over to Sid and placed his hand on his shoulder. 'How you feeling, Sid,' he asked.

"'Oh, Coach Bryant, my head's still hurting me bad, I hear ringing in my ears, sounds like a telephone ringing.'

"'Well, Sidney, next time it rings, you answer it, because it's me telling you to get your fat ass out to practice.'"

Laslie's input gave the impression of balancing out the sometimes overzealousness of the head coach, and he and Bryant used it to their advantage. They both agreed on what was required of players. But Bryant knew if Laslie was convinced of the merit of a player or an assistant coach's idea/suggestion/concern, it was likely something to pay attention to. It was true that no one got to the head coach except through Carney Laslie. But there was always room for new players to see what they could get by their coaches, especially when it came to the grueling practices.

One player reminisced about an incident on the field during Bryant's first year at Alabama that highlighted how Bryant and Laslie dealt with injuries: "Coach Laslie used to handle the wounded-type guys," he said, "and they were all out in sweats, and one day Coach Bryant looked over there and he saw more guys in sweats than there were in pads . . . and he went over and talked to Laslie, and they started [them] running and they ran damn wind sprints the whole practice while we were over there scrimmaging, doing whatever drills . . . the next day, all them sonofabitches was back in pads."

But Laslie was no pushover. Along with the heat was the constant pressure as the coaches made sure the players felt they were pushing themselves to their limits. Many, if not most, were indeed pushed to their limits and considered quitting. The most dramatic defection occurred the second day of practice their first year, described by a player:

One group of players was running skeleton drills, sort of half scrimmages, with just one side of an offensive line running against a linebacker, defensive end, tackle, and guard. Most say that Coach Laslie was in charge of the drill. In the huddle between plays, Eugene Harris, a sophomore . . . repeatedly begged a couple of players to quit with him . . . Reaching his breaking point he made a decision, and as a play began, he rushed past the nose guard and took off toward the fence . . . Laslie yelled after him, "Come back here, boy," but Harris did not slow down . . . eye witness accounts say he hit the chain link fence about four feet off the ground, and vaulted over the top. Harris fled toward the dressing room shedding equipment on the way. Laslie inserted another player in Harris's place and continued the drill.

CHAPTER THIRTY-FIVE

Defense Wins the Game

TUSCALOOSA, ALABAMA
1958–1961

WHENEVER ASKED BY REPORTERS what constituted Alabama's success, Laslie would always point to Bryant as the driving force. "There is no one more disciplined," Laslie insisted. "He is the first one up and the last one at the end of the day." Even when some would give Laslie credit for a plan or play, he would not hesitate to point to his boss as the guiding force of their efforts.

Known for being an excellent speaker, Laslie would often fill in for Bryant at speaking engagements during their years together. Bryant was, understandably, a first choice as a speaker for many organizations, especially as his popularity grew. Calls came in regularly ranging from Kiwanis Clubs to high school awards banquets to corporate events looking for a popular headliner as a draw. Often the organizers were disappointed when Bryant was unavailable, and his second in command was sent. But as Bryant, Jr., revealed in an interview, Laslie spoke at many events, and was known for being an excellent speaker, sought after around the country. Although Coach Bryant was glad to have Laslie fill in for him at a speaking engagement, he didn't like it if the same group came calling again and asked for Coach Laslie as their first choice.

Bryant's talent for coaching, aided by his phenomenal capacity for hard work, was matched by his exceptionally efficient use of time. For example, one reporter noted he was known for avoiding long telephone conversations, particularly long-distance calls charged to his budget, a tactic no doubt emphasized as well by the keeper of the athletic department's purse, Coach Laslie. Bryant was able to devote his time to those areas he was exceptionally adept at because he could rely on Laslie.

Ed Conyers, longtime practice field official, remembered the afternoon he was called upon to fill in to officiate a practice game. Laslie, he said, reached him in a panic trying to locate the missing ref. "He asked me if I officiated and when I said yes, he said, 'Well, get on out here.' Then I asked him how much I would be paid. 'Do you want to ask Coach Bryant that? Because I won't ask him that. Or do you just want to get out here and officiate?'" Conyers officiated for the next ten years free of charge, over which time he says he says Bryant didn't even know his name. When the NCAA mandated that anyone on the practice field who had an advisory role be paid, Conyers' pay was upped to $10 per practice. "With the Lord as my witness, when I first heard about the rule, I thought I was going to have to pay them $10," he says. "I thought, I only have $5 on me, I hope they'll still let me go. I'd probably still pay if I had to."[147]

Laslie and Bryant divided up the tasks to capitalize on their strengths and to position Laslie where he could apprise Bryant of both player and coach strengths and weaknesses. Having adminstrative expertise, he used his position to glean as much about the players and coaches as possible. One player would later describe Laslie as being one who knew a lot more than he appeared to, hence his nickname, the Silver Fox, his discretion in all things well respected. For example, Coach Laslie personally doled out the monthly cash stipends many players on financial assistance received, and was known to take a keen interest in the managers and student trainers.

Laslie's role at Alabama expanded by virtue of the success of the program. But he was also called upon to help handle the most sensitive of issues. He worked tirelessly in the background protecting, promoting, and quietly influencing Bryant, a model not lost on the other assistants who grew to understand, like Coach Stallings explained, that to get an idea in front of Bryant, one had to go through Laslie to get heard. It was a partnership that Coach Johnny Majors at Tennessee envied. Bryant, he explained, not only had the loyalty of Laslie, but also a voice of expertise he trusted and could rely on, leading Majors to describe the duo as the closest coaching collaboration known in the history of the sport.

But it was not only a matter of loyalty bound in friendship. Laslie remained committed to Bryant because of his belief in Bryant. The two were on track for a goal they had both sought for sixteen years. They had told the players when they first arrived at Alabama, "You do what we say and in four years we'll win a National Championship." They knew they could do it with the right players. And they knew they could do it together. They needed each other to make it happen.

Morning, noon, and night, as Mary Harmon Moman, Bryant's granddaughter, remembered, "Uncle Carney" and "Poppa" would huddle at the back of the Bryants' lake house, where they spent their summers. There they would review game films and go over game plans, training schedules, and player rosters, strategizing for the upcoming season. Bryant would later describe Laslie's staying power and influence in his autobiography. "In all those years, he never faltered," he wrote in his succinct tip of his hat to what many in the realm of coaching knew: that Laslie was not only a player's coach but a coach's coach. But more to the point: *The* coach's coach. Coaches Gene Stallings and Jack Rutledge, both players and coaches under Bryant and Laslie, would also refer to Laslie as having that rare ability to connect with both players and coaches to instruct, encourage, and facilitate individual growth. "Do you understand what I'm saying?" Coach Rutledge emphasized in a phone interview.

When the first game of their first year at Alabama rolled around, it would be against Louisiana State University coached by Paul Dietzel as the head coach. As in many programs in the SEC, there were ties between the coaches that made their going up against each other a personal rivalry as well. Dietzel had been assistant under Bryant at Kentucky and an assistant with Laslie at West Point. They knew what they were up against with the LSU team, which was favored by twenty points. Bryant, as ever understated with the press pre-game, emphasized what the coaches were looking for in their players: drive and focus. "If these boys go at it with everything they've got, I'm not worried about winning or losing. We'll get our fair share."[148] They lost to a powerful LSU team, 13–3.

By the end of their third season, Alabama had once again established itself as a force to contend with. Many wondered what the secret was in Tuscaloosa. "We have a reputation in football for demanding a lot from our players. Sure we do," said Laslie, "but we consider that a compliment to their ability and they consider it a challenge. To be the best, you must get the best from your men, and there is no substitute for work." He added, " [W]e are probably the smallest team in major football. But we always tell our boys that 'bigness is in your heart and not body.'"[149]

There was a lot of heart in Tuscaloosa.

After three consecutive winning seasons, the Crimson Tide arrived on the cusp of a National Championship in 1961. It was also, however, a team steeped in controversy related to the accusations of brutality in training and play. It wasn't long before the tenor of criticism about Alabama's play on the field grew strident, and controversy exploded with an incident that occurred in a game between Georgia Tech and Alabama late in the season of 1961. When the November 17, 1961, *Time* magazine went public, characterizing Bryant as one of college football's "bad guys," just two days prior to the game, all of college football—particularly his rivals—was ready to pounce on the controversial coach. (In spite of the harsh characterization of Bryant, the article went on to laud him as inarguably one of the best coaches even at that time.)

The game, played on November 19, 1961, later became known as the Holt-Graning Incident and was exemplary for several reasons. Linebackers Lee Roy Jordan and Darwin Holt were breaking records— their last three opponents had been scoreless. Upon entering the stadium that day, not only was Alabama a promising pick for the SEC Championship, but many predicted Alabama was also well on its way to winning the National Championship. But it was also a game where the tough play of the Crimson Tide squad drew the ire of Alabama's rival coaches. In a chorus of criticism, they called out Alabama for the incident, a tackle they decried as "brutal play," the incident serving as the poster play for such and the basis of an article in *The Saturday Evening Post* titled "College Football is Going Berserk":

> Billy Richardson was back to field the punt for Alabama. One of his blockers was Darwin Holt, a senior from Greenville, Texas. Leading the Tech (Georgia) players covering the punt was halfback Chick Graning. Richardson signaled for a fair catch at the Alabama thirty-one-yard line. Graning was racing toward him about ten yards downfield when Richardson made the catch. Holt then crashed his forearm into Graning's face, beneath his mask. Graning fell backward, unconscious. Holt ran to the sidelines. The partisan crowd fell silent as Graning was carried off the field on a stretcher.[150]

No penalty was called, despite the outcry of Georgia Tech fans and coaches that day. Bryant, too, acknowledged after the game that the lack of a call was clearly remiss. The incident drew little attention in the Sunday newspapers' account of the game. Then the severity of Graning's injuries became known.

The *Atlanta Constitution* reported on the injuries, adding that Georgia Tech's physician had called it "the worst facial injury he had ever seen in athletics: (1) fracture of alveolar process (facial bones); (2) five missing front upper teeth and the majority of remaining front teeth broken (will eventually lose other upper teeth); (3) fracture of nasal bone; (4) fracture of right maxillary sinus and sinus filled with blood; (5) fracture of right zygomatic process (bone beneath right eye); (6) cerebral concussion; (7) possible fracture of base of skull."[151]

Wire services picked up on the story, which competed with the news that the victory over Georgia Tech had catapulted Alabama into the number one position in the national ratings. Tamping down the criticism, Bryant "called in the press, showed the game film, and pointed out that the Tech team was guilty of more infractions than his."[152] The devastating hit was an accident, a deeply remorseful Holt repeatedly said, not a deliberate or coached technique. Between the lines on every football field is physical confrontation. Outright brutality is the hallmark of the game. Football is, after all, a contact sport between young, zealous, and physically conditioned, strong athletes. Accidents happen. A sentiment expressed by many of those with firsthand experience, namely players and coaches.

The press agreed, although some rivals in the college coaching ranks characterized the use of the game tapes as manipulation. It also seemed that rival coaches, like Ralph "Shug" Jordan, head coach at Auburn, had no other reason for Alabama's success than to point to Bryant's growing controversial, painted as a new "hell-for-leather, helmet-busting, gang-tackling brand of football," being demonstrated by the Bryant-coached Alabama team.

Sports journalists continued to inflame fans with accusations that Bryant's coaching intent was to knock players senseless, giving rise to the sentiment expressed by more than one coach in the SEC that since Bear Bryant came back into the Conference, the only kind of game any opponent could win was to match the vicious play. Such accusations seemed more self-serving than not. Time would tell for this coach whether that would hold true. Those that reviled the so-called poster child for being the "most brutal coach" pointed to that as the reason for his winning record. Laslie's mantra had always been that defense wins the game. In 1961, it would be a signature characteristic of the team.

Laslie had distinguished himself as a defensive coach of national acclaim who had joined Bryant directly from his tenure at West Point as assistant head coach to one of the toughest head coaches in the academy's history. He pushed for tough, defensive, "take no prisoners" play. His techniques had won him acclaim in the past. But it seemed Alabama was now a lightning rod for criticism related to the resurgence of what many characterized as the brutality of the sport. Bryant was an easy target; the stigma of his first year at Texas A&M and the infamous Junction Boys never left, enabling his rivals to cast him in a less-than-favorable light for many reasons, including the recruitment of players. There were already on the scene a number of coaches such as Darrell Royal at Texas and Frank Kush at Arizona State who became far more notorious for "their grinding workouts and pitiless retribution against players who displeased them"[153] when compared to Alabama's Bear Bryant.

But it was Bryant's ego that also tended to trip him up. It was the elephant in the room for those who really knew him. They were forgiving at best, and at the least tolerant of how unconcerned he was of the repercussions of his actions. Its most benign manifestation was what Laslie used to refer to as the "I LOVE ME WALL," a popular way to describe when a wall was the designated place holder devoted to pictures of someone alongside politicians and celebrities. But it was Bryant's ego, his love of being in the headlines, his disdain for critical sportswriters, and ultimately his arrogance that dropped trouble at his doorstep on a seemingly regular basis. For this, Carney's gentler, behind-the-scenes presence was even more necessary.

The barometer of public opinion swung from one extreme to the other: Bryant was either loved or despised. All could agree, however, that Bryant had a genius for self-promotion, going back to his early days. He was described as a natural showman by friends and teammates alike. Self-promotion without results didn't attract much attention. Alabama was winning and on the proverbial map once again.

Standing in front of the "I Love Me" Wall at the Bryant home: L-R: second, Mary Harmon Bryant; fourth from Left, Paul Bryant, Alice Laslie, Carney Laslie.
© *Catapult Sports*

CHAPTER THIRTY-SIX

Kill or Be Killed

"Coming into the huddle, he dropped to one knee. 'Kill, or be killed,' he said between gritted teeth, shaking his fist for emphasis. Was he making a joke? We didn't know whether to laugh or not. But— we won."

—Bill Battle, University of Alabama,
describing a pep talk from Coach Laslie before a game

TUSCALOOSA, ALABAMA
1961

WHEN BENNY MARSHALL DECIDED to interview Alabama players for his book *Winning Isn't Everything*, many of them from the team of '61, he was impressed with the group overall not looking, speaking, or acting like the thugs they were portrayed. "They didn't look brutal. Most of them didn't look like football players, even. They didn't sound brutal. They sounded like intelligent young men who knew whereof they spoke,"[154] wrote Marshall.

Marshall gave them plenty of room to say whatever they wished about collegiate brutality in general and the Bryant brand that had been so demonized in the press. Bryant's own players, like Gary Phillips, a 185-pound tackle who played on the team in '61 and who later went into medicine; Pat Trammell, who quarterbacked the team; and Leon Fuller, who never weighed more than 170 when he was an Alabama back-fielder and who stayed for post-graduate work at the university, had a decidedly different opinion of how they were coached built on their firsthand experience.

"Coach Bryant brutal? He must not have been too brutal," Pat Trammell told Marshall. "Phillips, a tackle at 185 pounds and less, played. Actually, he's hard on people who play dirty football. He doesn't like penalties."

"There's a difference between being tough and being dirty," Phillips added. "I remember an end who got three fifteen-yard penalties Coach Bryant's first year. He never played any more."[155]

Jim Blevins, captain of the 1959 team at Alabama and who later became a high school and college coach, commented on the importance of playing within the rules. "There were three 'musts' you learned in Alabama football. You must not bust signals, you must block your man, you must not get penalties."[156] They were not coaching their boys to engage in risky play—late tackling, piling on, or butt blocking— tempting but not violating regulations. It was totally against their principles of fair play and never condoned.

Marlin Dyess, a 145-pound halfback, later an engineer in the space program, commented when asked about Coach Bryant and sportsmanship. "There's not a one in here who can't tell you the lessons Coach Bryant taught. Turn away from a fight, he'd say. That takes a man. I don't know how many he's snatched out of a game for doing something wrong."

Though they wouldn't tolerate dirty play, they did demand tough play.

Other than one freshman player from Whitworth's last season, the roster of '61 had no players from the Whitworth days. Eighty percent of the players were from the state of Alabama. And though they were overall a small group, they were described by the press as being lightning quick. The previous three seasons had been remarkable for emphasizing strong defense and mistake-free plays and included a victory over rival Auburn. Their appearance at the Liberty Bowl in '59, which they lost, marked their first bowl game in six years. But now, a National Championship seemed to be within reach.

Retrospectively, the two coaches' win at Kentucky over number one Oklahoma on New Year's Day nine years before had been one for the record books. But though the bowl game win gave them both a large measure of professional pride, the two still couldn't claim a National Championship given Kentucky's standing in the polls prior to that game.

But it was the loss to Tennessee a decade before that remained one of Laslie's biggest disappointments upon leaving Kentucky. Their loss to Tennessee at the Gator Bowl while the two were at Texas A&M also stung badly. Now, in one of the season's most anticipated games in Tuscaloosa, the Tide had an opportunity to give Laslie the retribution he was looking for against the Tennessee Volunteers.

When the Tennessee players arrived in Birmingham for a televised game against Alabama, everyone was hyped and ready. Alabama hadn't beaten a Tennessee team at home in sixteen years, since 1954. Now back at their alma mater, Bryant and Laslie were poised and ready to deliver a one-two punch to their arch rival Tennessee. Although they wouldn't have the satisfaction of presenting General Neyland's head on a silver platter, he was still Tennessee's athletic director and any win against him would still be personally satisfying.

The night before the game, Coach Laslie, as was his tradition, took a group of his players to the movies. Walking back to their hotel after the show, he and the Alabama players passed a group of Tennessee players.

Back and forth pre-game smack talk ensued as they passed by each other, the taunting Tennessee players not noticing that the Alabama players were accompanied by their coach, Coach Laslie letting them all have their say. Once they had passed but still within earshot, the white-haired coach, walked into the middle of the street and had the last word. At the top of his lunges he shouted, "You sons of bitches will never win in this town as long as Bryant and I are here!"[157]

The initially stunned Alabama players quickly found their voices. Fists raised, they hooped and hollered back at the Tennessee players, saving the last of their gusto for their approval of their coach. As for Coach Laslie, he couldn't hide a quiet smile.

When the game started off with a fifty-four-yard field goal by Tennessee, it felt all too familiar. Hearts sank. But the Crimson Tide quickly rallied. For the remainder of the game, they smothered the Vol's, decimating Tennessee with their defense. Alabama held the Vol's to sixty-one yards of total offense, Laslie's defense dominant, and racked up thirty-four points of their own. The final score: Alabama 34, Tennessee, 3.

The coaches now began the arduous task of keeping their team focused in the face of all the favorable press coverage. It was hard not to feel like they were riding the crest of a wave. The first five games resulted in one shutout with a total of only three touchdowns given up. Alabama would end the season with six shutouts and only twenty-five points scored against the team in eleven games.

Sixty-one years later, the '61 defense is still said to be one of its best, stopping opponents at the goal line a hallmark of their play. "I don't know how many times we made goal-line stands, but we brought that back," player Tommy Brooker said in an interview in 2011. "We'd sit on the bench for two quarters, and if someone threatened to score a touchdown, [Bryant] would say, 'Give me the red bunch.' And we came off the bench cold, and nobody could score." Loaded with talent, the team of 1961 had a roster of players that included Bryant's all-time favorite player, Pat Trammell, Lee Roy Jordan, a linebacker who went on to become Alabama's Player of the Decade, and five seniors on the team who went on to become draft picks for the NFL and AFL.

Senior Trammel, playing his third year at quarterback in '61, was soft-spoken. Despite his gentle manner, he was known for his hard-driving play and for being a quarterback who loved to run with the ball. Bryant admired Trammel's desire to win above all else, referencing his abilities with a less than stellar compliment of he "didn't run well or pass well".[158] But it was Trammel's fight off the field that earned him Bryant's love and respect when he went on to graduate from medical school in Birmingham, ultimately losing his fight with cancer at age twenty-eight.

Lee Roy Jordan, a junior that year, played both center on offense and linebacker on defense. Compared to most players in those positions, Jordan was small, standing just six foot two and weighing in at just 200 pounds. Jordan, an All-American, was the Dallas Cowboys' top pick in 1963, a key player on that team's famed "Doomsday Defense", and played for Dallas for fourteen seasons.

They continued to apply what the coaches had drilled into them, remembering their words when they arrived: do what we say, and in three years you'll be national champions. This included superstitious routines that this particular team inserted into the season. From wearing the same pair of socks (without washing them in between games) to having a lucky number, many athletes agree that repeating a habitual behavior associated with a win is a common practice. Coaches, too, have their superstitious routines. Laslie had been notoriously superstitious, incorporating a variety of routines over the years he adhered to both personally and with the players. Before each game, after the last word of prayer had been said, it was Coach Laslie who got in the huddle with the squad, giving them final words before they broke and headed to the field: "You've got to get in there and block for sixty minutes and tackle for sixty minutes."

"I remember once when we were playing one game . . . and Coach

Bryant asked the assistant coaches if they had anything to say. Coach Sam Bailey said he didn't and neither did Howard Schnellenberger. And he asked Coach Laslie," remembered Bill Battle, former player and athletic director at Alabama and coach at Tennessee. "Coach Laslie jumped up and came to the huddle. He said he just wanted to remind us of something they used to say in the Army."[159] Evoking the intensity of a battle-cry, he shook his fist for emphasis, "'It's kill, or be killed,' he said. Some of the guys didn't know what to think. Some laughed, thinking he was kidding. But we won the game."

Mal Moore, later the athletic director at Alabama, remembered the customary routine players followed on game day:

> When I was playing, Carney would be in the dressing room and he would lead the team out going onto the field to start the game. Once on the sideline, he gathered everybody around him and he would always say "you've got to block and tackle like you've never blocked and tackled before. Then he'd kneel down, and with all the players gathered around, and they would grab his hat and wad it all up and throw it up in the air. Then he'd go to the trainer and say "Give me some oxygen, Jim!" because he would have run out on the field. And he would do the same thing every game."[160]
> Chuckling, he added, "Players loved it."

It is unknown how many hats he went through by the end of season.

The victory over Tennessee in '61 became the first since Bryant and Laslie arrived in '58. Somehow, it was this victory over Tennessee that many attribute the introduction of the tradition of smoking of Cuban cigars. However, the "tradition" was actually begun by Coach Hank Crisp, who gave out cigars after the 1935 game when Alabama beat Tennessee. Much later in 1957 when Bryant was at Texas A&M, Bryant asked head trainer Smokey Harper, who had been at Kentucky with him and Laslie, to get cigars to have on hand for the expected victory over Tennessee at the Gator Bowl. But they lost. The players didn't get the cigars. Then, in 1959, Bryant again requested cigars for the game against Tennessee. Fred Sington, Jr., son of a teammate from his and Laslie's playing days at Alabama, missed a field goal that cost them the game. Bryant gave them cigars anyway as a consolation for the loss.

But it is Jim Goostree to whom the tradition is attributed to, a victory over their rival still celebrated in the Alabama locker room as well as among fans, with a Cuban cigar. Depending, of course, upon the status of US relations with Cuba, sometimes resulting in a boycott of Cuban products. In that case, an alternative would have to suffice.

Many players arrived at the university with nothing more than what could fit into one suitcase, and that consisted of mainly a few changes of clothes. They were from poor working families and relied heavily on any monetary assistance the university could offer. One such benefit was the fifteen dollars a month stipend that was given to players for laundry. Memorable to many players was the role Coach Laslie played in the lives of players who were recipients of the so-called "laundry money", which they sometimes used for their laundry, but most times, probably not. It was a rush to get to Coach Laslie's office at the designated time to collect. The resulting pandemonium was accompanied by the coach's good-natured jibes and jesting with the players as he grudgingly doled out the money to each player, no doubt along with a tongue-in-cheek comment, while painstakingly keeping track of the process.

Players gather round for their monthly
"laundry money" doled out by Coach Laslie. © *Catapult Sports*

In his role as assistant athletic director, Laslie was also the one who arranged for a few players to be hired for summer jobs available on campus. Players selected for these coveted jobs were those Coach Laslie hand-picked, offered to those whom the coaches wanted to keep tabs on, or those they wanted to keep on a stringent conditioning program, or, like Ray Perkins, to one of the few married players on the team. Or a combination of all three. In an interview with Perkins, then head coach of the Tampa Bay Buccaneers in 1991, he spoke of one such summer when Coach Laslie assigned him and Joe Namath the summer job of painting the bleachers in the stadium, which were in need of some sprucing. Coach Laslie measured their progress by the number of empty five-gallon paint cans at the end of every day. As Coach Perkins recalled, most days, when he became curious about Namath's whereabouts, he could find the future NFL Hall of Famer quarterback Namath napping under a canopied section of the stands, a few of his allotted cans of paint secretly poured down the drain, the empty cans used to prove his day's work to his coach.

Coach Laslie's affinity for the young student managers on the team was well known, starting from his early days at Kentucky. He knew they worked hard to support the team and gave them special attention. One student manager who survived being cut from the first season in '58 and who continued in various capacities in the athletic department until he retired in 1996 was Gary White.

A young man who was in the program on a partial scholarship, White described how Coach Laslie became like a second father to him, teaching him, among other things, to be self-reliant and resilient. One instance he remembered often loaned him grocery money at times when he would be down to his last nickel at school. But Coach Laslie always expected to be paid back, White said. Which White always did.

White—a young man not afraid of hard work—had undoubtedly caught the eye of Laslie. He would literally jump to the ready without complaint when called upon. Like the time when he was walking back to the dorm from class and, as he laughingly tells it, "Lo and behold here came Coach Laslie on a team bus. He opened the door and said, 'White, climb on in here. We have a game tomorrow we have to get to and we need you.' I said, 'But Coach, I don't have anything with me!' 'Well, son, you'll figure it out. Now get on in.' Well, I climbed in and he was right. It wasn't easy but I figured it out, even hitching a ride back to campus when the bus left without me after the game!"

Over the years, White became a trusted house-sitter for the Laslies whenever they were out-of-town, and later in life modeled the house he built for his own family on the Laslie's home. To this day he lovingly tends the gravestones of Coach Laslie and wife, Alice, in Tuscaloosa.

CHAPTER THIRTY-SEVEN

Undefeated

"Holding is much more important than kicking . . . trying to put the ball on the spot smaller than a dime . . . knowing [sic] that a victory might hang on the way he handled the ball."

—Leo Costa, kicker, Skycrackers

UNIVERSITY OF ALABAMA
1961

CARNEY LASLIE, A KICKER in high school and college in addition to his position as a linebacker, had always recognized the crucial role of the kicker and special teams. The season of '61 would showcase the place kickers as well as the defense that year.

Among Laslie's saved newspaper clippings from 1961 was a photo of Laslie with the quarterback and two kickers from the Alabama team. The clipping was sent to him by a friend named "Joe", and had been torn out of his local paper. Across the top of the faded yellow page was inscribed: "Lasko (Laslie's nickname): I knew you did a great job coaching Gain and Parilli but I didn't know you were responsible for pulling out the close ones for the Tide this year. Best regards to Alice, Paul, Pat, Jerry, Phil, Charlie.

Coach Laslie instructing players with #17 Steve Davis and #40,
David Ray in 1967. "Don't ever take your eyes off that lace on your
shoe, right there!" © Catapult Sports

Special teams member Tim Davis opened the season with his
first (and longest) of nine field goals in the first quarter against the
Georgia Bulldogs played on September 23rd, the final score, Alabama
32, Georgia 6.

Next up, was Tulane, where Alabama was said to have looked a
bit tired, but prevailed, and where Davis, once again kicked a field
goal, this time from 24-yards out. The final score, 9–0. Trouncing
Vanderbilt in their third game of the season, Alabama coasted to a win
by a comfortable twenty-nine points over the Commodores, 35–6. And

in game four, against North Carolina State, though Alabama trailed for the first time in the season, they rallied quickly and beat State by a score of 26–7.

Tennessee and Alabama played on Oct 21, and Davis kicked two field goals before the half, a 35-yarder and a 21-yard kick bringing the score to 20–3. Alabama held the Vol's to sixty-one yards of total offense, Laslie's defense dominated and Alabama racked up thirty-four points of their own. The final score: Alabama 34, Tennessee 3.

The last game of the season of '61 was its most emotionally charged game because it was played against Alabama's longest rival, Auburn. Die-hard Alabama and Auburn fans were known to base their decision to attend church on the following Sunday on whether their team won or lost Saturday's game. The Iron Bowl, as the Alabama-Auburn contest is known, would be of particular importance in '61. Auburn had the distinct opportunity as the last team to play Alabama in the regular season to rob Alabama of a perfect season, the possibility of delivering the blow to their nemesis further escalating the normally super-charged, emotional game.

Just prior to kickoff on the day of the game, Alabama was officially declared a Sugar Bowl contestant. Still, the Crimson Tide coaches, and players, wanted nothing less than a perfect season. The defense, ranked top in the nation, held once again at the goal line, the Alabama offense delivering a decisive defeat to Auburn, the final score 34–0. It was the first time in their careers to post a season with no losses and no ties.

Alabama was voted National Champions and SEC Champions for the year 1961, prior to their appearance in the Sugar Bowl on January 1, 1962. They were the first Alabama football team to win a consensus national championship in the poll era.

As the team prepared for their appearance in the Sugar Bowl on January 1, 1962, unsettling events swirled in the background. The Soviet Union's Premier Nikita Khrushchev had declared his country would do everything possible to avoid a nuclear war in 1962. That was little comfort when the Soviet trade paper *Trud* emphatically stated, "The world belongs to us . . . the doomed world of capitalism will be unable to defend itself even with nuclear weapons, from the immutable course of historical development."[161] Along with such pronouncements, which unnerved much of the country and lent a less-than-optimistic view of the coming year, was President Kennedy's announcement that the US would "provide increased assistance to help South Vietnam repel the threat of Communist guerillas."[162]

Despite such concerns, nothing could detract from the college football mania that gripped fans as the Sugar Bowl prepared for its twenty-seventh anniversary playoff in New Orleans in 1962. The state's business, too, would have to wait; Alabama's governor postponed office appointments while he attended the pre-game events in Louisiana.

Slated to play Arkansas, the ninth-ranked team in the nation, it was a matchup that, for Bryant and Laslie, held great import. Arkansas was the road not taken when WWII interrupted the dreams of greatness a foursome of young men, Bryant, Laslie, Moseley, and Walker, had envisioned for themselves; grand schemes to become the best coaching staff known in the sport. It was, after twenty-one years, down to the two of them.

The Sugar Bowl '62 ended with a score of 10–3, and Frank Broyles, in his fourth season as head coach for the Razorbacks, summarized Arkansas' loss in his postgame comments: "We knew when we went into the game that we were going to have trouble grinding out yardage against this team. But, we never thought it would be this hard. We just couldn't get our offense going. I guess the main reason was Alabama's great defense. Bama's offense was just what we expected, tough and aggressive. Our boys were tight and uneasy in the first half. That didn't help, but when you're playing the number one team in the nation, you expect that. In the second half, I thought we did a respectable job."

It was a perfect season for the Crimson Tide, finally the coveted National Championship. Despite the heartache and losses delivered by a war that could have undone the very fabric of their lives, they had prevailed. It was a bit of reflection that would have to wait, savored in private. This was a victory for the boys who had fought hard for four years. And they had delivered.

Two weeks after the win, in a handwritten note to Frank Moseley, Bryant wrote,

Dear Bull,

No way of saying how much I treasure and appreciate your loving and warm friendship.

Paul Bryant, January 15th, 1962

Epilogue

DAVID NELSON'S *ANATOMY OF a Game* is a hardcore chronological look at the changes in the rules of college football and how they played out in the way the game on the field evolved over time. In America, football changed so radically and rapidly because it was a purely invented sport with no folk antecedents. Pre-NCAA, significant changes to the game could be made without worrying about too much pushback from fans. Later, when the NCAA would initiate a change, for example, to the forward pass, fans weren't so agreeable, not wanting the game they had grown up playing changed. For those inclined to tackle the 599-page tome (no pun intended), it is a critically acclaimed reference for those wanting a more detailed understanding of precisely how certain strategies, formations, plays, and oddball rules actually played out on the field. The prohibition of coaching from the sidelines is just one of many examples, as are the substitution rules that varied over time. Alabama, for example, could use 200-pound linemen in the '50s and early '60s because they had to play both ways for most, if not all, of the game but, according to many students of the game, stayed with that too long, which is one of the reasons why the team's performance declined in the late '60s. But there are, of course, other reasons as well.

In 1968, two years prior to Carney Laslie's death, a no. 7–ranked Alabama would play Virginia Tech in Birmingham, Alabama. It would be the beginning of play between the two schools, who normally would not meet in any given year, as a nod of thanks to Moseley, who by this time had been athletic director at Virginia Tech for almost ten years. The two would play against each other several more times prior to Bryant's death. Their second meeting, the season opening game of 1969, was played in Blacksburg, Virginia, in front of a crowd of 42,000. It would be the largest crowd ever to attend a Virginia sporting event during that decade. The thirteenth-ranked Alabama defeated Virginia Tech 17–13. It was also notable as being the hundredth consecutive game in which Alabama had scored, never being beaten without having points on the scoreboard.

With Jerry Claiborne's departure in 1970, Moseley then hired Charlie Coffey. Coffey quickly became a controversial figure for a number of reasons. He quickly adopted a passing game, as opposed to the running game tradition that Virginia Tech had long established. And he was intent on improving Tech's image overall in a number of ways that required large monetary investments by the university. After two losing seasons, Coffey was out and retired from coaching college football altogether at the age of thirty-nine.

Moseley called on his old friend Coach Bryant to get his input on who he should hire for the head coach vacancy at Virginia Tech. Bryant recommended Jimmy Sharpe, an offensive line player for Alabama on the '61 team and assistant coach for twelve years at Alabama. Sharpe had similar roots to Frank. He grew up in Montgomery and went to Sidney Lanier High School, Frank's alma mater. Moseley knew from whence Sharpe came. After four seasons considered anything but stellar by the Hokie fandom, Jimmy Sharpe was summarily fired by the president of the university days after the '77 season's end. Moseley immediately submitted his resignation. He died a little over a year later.

He left behind a legacy that included a new stadium and coliseum. He was inducted into the Virginia Sports Hall of Fame in 1979, and the Virginia Tech Sports Hall of Fame as an inaugural member in 1982. He has a practice field at Virginia Tech, Moseley Field, named after him.

After their first National Championship won in '61, Bryant and Laslie went on to lead Alabama to 'number one' with two more National Championships in 1964 and 1965. Their tenure together brought Alabama back into the prominence enjoyed under coaches Wallace Wade and Frank Thomas and ushered in a decade during which the two came to be known as one of the closest, most collaborative coaching partnerships in the history of the sport. Led by the Bryant-Laslie partnership until 1970, the University of Alabama and its football program became the center of one of the most tumultuous times in our nation's history.

With the civil rights movement raging, the state's segregationist policies were scrutinized as governors across the nation moved to desegregate schools. Alabama's controversial governor George Wallace, however, declared in his inaugural address in January 1963, "Segregation now! Segregation tomorrow! Segregation forever!" Infamously known as "The Stand in the Schoolhouse Door," a blockade formed to bar Black students from enrolling at the University of Alabama took place at the university's Foster Auditorium on June 11, 1963. It was only the threat of the National Guard being called in that forced the governor to shut down the blockade and allowed James Hood and Vivian Malone to register. Publicly, Bryant remained silent about the university's staunch opposition to the integration of the football team. As a state university, Alabama was funded by a legislature that was adamant about keeping sports programs segregated. Privately, he and Laslie bemoaned the governor's stance, foreseeing an uneven playing field of competition between Alabama and other teams around the country, which had the advantage with their ability to recruit top talent, Black or White.

In 1966, Alabama was the only undefeated collegiate football team in the nation. Surprising to many, the AP Poll (the system used at that time) voted Notre Dame the national champions with Michigan State in second place. When Alabama finished in third place, some saw it as a resounding message of solidarity among sports reporters for their condemnation of Alabama and its segregationist policies, particularly as related to collegiate football. Others pointed to the schedule of teams played that year, a slate that was not held to be worthy of a number one vote.

Southeastern Conference Commissioner Bernie Moore (seated in the center) to honor Coach Wallace Wade at the University of Alabama, in 1966. Former players included: seated, L-R: Paul Burnham, Carney Laslie, and John Cain. Standing, L-R: Babe Pearce, Frank Howard and Newt Godfrey. © Catapult Sports

When Alabama's then Lieutenant Governor Albert P. Brewer became acting governor in 1968 after Governor Lurleen B. Wallace died of cancer sixteen months into her term, there was a departure from the contentious bullying, race-baiting tactics still associated with the governor's office. Mr. Brewer enacted ethics reform, increased public funding for schools, and created an economic development office. Under his leadership, the door was cracked to the possibility of integrating the football team, and Bryant and Laslie continued to work quietly behind the scenes, strategizing a plan to integrate the state's most popular sport. In 1969, the Crimson Tide lost soundly on its home field in Birmingham to archrival Tennessee with a score of 41–14. The Volunteers did so with two Black players in their starting lineup. As a result, as early as late 1969, after years of effort, the coaches began in earnest to recruit Wilbur Jackson, a Black running back from Ozark, Alabama, who was given a scholarship and entered as a freshman in the fall of 1970.

It is the game against the University of Southern California (USC) in September 1970, four months after Laslie's death, that is credited with turning the tide of segregation at Alabama. The game was reportedly scheduled after a meeting months before between the two head coaches, Bryant and John McKay, head coach of the Trojans. The two agreed the teams would meet for the first game of the season to showcase, to Alabama fans in particular, what the university was ignoring by remaining closed to Black players: talent. Alabama's Wilbur Jackson, a freshman, watched the game from the stands as he was deemed ineligible to play for Alabama that year under NCAA rules.

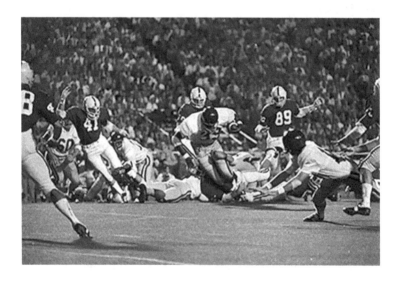

With super human effort USC's Sam Cunningham wowed fans as he managed to break free from every lineman's attempt to stop him.

Soundly trounced by a fully integrated USC team, it was perhaps the reason Alabama's game against Tennessee didn't make as much of an impact, since Tennessee played only two Black players in their matchup the year before. All six touchdowns made by USC were by Black Americans, the Black running back Sam "the Bam" Cunningham demoralizing the all-white Alabama squad in a powerful display of talent. The final score was 42–21. That next year, John Mitchell would be the first Black player to start for Alabama and later became the first Black assistant coach at the university.

One of many black tie affairs: L-R: Alice Laslie, Carney Laslie.

The success in their football program meant success throughout the university, and growth in the work and responsibilities overall related to the running of the athletic department grew as well. Coach Laslie could now preside over some expenditures that in previous years were considered non-essential and out of their budget. Artificial turf, for example, was spearheaded by Laslie for its cost-saving properties and adopted by the university in 1967. He was appointed to the Building Committee by the Board of Trustees and oversaw the construction of new buildings related to the athletic department. Representing Bryant at many annual meetings, like the annual meeting of coaches in the SEC, and NCAA business meetings, he became the face of the team behind the scenes. By 1968, he was fully entrenched in responsibilities related to the athletic department. The load was heavy enough, as Bryant, Jr. revealed, for Laslie to be considered the school's athletic director, even though in title he was officially the "assistant" athletic director.

Other than their first season at Alabama, '69 and '70 were the worst of Bryant's tenure. Some attributed the lackluster performance of those years with Alabama's reliance on their use of linemen who could play both ways for most, if not all, of the game. Others have suggested that Bryant relied too much on advice from his assistant coaches during those years. But there are other factors as well.

Coach Laslie posing while artificial turf is first iinstalled at the practice field at the University of Alabama. © Catapult Sports

Even with his administrative responsibilities pressing, according to Mal Moore—who went from player, to coach, and finally to athletic director at Alabama—Coach Laslie never missed a practice. "I can still see Coach Laslie making his way to the practice field, hands in his back pockets, whistling a tune," he said, adding wistfully, "I will always miss him."

It was on the practice field in April of 1969 that Laslie sustained an injury that would, a little over a year later, cause his death. Standing on the back of what is known as a "charging sled," he poised himself to steady the sled while the linebackers and tackles rammed against the padded apparatus during spring practice. One well-placed and forceful charge caused the sled to topple and along with it the coach, the metal frame delivering a hard blow to his leg. Players recounting the event many years later would tell of their revered coach, who seemed embarrassed by the foible, jumping up off the ground and with blood dripping down his leg from a nasty cut staying on the field until hobbling off at the end of practice with the rest of the team. Later that summer, he suffered what he referred to in a letter to Coach Hank Crisp as a "coronary." Sidelined by his doctor, he wrote, he was encouraged to forego too much excitement. With his son-in-law in Vietnam, Carney and Alice kept the news to themselves, not wanting to worry their daughter.

A photo of Clemson's coach Frank Howard, the so-called 'Bear' Bryant of South Carolina, as a young football player was found among Laslie's effects. On the photo, Howard had hand written the date, October 24 1969, the eve of the Clemson vs. Alabama game, and the message "To my ex-roommate Carney Laslie, from Frank Howard. The only member of the 1930 Ala [sic] Squad who is still a

Head Football Coach & AD."

Howard's assertion stated bluntly, though rather cryptically as well, is what many of the coaches in the SEC suspected at the time: that Laslie was shouldering much of the weight of directing the coaching staff and administrative responsibilities of the athletic department at Alabama. In turn, Coach Laslie leaned on the team's assistant coaches to pick up the load during such a time when both he and Bryant were dealing with their own health and personal problems. They beat Clemson the next day, but it was notably one of only six wins that season. Despite the able and loyal assistance of the other assistant coaches, the season of 1969 was their worst since '59.

In the wee morning hours of January 23, 1970, immediately following the honorary dinner given on the eve of his induction in the Alabama Hall of Fame, Coach Hank, beloved coach and stalwart member of the University's athletic staff for forty-six years, died of a heart attack. Coach Laslie, who had been instructed by his doctors to avoid any extraneous celebrations due to worries about his heart, had been unable to attend. He learned the news while penning a letter he planned to give to his friend and old Coach upon his return:

Dear Coach Hank:

I had wanted to be present for the Hall of Fame banquet tonight, when you received an honor which you prized more highly than your membership in the National Football Hall of Fame, or a similar recognition by sports lovers in Virginia, your native state. Most of your adult life has been spent in Alabama, and you had grown to love it almost as [much] as we love you! However, I am still convalescing from a coronary sustained last Summer, and my doctor has declared elaborate occasions "OFF LIMITS" for me! But I am thinking of you and rejoicing with you! . . .

Kathryn just called and shared the shocking news that

you left suddenly early this evening on a mysterious voyage, across the immortal sea, from which no voyager returns! So, I will continue my letter to you, with faith that you will receive it! Kathryn told me that this had been the happiest day of life. There could not, I think have been a better day to begin the journey nor a better way! Could anything have pleased you more than to have Hank, Junior come forward at the banquet to receive your "HALL OF FAME" Plaque? You had every reason to be proud of him.

I've thanked you before, by letter and in person, for the lessons you taught me in self-discipline. Many of us whom you coached were not greatly talented, but we WOULD fight a buzz saw, and that was the quality you admired most of all in "your boys."

How you ever found time to serve as counselor and guide, I will never understand. But any of us who went to you in time of trouble always received your undivided attention and consolation. On numerous occasions, you bailed your boys out of trouble with crumpled bills extracted from your pocket, and for which you were never recompensed.

By that April, Coach Laslie appeared to be recovering well from his heart issues as well as from the gash on his calf. Dr. Ernest C. "E. C." Brock, orthopedic surgeon and Alabama's team doctor, checked on his injured leg regularly, stopping by the Laslies' home after work. After personally inspecting the wound site, he would then enjoy a cocktail (or two) and exchange the news of the day before driving to his own home just up the street. He was satisfied there appeared to be no outward signs of a complication. But by May of 1970, just to be certain, Dr. Brock encouraged Laslie to check himself into Tuscaloosa's Druid City Hospital to have the leg checked for any blood clots. It was there at the hospital while Coach Laslie walked down to the hallway toward the hospital barbershop that the clot from his leg broke loose, causing a massive pulmonary embolism. He died exactly five months to the day after their beloved Coach Hank, on May 23, 1970.

After his friend's death, Dr. Brock found it unbearably painful to pass the Laslies' house on his way home. So much so he decided to move to a different neighborhood altogether.

I was thirteen years old, the oldest of my grandparents' four grandchildren, when my grandfather died. The day after we got the news, our family boarded a University of Alabama ten-seater jet sent to take us from Washington, DC, to Birmingham as fast as possible. We landed that night to find a police escort waiting. Cruiser lights flashing, we sped down Highway 59 at ninety miles per hour all the way to Tuscaloosa.

We arrived late that night at my grandparents' modest ranch-style home located in Tuscaloosa's Woodland Hills neighborhood. Inside, the house was crowded. Large men dressed in dark suits and ties balanced a drink in one hand and small plates of food in the other, huddling in small groups around the house. Some gathered in the living room around the upright piano; two steps down into the den another group sat on the sofa with one man perched on the sidearm; another group congregated in front of Poppa's green leather recliner. Their conversations were low rumblings, inaudible but punctuated occasionally by soft laughter presumably over some shared humorous memory. Mixed with the profound grief was a prevailing mood of uncertainty, the unexpected and sudden loss of the university's acting athletic director, Bryant's "right-hand" man, his "wing-man" gone forever, not quite setting in. For me, as I processed the scene from my corner in the living room, the enormity of our own family's loss seemed overshadowed, secondary to these large and larger than life men and the huge organization that mourned his passing.

Periodically, from the various small groups conferring around the room, one of the men would lift his head and cast a furtive glance toward the large figure of a man, who I knew as Uncle Paul. Standing a little over six feet four inches, Coach Bryant seemed huge, a big man with broad shoulders, and large hands. By all accounts his was an intimidating presence both physically and mentally. When he walked into a room, he evoked confidence among his staff. Confidence because they knew he was always supremely prepared in every situation. This was obviously not in the playbook. Was he prepared?

He was visibly shaken. They all were. His staff wondered what would come next. What would be the game plan for a deficit that would be felt so deeply, resonating from the top echelon of the university itself to the newest freshman on the team? Little did they realize that Bryant would suffer an identity crisis all his own. Characterizing what the loss meant to him in an interview in the *Tuscaloosa News* several days later, Bryant declared that what "was a sad day for many, was a tragic one for me." It was a personal loss. His closest confidante and a friend whose absence would be felt till the end of his days.

The city, too, mourned my grandfather's passing. Scores of police in their dress blues lined the streets of Tuscaloosa along with loyal fans, saluting his hearse as it passed. He was sixty years old.

My grandmother, Alice Laslie, heartbroken, passed away two years later. Tuscaloosa Academy, founded in 1967, would go on to honor my grandparents with an athletic award established in both their names that is still one of the school's most prestigious awards. The annual Carney G. Laslie Award goes to the school's top male athlete, and the annual Alice B. Laslie Award goes to the top female athlete. Voted on by their teammates, the winners must possess qualities of character, drive, and leadership in addition to athletic ability. When the first Carney Laslie Memorial Award was given out in 1971, the principle speaker at the banquet, Alabama head basketball coach C. M. Newton, said, "Too much emphasis is put on how to be successful. It is more important to know why, then the how will follow naturally."

The football season of 1970 was a replica of 1969, with one

exception: Carney Laslie was not on the sidelines. When an assistant coach informed Coach Bryant of Vince Lombardi's passing that September 3, Bryant spoke candidly of regrets he had, a shocking statement for Bryant to make. It was the only time this man said he had ever heard Bryant express anything that resembled self-doubt or regret. It was then he realized that Coach Bryant was a lonely man.

That seasons record of six wins, five losses and one tie at the Astro-Bluebonnet Bowl would usher in what some called a crisis point in Bryant's career. Bryant certainly gave consideration to quitting college football and moving into a coaching position in professional football. But it was short lived. The best thing he could do was to continue to honor those who had gone before him: Jimmy Walker, Coach Hank, and now Carney Laslie. And he would do it with all the toughness and lessons learned from all three that he could muster. In 1971, he introduced the wishbone, a variation of a T-formation offense that incorporated a lateral pass, and the next decade would produce another three National Championships.

During his last decade of coaching many described Bryant as a man who had mellowed with the passing years. Two years before his death, Bryant started reading a devotional: when tomorrow comes, this day will be gone forever, leaving something in its place I have traded for it. "I wish I'd read this devotional thirty years ago," he later told a friend. "I wouldn't have wasted so much valuable time."

Edy Moseley passed away at the age of seventy-eight in June of 1993. A member of the Lutheran Church, she too had a spiritual awakening, a frequent visitor to Blacksburg Christian Fellowship, and regular participant in Bible Study Fellowship. She, like Bryant, expressed many times to friends and family her wish that she had known earlier what she had discovered so late in life.

My grandfather's death marked the end of college football's closest coaching partnerships. He would not have been surprised, however, by the myriad of achievements and legendary success of Bryant and the Crimson Tide as they moved through the next decade. Bryant and his coaching style would go on to become a brand, and the man wearing the houndstooth hat an iconic legend, one equated with winning and the pure drive and sacrifice it takes to be "a winner." It can be said that both Coach Bryant, and my grandfather, Coach Laslie, realized the dream they had envisioned for themselves in their youth. And for that, there were no regrets, their accomplishments outliving them both, their legacy a generation of men they inspired to realize their own potential, who they taught how to both lead and to follow, and the importance of being part of something bigger than themselves. Those men would go on to pass those ideals on to a future generation of young men and women: their own sons and daughters, business colleagues, or as coaches themselves to their players.

Many who remember Coach Laslie today are those who acted as the managers and trainers for the Alabama football team. He had a special place in his heart for those young men. He supported them as valued members of the team and encouraged the whole team to see them as such. He knew it was a hard position to have on the team: in the background as ancillary support and seemingly not acknowledged by fans.

Manager Jerry Glover related his forgetting to unlock the locker room door prior to the team coming in from halftime. Before the manager could get there to unlock the door, an angry Coach Bryant rammed his hand and shoulder against the door and broke it open. Coach Bryant didn't tolerate slip-ups like that at all. But if Coach Laslie thought a manager needed a second chance, he was the first to make the case to Coach Bryant. Years later, the manager related, he was surprised when Bryant had called him into his office and calmly told him he was giving him another chance but not to make the mistake again. Coach Laslie, too, he wrote, had pulled him aside and gently admonished him. "Don't let that happen again, Jerry," Coach

Laslie told him. "Paul could have broken his hand breaking down that door."[163] By using Coach Bryant's first name, Laslie made the revered coach a real person—someone who was not larger than life but rather flesh and blood. In this way, he was able to communicate to the manager that the coaches and players alike were all just people.

Coach Laslie had an affinity for the managers and trainers and understood their importance in the hierarchy of the team. Their respect and admiration for him was recognized in a scholarship fund in his name dedicated to the future trainers and managers of the Crimson Tide. To learn more, email stewardship@advance.ua.edu about the Carney Laslie Quasi-Endowed Scholarship Fund in the Athletic Training Education Program. A percentage of the proceeds from this book will go to support the fund.

Acknowledgments

I am extremely grateful to so many who offered invaluable help, support and encouragement over the years. To the Moseley family, in particular Alene Moseley Danby, I am deeply grateful for your entrusting me with your family's treasures: memorabilia and letters that provided a robust and personal voice to the narrative. And to Nancy Moseley, who along with MountainHouse Productions, shared her talents in media to construct a great video used to gauge overall interest in the story early on. To Stephen and Claire Keefe, your vision for *A Tide of Dreams* as an MBA project which focused on the publishing industry undertaken during one of the busiest times in your lives was never taken for granted. Armed with the results of your work I was better prepared to deal with what became an eight-year journey. Not to mention the memories created along the way. A priceless contribution.

A hearty thanks to Will Crisp, Coach Hank Crisp's nephew, who entrusted me with the Crisp family's historical documents and, himself a seasoned writer, met with me to encourage my pursuit and writing of the story. And to Greg Fields; John Koehler; and the team at Koehler—my sincere thanks for all your contributions in bringing this to fruition.

Many thanks as well to those associated with the University and the football program, past and present, who shared their memories and anecdotes with me.

There were many who shared their talents and overall knowledge in various capacities and to whom I'm deeply grateful. Their contributions in those earliest days were never taken for granted and included early readers Candy McPhee, Cliff Garstang, Carol Lemons, Ben Reitz, Julie Stevens, the late Martha Woodruff, and Peggy Ward's book club in St. Petersburg, Florida. Thank you all for being willing to read those fledgling attempts while I figured out how to best tell the story. To Andrew Doyle, who generously gave of his time early on, both in conversation and through his articles, his expertise in Southern football well known, thank you for helping me to understand from an academic point of view the impact and importance of the sport to the South. And to John Watterson, who at the eleventh hour kindly lent his expertise with an eye toward helping me correct errors of every sort, the result a more accurate and better construct of the manuscript. I can't thank you enough.

Many thanks to Jane Johnson, whom I consulted in the latter stage of writing and is truly a kindred spirit, and who also happened to be a researcher extraordinaire whose assistance I could not have done without. And a special thanks to Adele Kellman, a Laslie cousin, who applied a keen eye to the manuscript as well as to ancestral facts. I am also eternally grateful to Anne Keene, author of *The Cloudbuster Nine: The Untold Story of Ted Williams, and the Baseball Team that Helped Win WWII*, and granddaughter of the commander of the US Navy Pre-Flight School in Chapel Hill, NC, whose generous sharing of research done on the pre-flight Navy program was heavily relied upon, our shared passion to bring the little-known story of American sports and its impact on WWII into the public eye making us fast friends. And to Brenden McHugh, thank you for sharing your amazing gifts of editing to the advanced copy. Your insight into the deeper themes of the narrative was spot on, and it was more than gratifying to know it touched your heart.

Other champions of this work whom I could not have done without include Denise Goodwin, fellow road warrior and cheerleader from the very beginning. Always there to help bolster my confidence and whose fearless approach to life is inspirational are Ellen and Lee Vaughn, who, along with Jamie Longo, a visionary-extraordinaire, prodded me to "finish the book!"—adding a great amount of energy to getting it off my desk and out the door.

I am also grateful to Paul Bryant, Jr. Thank you for the time you spent with me over the phone, answering questions, sharing memories and being available when I needed clarification on some aspect of the story. It was truly a pleasure.

The support of family and friends who had faith in my ability to tell this story was a forever gift. To the Kings, Nell and Billy; my Bendini sisters (Barb, Linda, Pattie, Peggy, and Trudi); the Stevens and Tranquillos; Susie Moses; and John and Cindy Griffin, who never doubted, despite my own doubts—thank you. And of course, Robert Keefe and all the Griffin clan—Carter, Justin, Wes, Harper, Juliet, and Wills—along with Hannah and Hunter Keefe, who continue to help us all to keep "the main thing, the main thing."

Finally, to my mother, whose guidance in all things I will be forever grateful for and whose storied life as the daughter of a football coach prepared her for the challenges and adventures of being an Army wife, an example of grace and strength to all her children, grandchildren, and great-grandchildren. And to my father, who quipped, "You should be a writer!" when I was eleven years old, and who I miss so very much. His life reflected a deep sense of patriotism and love of country, a principled man who was admired and loved by so many. His life gave me a great appreciation for the huge sacrifices he and all those who serve our nation in the military make—an appreciation that was enlarged and rekindled during the process of writing this story.

Saving the best and most important for last, my husband,

Stephen, love of my life, who gave me the push I needed to embark upon a writing life with a litany of life adventures shared to draw material from and the unbridled support I needed to pursue it. He was always the first to evaluate a new chapter, listened attentively to every new draft, multiple times, with nary a complaint, and offered insightful opinions or suggestions that were always constructive. For those, and many other reasons too many to list, it goes without saying, but I'll say it anyway: I could not have done this without you.

Endnotes

1   Building a Championship Team, by Paul W. "Bear" Bryant and Gene Stallings, page 3.

PROLOGUE

2   Dave Kindred, "The Bear Ain't Ready Yet to Hibernate," *Washington Post*, Sunday, November 29, 1981, page D4.

3   Interview with Coach Laslie appearing in the *Charlotte Observer* in 1965, Garrison, Wilton, "Getting Gridders Ready Without Overworking Them Big Problem."

4   Bryant's comment about his coaching football because he wasn't able to do anything else has been documented in several sources: his autobiography, and televised as well as newspaper interviews.

5   Bill Curry, *Ten Men You Meet in a Huddle*, p 8.

6   Paul Bryant, Gene Stallings, *Building a Championship Team*, 1961.

7   Tommy Ford. "Laslie's Long-Gone National Championship Ring Finds Its Way Back Home," Alabama A-Club article.

8   Ibid

CHAPTER TWO

9   Hamilton's remark was made in 1978 upon being awarded the
     Legion of Merit with the following citation: For exceptionally
     meritorious conduct in the performance of outstanding services
     to the Government of the United States as Officer in Charge,
     Physical Training Section, Naval Air Training Division, Bureau
     of Aeronautics, December 1941 to June 1943.
10   Thomas Hamilton's Original Plan for Pre-Flight Training, V-5,
     page 1.
11   Ibid
12   Interview of Thomas Hamilton by the Navy. US Naval Institute.
     *The Reminiscences of Rear Admiral Thomas J. Hamilton, US
     Navy,(Ret.)* Annapolis, Maryland. 1983.
13   The Hamilton papers, 32–33
14   Ibid
15   Ibid
16   The Hamilton papers, 32–33
17   Page 10, The Hamilton Papers
18   Ibid
19   Tentative Proposal, Hamilton, page 10
20   Ibid
21   Hamilton Papers, page 65.
22   Ibid
23   Ibid
24   Hamilton Papers, page 65.
25   Ibid
26   Ibid
27   Hamilton Papers

CHAPTER THREE

28   Layne Baker, "The Sky's the Limit: US Navy Pre-Flight School,"
      NC Collection/UNC-CH Library
29   *The Navy's Air War*, by the Aviation History Unit, OP-519B,
      DCNO, Harper and Brothers Publishers, New York and London,
      1946. Chapter 28, page 307–311
30   Navy Football Handbook, page 6–8
31   Hamilton Papers
32   Ibid
33   Hamilton Papers
34   Football! Navy! War! Location 367
35   The Bomb, VMI Yearbook, 1942

CHAPTER FOUR

36   AP. *Athletes in the Navy to get Combat Duty, Physical Instructor
      Group will be Trained in Gunnery,* June 12, 1942.
37   Autobiography, page 83
38   Michael Geflan's thesis, *Tomorrow We Fly: A History of The
      United States Navy Pre-Flight School on the Campus of The
      University of Georgia, Athens, Georgia*, p 59
39   Reed, Delbert. *When Winning Was Everything: Alabama
      Football Players in World War II.* (Tuscaloosa: University of
      Alabama Press, 2013)

CHAPTER SIX

40   Memoirs, Col. Donald E. Marousek, 2013.
41   Memoirs, Col. Donald E. Marousek, 2013.
42   *Cloudbuster*, "Doctor Turned Soldier," Saturday March 25, 1944,
      page 1.
43   Ibid

44   Ibid

45   *Cloudbuster*, "Navy Secretary Praises Combat Value of Football."

CHAPTER SEVEN

46   Reed, Delbert. *When Winning Was Everything: Alabama Football Players in World War II.*

47   Ibid

48   Interview with Coach Laslie, Lexington-Herald, 1954.

CHAPTER EIGHT

49   Al Browning Interview, *The Tuscaloosa News.*

50   Historical Homes of Tuskegee, description of the Cobb-Laslie Home.

51   E. A. Bethea, *The Establishment of a Natural Cultural Center in Tuskegee, Alabama, A Feasibility Study*, Industrial Development Division, Georgia Institute of Technology, Atlanta, GA, 1975

52   https://news.ncsu.edu/2017/05/boll-weevil-war-2017/

53   Letter written by W. T. Laslie was located in the Alabama Department of Archives and History located in Montgomery, Alabama, the official repository of archival records for the US state of Alabama.

54   Acts of the Legislature, State of Alabama, Session of January 1919; Montgomery, Alabama, Brown Printing Company, State Printers and Binders, 1919.

55   http://www.remington.com/pages/our-company/company-history.aspx

CHAPTER NINE

56   The quotes about Dr. Laslie were taken from his obituary, Montgomery Advertiser, 1953.

57 Ibid.

58 Isabelle's active role in high society Montgomery was noted in Iva Cook's Society column, page of the *Anniston-Star*, on March 30, 1920.

59 Ibid

CHAPTER TEN

60 Charlotte Central High School Yearbook, 1928

CHAPTER ELEVEN

61 *Alabama Football Tales: More Than a Century of Crimson Tide Glory* by Lewis Bowling

62 *Alabama Football Tales: More Than a Century of Crimson Tide Glory* by Lewis Bowling

CHAPTER TWELVE

63 http://www.nytimes.com/1996/01/27/sports/frank-howard-86-the-coach-of-top-clemson-football-teams.html and https://nsjonline.com/article/2020/01/hill-frank-howard-founding-father-of-clemson-football-and-the-acc/

64 Ibid

65 Ibid

66 Edson, James. *Alabama's Crimson Tide*. (Montgomery: The Paragon Press, 1946): p. 161

67 http://library.duke.edu/rubenstein/uarchives/history/articles/wade

68 Hamilton, Guy, "Southern Conference Will See Many New Linesmen in Action." AP, Sept 23, 1930.

69 Quotes came from the Alabama Yearbook, *The Corolla*, 1931

70 Ibid

Information about games, season, players were referenced from University of Alabama 1929 yearbook, *The Corolla*, page 339–345.

The team of 1930 was the finest Wade ever coached and one of the best in Alabama's history and was documented in *Southern Football*, by Zipp Newman.

71   *The Corolla*, 1932

CHAPTER THIRTEEN

72   Ibid

73   *The Tuscaloosa News*, Nov 17, 1931, "U of A Player Dies of Injury," page 4.

74   *The History of College Football*, Watterson.

75   Ibid

76   "Bear Remembers Moseley, Room 9," Reprinted from *The Huntsville Times*, Huntsville Alabama, in Tech Sports, Sept 4, 1979 on page 3

77   Bryant autobiography.

78   "Blytheville '11' Seeks Grid Tilt With Pine Bluff, Associated Press, *Blytheville Courier*, November 19, 1935.

CHAPTER FOURTEEN

79   Blytheville '11' Seeks Grid Tilt with Pine Bluff." Associated Press. *Blytheville Courier News*, November 19, 1936.

80   All sports quotes in this chapter, including this one, are from the *Blytheville Courier News*, September 1934–December 1936 and include the following:

22, Nov, 1934, page 4.

Sat Oct 13, 1934, page 6.

Nov 28, 1936, page 6.

Dec 5, 1936, page 2.

January 14, 1937.

81   President Roosevelt's quote was published in *The Blytheville Courier News*, 20 Oct 1934, page 1.

82   The Blytheville Courier News, 20 Oct 1934, page 1 reported that the 1924 Blytheville High School team, which included Laslie friends and former Alabama teammates Jess Eberdt and JB Whitworth, could not claim an undefeated season due to forfeiting a game in their otherwise "fine record", upsetting any claims of an undefeated season.

CHAPTER FIFTEEN

83   *Alumni Review*, Spring 1975, page 75, B. M. Read.

84   Original recipes provided in Chapter Notes.

CHAPTER SIXTEEN

85   Unless noted otherwise, quotes are from the Moseley Letters.

CHAPTER SEVENTEEN

86   *The Courier-Journal*, Tue, Dec 1939 Page 1, "Shine in Kentucky, Moseley Tells Stars," by Earl Ruby, Sports Editor

CHAPTER EIGHTEEN

87   The Original 'Cracker Jack' term was a snack of molasses covered popcorn that got its name when a salesman who tried it for the first time exclaimed "Cracker jack!" which at the time meant "awesome" or "wonderful."

88   *The Kentucky Alumnus*, February 1946, VOL XCII, Number 1, page 10 News

89   *VPI to State University: President T. Marshall Hahn, Jr. and the Transformation of Virginia Tech.* page 135

CHAPTER NINETEEN

90   All quotations in this chapter are taken from Frank's letters to
      Edy written during this time.

CHAPTER TWENTY

91   George Christian *The Corolla Yearbook*, 1933
92   Ibid
93   *Atlanta Constitution*, "Miss Alice Louise Backus to Wed Mr.
      Laslie in Cartersville Ceremony," March 30, 1935.
94   *History of College Football*, Watterson, page 181.

CHAPTER TWENTY-ONE

95   *Time Magazine*, November 17, 1961.
96   Laslie describing his boss in an interview with *The Lexington
      Herald-News*.
97   *The Courier Journal.* "Phooey! Ex-half back claims that Bear
      didn't want me to look good, ran a lot of good players off," Jan
      27, 1975, page 21.
98   Ibid
99   *The Lexington-Herald.*
100   "Phooey! Ex-half back claims that Bear didn't want me to look
      good, ran a lot of good players off," Jan 27, 1975, page 21.

CHAPTER TWENTY-TWO

101   *Courier Journal*, Louisville, Kentucky, Sat Nov 19, 1949,
      "Kentucky Plays Tennessee Today For 45th Time," by Larry
      Boeck, page 14.
102   Ibid

103 *Courier Journal*, Louisville, Kentucky, Sat Nov 19, 1949, "Kentucky Plays Tennessee Today For 45th Time," by Larry Boeck, page 14

104 Ibid

105 *The Advocate-Messenger* (Danville, Kentucky) 24 Jan 1950, Don Phelps Wins Letter At UK, page 8.0

CHAPTER TWENTY-THREE

106 *Courier-Journal*, April 20, 1950 page 35

107 *The Courier-Journal*, 17 Sep 1950 page 19, "Kentucky shows Little."

108 *Courier-Journal*, Thu Sept 28, 1950. Larry Boeck, "Iron U.K. Defense To Get Stern Test."

109 Ibid

110 Ibid

111 *Courier-Journal*, 25 Nov 1950, page 13.

112 *The Courier-Journal*, Wed Dec 27, 1950

113 Bryant autobiography, page 103.

CHAPTER TWENTY-FOUR

114 *History of College Football*, Watterson, page 266

115 *New York Times*, Judge Streit

CHAPTER TWENTY-FIVE

116 *Lexington Herald*, "It Says Here," December 12, 1950.

117 John Watterson's *College Football History*, page 223.

118 *Courier-Journal*, March 20, 1952, Ruby Report, sports section 2, page 8.

CHAPTER TWENTY-SIX

119   "Army Was Right in Grabbing Dietzel" by Dan Daniel, *N.Y. World Telegram-and The Sun* January 1962
120   "Alabama's Laslie talks about a colonel he knew." *Birmingham News*, Jan 23, 1958, *Benny Marshall says.*
121   Frances Baker, "Daughter of West Point Coach Answers the 'Dating' Question, Highland Falls, 1954
122   Ibid
123   https://www.nytimes.com/1999/01/03/magazine/the-lives-they-lived-russell-p-red-reeder-born-at-reveille.html

CHAPTER TWENTY-SEVEN

124   "Irving Calls Ousted Cadets an Organized Ring," by Edward O'Neill. *Daily News* (NY,NY) Thurs Sept 6, 1951.
125   *The Courier-Journal*, 11 Aug 1951. "Army's Squad of 31 Includes 19 Sophs."

CHAPTER TWENTY-EIGHT

126   *For What They Gave.* The quotes used in the accounts of this game were taken from the online postings on the website http://www.ForWhatTheyGaveonSaturday. Unless otherwise noted.
127   "Power Gives Duke Edge," page 97, *Daily News*, NY,NY. October 15th, 1953.
128   ForWhatTheyGaveonSaturday.com
129   "A United 'Army' Wins Its Greatest Victory," *The Pointer*, 1953.

CHAPTER TWENTY-NINE

130   www.ForWhatTheyGave.com

131 George Munger, *The Philadelphia Inquirer*, Sunday, Nov 29, 1953. Page 77.

CHAPTER THIRTY

132 *Birmingham News*, Wed, March 9 1960
133 Coach Gene Stallings Interview, Montgomery, Alabama, October 15, 2015.

CHAPTER THIRTY-ONE

134 *Bryan Daily Eagle*, "A&M Restored To Full Rights By NCAA" AP, Jun 2, 1957.
135 *The Austin American*, "'Depth-Shy' Aggies Will Open Spring Grid Practice." Monday. Sun Feb 1957.

CHAPTER THIRTY-TWO

136 *The Birmingham News*, Sunday December 1, 1957, "War Eagle gives final proof," by Sid Thomas
137 Ibid
138 *The Birmingham News*, Sun Dec 1, 1957, "Benny Marshall says . . . " page 59.
139 *Birmingham News*, Sun, Dec 1, 1957, "Whit thanks his troops and wishes them well," by Alf Van Hoose.
140 https://www.knoxnews.com/story/shopper-news/bearden/2020/11/05/no-one-wanted-play-us-former-bearden-coach-smelcher-reminisces/6083266002/
141 https://www.wbir.com/article/sports/not-a-normal-game-tennessee-and-the-1957-gator-bowl/51-10a271c8-45a7-4072-98329b38ff85a7a4#:~:text=More%20than%2060%20years%20after,0%20win%20over%20Texas%20A%26M
142 Ibid

143 Ibid

144 Ibid.

CHAPTER THIRTY-FOUR

145 Moseley would confer with Bryant on a couple of other occasions when seeking a hire for his head coach position at Tech, further noted in the epilogue.

146 *Birmingham News*, "Hard to Say Goodbye," Looking with Charles Land

CHAPTER THIRTY-FIVE

147 https://www.tuscaloosanews.com/article/DA/20101215/News/605318482/TL

148 *Birmingham News*, "Tide needs luck tonight," by Benny Marshall, page 12, Sept 27, 1958.

149 *The Charlotte Observer*, Wilton Garrison, "Getting Gridders Ready Without Overworking Them Big Problem," Sunday, December 5, 1965.

150 Fumble, by James Kirby, page 1–2.

151 Ibid.

152 Ibid.

153 *History of College Football*, John Watterson, page 295.

CHAPTER THIRTY-SIX

154 All player quotes. Benny Marshall. *Winning Isn't Everything*, pages 53 and 54.

155 Ibid.

156 Ibid.

157 Interview, Jimmy Dellinger, 2012

158   Pat Trammel Remembered, YouTube, Sept 30, 2014.

CHAPTER THIRTY-SEVEN

159   Benny Marshall. *Winning Isn't Everything, page 57.*
160   Interview, Mal Moore.
161   "World Greets News with Guarded Optimism," by Pierce Lembeck Jan 1, 1962, page 1.
162   *The Birmingham News*, Jan 1, 1962, "Aid program to Viet Nam to be Outlined," page 3. Assoc Press.

EPILOGUE

163   *Play to Win: Keys to Victory in the Game of Life* by Jerry Glover. https://www.espn.com/espn/otl/story/_/id/7956658/thirty-years-bear-bryant-final-season-man-knew-best-billy-varner-struggles-remember-legendary-alabama-coach.

Bibliography

BOOKS

Barra, Allen. *The Last Coach: A Life of Paul "Bear" Bryant*. New York: W.W. Norton & Company, 2005.

Bryant, Paul W. *Building a Championship Football Team*. Englewood Cliffs, N.J.: Prentice-Hall, 1960.

Bryant, Paul W. and John Underwood. *Bear: The Hard Life and Good Times of Alabama's Coach Bryant*. Boston: Little, Brown and Company, 1974.

Burnes, Robert L. *50 Golden Years of Sports*. St. Louis, Mo.: Rawlings Manufacturing Company, 1948.

Curry, Bill. *Ten Men You Meet in The Huddle: Lessons from a Football Life*. New York: ESPN Books, 2009.

Daniel, Pete. *Standing at the Crossroads: Southern Life in the 20th Century*. Baltimore: John Hopkins University Press, 1986.

Dunnavant, Keith. *Coach: The Life of Paul "Bear" Bryant*. New York: Thomas Dunne Books/St. Martin's Press, 2005.

Dunnavant, Keith. *The Missing Ring*. New York: St. Martin's Press, 2006.

Edmundson, Mark. *Why Football Matters: My Education in the Game*. New York: Penguin Press, 2014.

Edson, James. *Alabama's Crimson Tide: A History of Football at the University of Alabama for the Period of 1892 Through 1945 Covering Each and Every Schedule Game Played and Containing Statistical Data with Reference Thereto*. Montgomery, Ala.: The Paragon Press, Montgomery Printers, 1946.

Glover, Jerry. *Play to Win: Keys to Victory in the Game of Life*. Bloomington, Ind.: iUniverse, 2008.

Gregg, Julia. *Wild Sweet Orange Ride*. Edgartown, MA: Vineyard Stories, 2014.

Keene, Anne R. *The Cloudbuster Nine: The Untold Story of Ted Williams and the Baseball Team That Helped Win World War II*. New York: Sports Publishing, 2020.

Kirby, James. *Fumble: Bear Bryant, Wally Butts, and the Great College Football Scandal*. New York: Harcourt Brace Jovanovich, 1986.

McCollough, Dr. E. Gaylon. *The Long Shadow of Coach Paul "Bear" Bryant*. Gulf Shores, Ala.: Compass Press, 2008.

Maraniss, David. *When Pride Still Mattered*. New York: Simon & Schuster Paperbacks, 1999.

Marshall, Benny. *Winning Isn't Everything (but it beats anything that comes in second)*. Nashville, Tenn.: The Parthenon Press, 1965.

New York Writers Workshop. *The Portable MFA in Creative Writing*. Cincinnati: Writer's Digest Books, 2006.

Newman, Zip. *The Impact of Southern Football*. Montgomery, Ala.: Morros-Bell Publishing, 1969.

Reed, Delbert. *When Winning Was Everything: Alabama Football Players in World War II*. Tuscaloosa, Ala.: Paul W. Bryant Museum, 2010.

Stoddard, Tom. *Turnaround: Paul "Bear" Bryant's First Year at Alabama*. Montgomery, Ala.: Black Belt Publishing, 2000.

Strother, Warren and Peter Wallenstein. *VPI to State University: President T. Marshall Hahn, Jr. and the Transformation of Virginia Tech*. Macon, Ga.: Mercer University Press, 2004.

Watterson, John Sayle. *College Football: History, Spectacle, Controversy*. Baltimore, Md.: The Johns Hopkins University Press, 2000.

NEWSPAPERS AND PERIODICALS

Alabama AAA Alumni Magazine. Ford, Tommy. "Championship Ring Returned To Family." Tuscaloosa: 2015.

Amarillo (Tex.) Daily News
"Kentucky Starts NCAA Title Defense." March 20, 1952, p. 45.
"Laslie To Go To West Point." March 20, 1952, p. 45.

Anniston (Ala.) Star. AP. "Tide 11 Stops In Washington To See Sights." Dec. 22, 1959, p.18.

Austin (Tex.) American
AP. "'Depth-Shy' Aggies Will Open Spring Grid Practice Monday." Feb. 24, 1957.
UP. "Bear Hires Line Coach From Army." Jan. 26, 1957, p. 10.

Baltimore (Md.) Sun. AP. "Texas A&M Picks Coach." Jan 26, 1957.

Birmingham (Ala.) News
AP. "All over —Whit thanks his troops and wishes them well." Dec. 1, 1957.
Thomas, Sid. "Roosts all-victorious— War Eagle gives final proof it is No. 1 bird." Dec 1, 1957, p. 61.
— "Bryant to announce first hiring tomorrow." Dec. 4, 1957, p. 33.
"'Ready' if Alabama needs him." Dec. 1, 1957, p. 56.
— "Where was the Bear? Getting himself a deer." Dec. 1, 1957, p. 56.
— "You'll have to travel a far piece to find a better man." Dec. 2, 1957, p.18.

Blytheville (Ark.) Courier News
Various issues Feb. 1934-June 1937 and 1954
Between You and Me. "Carney Laslie Kids Boss Man; Mantle Sulks over His Blind Spot." May 12, 1954, p. 11.

Bryan (Tex.) Daily Eagle
AP "Aggies Start Informal Footall Workout Today." Dec. 5, 1957, p. 6.
— "Aggie Coaches to Be Guests at A&M Club Meet." July 14, 1957, p. 7.
— "A& M Restored to Full Rights By NCAA." June 2, 1957, p.8.

— "Pat James Added to Alabama Staff." Dec. 7, 1957, p. 8.
— "Athletic Trainer Smokey Harper Welcomes Laslie to A&M." Feb. 15, 1957.
Carder, Charles. "Grid Champs Feted: Drills Open Monday." Feb. 24, 1957, p. 4.
— "Back Together: Smokey Harper and Carney Laslie." Feb. 15, 1957.

*Charlotte (N.C.) Observer.*Garrison, Wilton. "Getting Gridders Ready Without Overworking Them Big Problem." 1965.

Cloudbuster (Pre-flight Naval Training School newspaper, Chapel Hill, N.C). Vols. 1-4, Sept. 1941-Oct. 1945

Colby Quarterly. Doyle, Andrew. "Bear Bryant: Symbol for an Embattled South." March, 1996, Vol. 32, pp. 72-86.

Corpus Christi (Tex.) Caller Times
AP. "A&M Starts Spring Training Monday." Feb. 24, 1957, p. 33.
— "Bryant Given New Cadillac." Feb. 24, 1957, p. 33.

Decatur (Ala.) Daily. AP. "Bryant Gets 1st Look At Alabama." Dec. 9, 1957, p. 8.

Fairborn (OH) Daily Herald. AP. "New Line Coach at West Point." March 20, 1952, p. 6.

Fort Worth (Tex.) Star-Telegram
AP. "New Aggie Assistant." Jan. 28, 1957, p. 9.
Gregston, Gene. "Sports Report." Sept. 17, 1957, p. 27.
— "Mrs. Bryant Sets 'Bama House Hunt.'" Dec. 2, 1957.

The Georgia Historical Quarterly. Dooley, Vincent. "A Year Like No Other: Football on the University of Georgia Campus, 1942." Georgia Historical Society. Volume XCVIII. Fall 2014. Number 3.

Harrisburg (N.Y.) Daily Register

Haverstraw (N.Y.) Rockland County Times

Huntsville (Ala.) Daily Democrat. AP. "Crimson Tide Lost Stars and Coach But Expect a Strong Entry in South For This Fall." Sept. 1, 1931.

The Kentucky Alumnus. Ruby, Earl. "Shiveley Continues as Director of Athletics with New Grid Staff." Feb. 1946. Volume XVII. No. 1.

Kingston (NY) Daily Freeman. "Fifty Players Report for First Army Grid Drill." *Kingston Daily Freeman*, Aug. 30, 1952, p. 9.

Lexington (Ky.) Herald
    AP. "Blue, Gray Gridders Work on Passes for Saturday Meeting." December 25, 1947, p. 5
    "UKAA Board Gives Bryant Release, Appoints Committee To Pick Successor." Feb. 8, 1954, p.1.
    "Donovan Won't Recommend Breaking Bryant's Contract." Feb. 6, 1954, p. 1.

Lexington (Ky.) Sunday Herald-Leader. Ashford, Ed. "Paul Bryant Is Confident of Release, Says He's Definitely Through at UK." Feb. 7, 1954, p. 1.

Louisville (Ky.) Courier-Journal
    Various issues, Jan. 1946 - Sept. 1955.
    Dent, Heggy. "Ring Roundup." Dec. 22, 1939, p. 5.

AP. "UK Scouts Say Bama Now 'Best.'" Oct. 28, 1947, p. 2.

Steinfort, Roy. "Neyland Praises Defense In Vols Win Over Wildcats." Nov. 20, 1949, p. 29.

AP. "Kentucky Plays Tennessee Today For 45th Time." Nov.19, 1949, p.14.

— "Vols Make Three Other Scoring Bids While Cats Threaten Only Once." Nov. 19, 1949.

— "Coaches Also to Hold Meeting." Jan. 7, 1951, p. 23.

— "Santa Clara Beats U.K. in Orange Bowl." Jan. 3, 1950, p.14.

— "Iron UK Defense to Get Stern." Sept. 28, 1950.

— "Army's Squad of 31 Includes 19 Sophs." Aug. 11, 1951, p. 15.

— "Bryant Denies Rumor He Will Leave UK." Oct. 24, 1952, p.17.

— "Line Denies Any Part in fixing UK Scores." Feb. 21, 1952, p. 24.

—"U. of K. Appeals Donaldson Case." Aug. 12, 1952, p. 20.

— "Spivey's Trial to Begin in New York." Jan. 11, 1953, p. 26.

— "Lifting of Ban Expected Later Today." Aug. 16, 1953, p. 34.

Montgomery (Ala.) Advertiser

Montgomery (Ala.) Journal. Nelson, Jimmy. "Claiborne Arrives at Campus to Begin New Alabama Setup." Dec. 5, 1957, p. 5.

Nashville Tennessean. "Aggies Check UT Movies." Dec. 22, 1957, p. 25.

New York (NY) Daily News

Pacific Stars and Stripes (military newspaper)

Red and Black (University of Georgia student newspaper). July 1942 – Oct. 1942.

Richmond (Va.) Times Dispatch

Roanoke (Va.) Times

Rockland County Times (Haverstraw, N.Y.)

Saranac Lake (N.Y.) Adirondack Daily Enterprise. Grayson, Harry. "Blaik's One Game Season Finds Clock, Navy as Foes." Dec. 11, 1956, p.8.

St Louis (Mo.) Sporting News. "Coach of the Year." Nov. 24, 1954, p. 33.

Saturday Evening Post. Wallace, Francis. "Test Case at Pitt." October 28, 1939.

Tuscaloosa (Ala.) News. "Parents and Coaches Present at Death Bed." Nov. 17, 1931, p. 1.

Waco (Tex.) News-Tribune
    "Titles Enough to Go Around, Dec. 17, 1957, p. 8.
    Campbell, Dave. "On Second Thought." April 16, 1957.

Washington Post

OTHER PUBLICATIONS

Aviation Training Division, Office of the Chief of Naval Operations. *The Naval Aviation Physical Training Manuals: Football.* Annapolis: U.S. Navy, 1943.

Baker, Mary Layne. "The Sky's the Limit: The University of North Carolina and the Chapel Hill Communities' Response to the Establishment of the United States Naval Pre-Flight School During World War II." Master's Thesis. UNC, 1976.

Bethea, E.A. "The Establishment of a National Cultural Center in Tuskegee Alabama, A Feasibility Study." Industrial Development Division, Georgia Institute of Technology, 1975.

Bethea, E.A. "A Feasibility Study for the Establishment of a National Cultural Center at Tuskegee, Alabama." Tuskegee: Economic Development Administration, U.S. Dept. of Commerce, Feb. 25, 1976.

Doyle, Andrew. "On the Cusp of Modernity: The Southern Sporting World in the Twentieth Century." Essay in *The American South in the Twentieth Century*. Athens: The University of Georgia Press, 2005.

Gelfand, Michael H. "Tomorrow We Fly: A History of the United States Navy Pre-Flight School on the Campus of the University of Georgia." Master's Thesis. Athens: University of Georgia, 1994.

Hamilton, Thomas. "Tentative Proposed Physical Training Program for Naval Aviation." U.S. Navy, Dec.,1941.

Hamilton, Thomas. Thomas Hamilton to Captain Radford, 1942. U.S Department of the Navy, Navy Historical Center, Naval Archives, Washington, D.C.

Hamilton, Thomas. "The Reminiscences of Rear Admiral Thomas J. Hamilton, U.S. Navy (ret.): An Oral Interview Transcribed." Annapolis, Md.: U.S. Naval Institute, 1983.

Lipscomb, Carol E. "Lister Hill and His Influence." Journal of the Medical Library Association, Vol. 90, 1, 2002, pp.109-10.

YEARBOOKS

University of Alabama *Corolla,* 1930, 1931, 1932, 1933, 1934, 1935.

Virginia Military Institute *The Bomb*, 1942.

Central High School (Charlotte, N.C.) Yearbook 1927, 1929.

Cartersville (Ga.) High School Yearbook, 1925.

WEB SOURCES

Ancestry. www.ancestry.com

Bank, Jimmy. "Fittingly, Paul "Bear" Bryant's first national title was led by his defense, and capped by a win against his home-state team." November 18, 2021. si.com/fannation. https://www.si.com/college/alabama/history/throwback-thursday-1962-sugar-bowl-alabama-arkansas.

Carter, Bob. "Rupp: Baron of the Bluegrass Sports Century Biography Special." ESPN.com. *http://www.espn.com/classic/biography/s/Rupp_Adolph.*

Fernandez, Louis. "Not a normal game: Tennesee and the 1957 Gator Bowl Game." *10 News NBC.* Jan. 2, 2020. https://www.wbir.com/article/sports/not-a-normal-game-tennessee-and-the-1957-gator-bowl/51-10a271c8-45a7-4072-9832-9b38ff85a7a4.

For What They Gave on Saturday Afternoon
    https://forwhattheygave.com/2007/10/14/bob-mischaks-tackle-1953-army-duke/
    https://forwhattheygave.com/2008/01/22/1953-football-team/

https://forwhattheygave.com/2010/01/15/class-nomination-letters-bob-mischaks-letter/
https://forwhattheygave.com/2009/02/11/bob-mischak-letter-to-west-points-hall-of-fame-selection-committee/points-hall-of-fame-selection-committee/

Google. www.google.newspapers.com

Koss, Maddie. Blogs.usafootball.com. March 16, 2018. "Why Assistant Coaches are Critical to Team Culture." https://blogs.usafootball.com/blog/5772/why-assistant-coaches-are-critical-to-team-culture

Nanavaty, Aaron. The Spun. *Sports Illustrated.* Oct. 21, 2017. "Photos:Alabama Fans Celebrate Win Over Tennessee with Customary Cigars." https://thespun.com/news/photos-alabama-fans-celebrate-win-over-tennessee-with-customary-cigars

New York Times. Jan 25, 1970. https://www.nytimes.com/1970/01/25/archives/hank-crisp-73-dies-coach-at-alabama.html

Newspapers. www.newspapers.com

Newspaper Archives. www.newspaperarchives.com

Numberbarn. Community Corral. "Phone History: All About Pary Lines." April 19, 2018. *Numberbarn.com.* https://www.numberbarn.com/blog/phone-history-party-lines.

Palmeri, Allen. Union University webpage."Remembing the Titans:Union's Football Legends Come Back Home." https://www.uu.edu/unionite/summer03/rememberingthetitans.html.

Pinto, Michael. The Bleacher Report. "The 50 Greatest Players in Alabama Football History." Dec 6, 2010. https://bleacherreport. com/aricles/536070-the-50-greatest-players-in-alabama- crimson-tide-football-history

Saturday Down South. "Johnny Majors." ttps://www.saturdaydown south.com/coaches/johnny-majors/.

Schexnaydar, C.J. SB Nation. An Alabama Crimson Tide Community. "'Ears' Whitworth: The Football Coach Alabama Forgot." June 10, 2009. https://www.rollbamaroll.com/2009/6/10/905275/ears- whitworth-the-football-coach.

Story, Mark. *Out of State Recruiting Ban Crippled UK Football.* August 22, 2010. https://www.kentucky.com/sports/spt- columns-blogs/mark-story/article44045568.html

Thompson, Wright. ESPN.com. *The Last Ride of Bear and Billy.* May 12, 2012. https://www.espn.com/espn/otl/story/_/id/7956658/ thirty-years-bear-bryant-final-season-man-knew-best-billy- varner-struggles-remember-legendary-alabama-coach.

Washington Post
https://www.washingtonpost.com/archive/sports/1981/11/27/ bryant/6bee457e-c978-4ccc-812f-52f3125b2a51/

Wikipedia. https://en.wikipedia.org.

AUTHOR INTERVIEWS

Louise "Lu Lu" McKinley Abernathy

Dr. E. C. Brock

Mrs. Hannah Brock, Nov.

Paul Bryant, Jr.

Ed Conyers

William Crisp

Alene Moseley Danby

James Dellinger

Col. William Eppley

General Thomas Griffin (ret.)

Lt. Col James R. Henry (ret.)

Mary Lou Laslie Henry

Lee Roy Jordan

Adele Kellman

Pete Manus

Lt. Fred Martinez

Dr. Gaylon McCollough

Mal Moore

Coach Ray Perkins

Jack Rutledge

Coach Gene Stallings

Dr. Gary White

TELEVISION INTERVIEW

CBS Sports. *Post-game interview with Coach Paul Bryant, Game 315 CBS* by Verne Lundquist, Nov., 28, 1981

Chapter Notes

PROLOGUE: THE WINNINGEST COACH

I relied on my memory of my trip to Blacksburg and confirmed my recollection of the conversation, snippets of which I include, with Alene Danby Moseley, the Moseleys' daughter.

I met Coach Curry at the University of Virginia where he was on a panel about football to talk about his book being showcased at the annual Festival of the Book in Charlottesville. Afterward, while signing my purchased copy of his book, I asked him if he remembered my grandfather, Carney Laslie. He stopped mid-sentence and looked up. "Everybody who was anybody in the Southeastern Conference knows who Carney Laslie is." Curry is a leader, coach, and speaker and was the head coach at Alabama from 1987 to 1990, winning the National Coach of the Year Award.

Colonel Blaik's autographed photograph with the slogan "There is no substitute for victory!" is hanging at the landmark Thayer Hotel at West Point. Bryant's quote, "There is no substitute for guts" was coined sometime after this, and can be found on any website for notable quotes, in this case https://www.allgreatquotes.com/authors/paul-bryant/

PART ONE, CHAPTER ONE: THE FIGHTING MEN OF VMI

In 1920, during General MacArthur's tenure as Superintendent at West Point, he had the words used to introduce Part I engraved over the entrance to the gymnasium in 1920. He continued to add to this book throughout the 1850s. Jackson was not (and never claimed to be) the author of most of these maxims; rather, he collected ideas and phrases from the books he read. This particular quote used to introduce the chapter is attributed to the Reverend Joel Hawes and first appeared in an 1851 work, *Letters to Young Men, on the Formation of Character & c.* Jackson's original notebook is located in the George and Catherine Davis Collection at Tulane University

The account of the day at VMI when Pearl Harbor was bombed was described in the VMI Yearbook, 1942.

The Corolla yearbooks, years 1933 and '34, were referenced for player information on the football teams.
Information for this chapter was drawn from interviews with Mary Lou Henry, Alene Danby Moseley, Bryant's biography, page 83, and VMI archival files, which graciously gave me access and copies which contained a wealth of information on all of the VMI coaches.

CHAPTER TWO: NAVY! FOOTBALL! WAR!

The title of this chapter came from Chapter II in Part I of the Navy's Football Training Manual, page 7

Post WWII, Rear Admiral Thomas J. Hamilton went on to serve as athletic director to the University of Pittsburgh from 1949 to 1971. He received many illustrious awards and also served on the US Olympic Committee from 1948–1964.

Descriptions of Coach Laslie were provided by interviews with Coach Johnny Majors of Tennessee, who described his impressions of Coach Laslie remembered from his attendance and leadership at Southeastern Conference meetings, a letter from a West Point cadet's letter written to Mary Lou when the cadet was recruited to West Point, and various newspaper articles written about him throughout his career, "Carney Laslie Leaving U.K. To Be Army Aide" by Larry Boeck, *The Courier-Journal Louisville*, March 20, 1952, page 8.

The scene in the Laslie house was recreated from snippets of images and people remembered by Mary Lou Laslie Henry and dramatized for the purposes of the narrative.

The number of troops in the military was referenced from Delbert Reed's *When Winning Was Everything: Alabama Football Players in World War II.* (Tuscaloosa: University of Alabama Press, 2013): page 67.

Found among my grandfathers' papers and books was the complete set of the Training Divisions Bureau of Aeronautics Manuals. Each sport had a manual devoted to graining the coaches on how to coach the sport uniformly throughout the Navy programs across the country. The Football Handbook covered everything from the history of football to the foundational elements of football, individual skills and team execution, and covered offense and defensive strategies in detail such as "Defense Against the "T" Formation (Using a Zone Pass Defense). It also included class football instruction complete with pictures and daily and weekly practice schedules.

The description of the Pre-Flight Program at Athens was taken from Vincent Dooley's *A Year Like No Other: Football on the University of Georgia Campus*, 1942.

Also referenced for this chapter was a thesis paper on file by Ms. Layne Baker held at the NC Collection |UNC-CH Library titled, *The Skies the Limit, US Navy Pre-Flight School*.

Michael Geflan's thesis, *Tomorrow We Fly: A History of The United States Navy Pre-Flight School on the Campus of The University of Georgia, Athens, Georgia* was also used extensively cross-referenced to supplement Hamilton's own description of the overall program.

The description of the physical qualifications needed to be accepted for the program were drawn from https://penelope.uchicago.edu/ Thayer/E/Gazetteer/Places/America/United_States/_Topics/ history/_Texts/AHUNAW/28*.html; Chapter 28, Training Naval Aviation's Manpower.

The value of establishing a varsity team was expounded on in Hamilton's original proposal, which was included with the transcripts of his interview given to the Navy and included this comment: The competitive drive was found to be "able to be developed at a higher degree, as was standard of perfection, the test of skill and character too desirably sterner. So too, the benefits in morale were considered to be infinitely greater for the whole student body on the campuses where the schools could be found, as they derived more pride and satisfaction from their interest in a Navy team."

Vincent Dooley's "A Year Like No Other: Football on the University of Georgia Campus 1942," page 192–216, gave an extensive overview of the Pre-Flight Program at UofG. Mr. Dooley is the retired head football coach and athletic director of the University of Georgia. His article included much about Bryant and Crisp, and their years at Athens, information he also sourced from Bryant and Underwood's autobiography, *The Hard Life and Good Times of Alabama's Coach Bear Bryant.*

In a response to requests that poured in from all over the country, the Navy designed a program specifically to coordinate physical training in private and public high schools and colleges with the Navy's physical training program. High school and college coaches were welcomed at the Pre-Flight School, put through the course for an abbreviated two-week course. Almost a thousand coaches across the country went through this training, enthusiastic new converts for the Navy's program.

A good overview of the program at Georgia can be found at https://digilab.libs.uga.edu/scl/exhibits/show/fightingspirit/navy_preflight

Also sourced for this chapter was *The Navy's Air War*, by the Aviation History Unit, OP-519B, DCNO, Harper and Brothers Publishers, New York and London, 1946. Chapter 28, page 307–311

Found among my grandfathers' papers and books was the complete set of the Training Divisions Bureau of Aeronautics Manuals. Each sport had a manual devoted to training the coaches how to coach the sport uniformly throughout the Navy programs across the country. The Football Handbook covered everything from the history of football to the foundational elements of football, individual skills and team execution, and covered offense and defensive strategies in detail such as "Defense Against the "T" Formation (Using a Zone Pass Defense). It also included class football instruction complete with pictures and daily and weekly practice schedules.

The description of the Pre-Flight Program at Athens was taken from

Vincent Dooley's *A Year Like No Other: Football on the University of Georgia Campus*, 1942

Also referenced for this chapter was a thesis paper on file by Ms. Layne Baker held at the NC Collection |UNC-CH Library titled, *The Skies the Limit, US Navy Pre-Flight School.*

Michael Geflan's thesis, *Tomorrow We Fly: A History of The United States Navy Pre-Flight School on the Campus of The University of Georgia, Athens, Georgi*a was also extensively cross-referenced to supplement Hamilton's own description of the overall program.

The description of the physical qualifications needed to be accepted for the program were drawn from https://penelope.uchicago.edu/Thayer/E/Gazetteer/Places/America/United_States/_Topics/history/_Texts/AHUNAW/28*.html; Chapter 28, Training Naval Aviation's Manpower,

The value of establishing a varsity team was expounded on in Hamilton's original proposal, which was included with the transcripts of his interview given to the Navy and included this comment: The competitive drive was found to be "able to be developed at a higher degree, as was the standard of perfection, the test of skill and character too desirably sterner. So too, the benefits in morale were considered to be infinitely greater for the whole student body on the campuses where the schools could be found, as they derived more pride and satisfaction from their interest in a Navy team."

Vincent Dooley's "A Year Like No Other: Football on the University of Georgia Campus 1942," page 192–216, gave an extensive overview of the Pre-Flight Program at U of G. Mr. Dooley is the retired head football coach and athletic director of the University of Georgia. His article included much about Bryant and Crisp, and their years at

Athens, information he also sourced from Bryant and Underwood's autobiography, *The Hard Life and Good Times of Alabama's Coach Bear Bryant*.

In a response to requests that poured in from all over the country, the Navy designed a program specifically to coordinate physical training in private and public high schools and colleges with the Navy's physical training program. High school and college coaches were welcomed at the Pre-Flight School, and put through the course for an abbreviated two-week course. Almost a thousand coaches across the country went through this training, enthusiastic new converts for the Navy's program.

A good overview of the program at Georgia can be found at https://digilab.libs.uga.edu/scl/exhibits/show/fightingspirit/navy_preflight.

Also sourced for this chapter was *The Navy's Air War*, by the Aviation History Unit, OP-519B, DCNO, Harper and Brothers Publishers, New York and London, 1946. Chapter 28, page 307–311

The report citing a 22.7 percent increase in the average cadet's physical fitness from the time of entrance to graduation, and that every cadet completing the program could swim and support himself in the water for hours was sourced from *Tomorrow We Fly*.

The section about the Black athlete came from Vincent Dooley's article, as well did information about Bryant's issues at Athens, page 212. Bryant also alludes to his "being full of himself" during this time period in Athens in his autobiography.

An interesting source outlining the expected behavior expected of a cadet can be found at https://media.defense.gov/2015/Sep/11/2001329827/-1/-1/0/AFD-150911-028.pdf.

CHAPTER FIVE: DEPLOYED

Much of this chapter was gleaned from the interviews with Mary Lou Henry, Alene Moseley Danby, and the many photos and other.

CHAPTER SIX: THE BOYS OF CHAPEL HILL

Most of the information pertaining to Chapel Hill Pre-Flight was sourced from the *Cloudbuster* publications from 1943–1945.

Colonel Donald E. Marousek's memoir was generously shared with the author by the Marousek family and provide a glimpse into life as a young cadet at Chapel Hill.

CHAPTER SEVEN: VICTORY AND LOSS

Information about Walker's death was included in archival records at VMI.

Al Browning's interview with Bryant about his first meeting with Wallace Wade in 1945 appeared in the *Tuscaloosa News*. Knowing that Laslie had, by the time of this meeting in 1945, a close relationship with Wade gives the most probable reason for his not saying anything during the time the three met. Laslie's comments in an interview over a decade later that he never took a position without first consulting with Wade also supports the nature of this meeting.

CHAPTER EIGHT: BEGINNINGS

Tuskegee's Historical Homes contains the description of the Cobb-Laslie House.

My visit to the Cobb House, now a beautiful bed-and-breakfast as of this writing owned by Sandy Taylor and Harvey Mottox, was especially memorable.

Ancestry.com was used to access census reports and birth and death records.

To learn more about Tuskegee University, go to https://www. blackpast.org/african-american-history/tuskegee-university-1881/#sthash.WWispkSq.dp

http://www.americaslibrary.gov/aa/index.php and http://www. buffalobill.org/PDFs/Buffalo_Bill_Visits.pdf; Buffalo Bill Museum, City and County of Denver, Rev October 12, 1912 was used to chart the Wild West Travelling Show itineraries through Alabama.

Pictured is the Laslie-Cobb House on South Main Street in Tuskegee, a home on the historic register since 1978. The house is now a bed-and-breakfast owned by Sandy Taylor and Harvey Mattocks, who have renovated it with beautiful furnishings echoing its grandeur of the past, the walls and bathrooms and kitchen updated to welcome guests to this historic town. To find out more, contact: The Historic Cobb House: (334) 226-1273, Sandy Taylor and Harvey Mattocks.

CHAPTER NINE: FAMILY TIES

Adele Laslie Kellman, granddaughter of Dr. Carney Laslie, and daughter of John Lewis Cobbs Laslie, Carney Laslie's first cousin.

Census reports and passport documentation found at ancestry.com established Dr. Laslie and Isabelle Laslie's honeymoon itinerary.

CHAPTER TEN: FAMILY WOES

Family scrapbooks, high school yearbooks, and articles in the *Charlotte Observer* from 1925–1929 were used for this chapter.

One article referenced for this chapter highlights the intensity of play and also how the bonds of friendship forged between players can produce results. Carney Laslie, linebacker and kicker, and Lowell Mason, quarterback for Charlotte Central High School, were close friends off the field, Mason accompanying Laslie to visit his uncle in Montgomery on at least one known occasion. In the 1927 game between Charlotte High School and Gastonia High, a game in which the Gastonia players were outclassed by Charlotte's better and heavier players a "knock down, drag out fight" ensued at halftime, with Gastonia high school girls joining hands and parading the field to offer a cheering section while their band accompanied the ruckus with "martial music." Not long into the second half, the dynamic duo of Mason and Laslie scored, Mason running the ball into the end zone and Laslie kicking the field goal. *The Gastonia Daily Gazette*, October 1, 1927, page 2. "Charlotte Walks Away With Gastonia At Stadium 43-0."

It is interesting to note, on the front page of the *Charlotte Observer* in 1928, directly above the congratulatory article about the athletes nominated for the All-Star football team, which included junior Carney Laslie, was a column highlighting the Orville Wright's visit to Kitty Hawk. Adjacent on the page is a small article noting a social event held by the Ladies "Swastika Club" of Charlotte. "The afternoon was pleasantly spent in sewing, following which the hostess served delicious Russian tea, sandwiches and doughnuts." *The Landmark*, Statesville, North Carolina, Dec 17, 1928. The Nazi threat not seen or acknowledged, a hint of the unbridled national optimism that existed at that time just one year before the stock market crash of October 1929.

Andrew Doyle's articles on the South and its love of football have been referenced extensively throughout this chapter, as were numerous accounts of the Rose Bowl of 1926 and '27 found in a variety of sources. Published by The History Press. Charleston, SC 2012.

CHAPTER TWELVE: COACH WALLACE WADE

Information about games, season, players were referenced from University of Alabama 1929 yearbook, *The Corolla*, page 339–345.

The team of 1930 was the finest Wade ever coached and one of the best in Alabama's history and was documented in *Southern Football*, by Zipp Newman.

CHAPTER THIRTEEN: TEAM PLAY

The contributions of Laslie's kicking abilities is once again referenced in this article in *The Anniston Star*, AP, "Alabama Wins 33-0 Victory Over Sewanee," Sunday, Oct 25, 1931, page 14.
Information about Max Moseley was generously provided by Patty

Moseley, Max's daughter. Articles referenced in the bibliography were also used to provide additional details.

"Alabama Crushes Florida Gators By 41 to 0 Score" was the headline in *Morning News*, Florence, South Carolina, on November 8, 1931. Players in this game included Frank Moseley at quarterback , "Ears" Whitworth, right guard, and Carney Laslie at right tackle, along with the illustrious fullback, Johnny Cain, a former teammate of Moseley's at Lanier High School in Montgomery. Whitworth, like Laslie, was a kicker, and in this game Whitworth kicked for three after touchdowns.

The Gastonia Daily Gazette, "Wealth of Stars in Football in the South," Atlanta, Ga, Nov 11, 1932 AP, page 2. Coaches were having a hard time coming up with picks for the All-Southern All-Star Team with all the talent they had to pick from. Solid candidates were listed for five possible teams, tackle Carney Laslie listed among the top choices.

Carney's senior year had him and Don Hutson badly battered and bruised from their game against Georgia Tech played on Saturday, Nov 12, 1932, in Atlanta, Laslie suffered from torn rib cartilages and Hutson, described as the "the flashy" sofphomore end, wa laid up with an injured foot that was reported as possibly severe enough to have him sidelined for the next game. *Anniston Star*, "Bruised Tide Working Out For Vandy Game: Badly Battered Capstone Players Begin Readying For Turkey Day Battle," AP Wednesday, Nov 16, 1932, page 10.

One paper, *The San Francisco Examiner*, in its sports column titled "Gingersnaps: Crimson Tide Today: Keeping the Crimson Rolling," described a key player—"'Little' Carney Laslie, 5'11", 210 pounds, and every bit a man, so they say down South"—in its issue on Wednesday, November 30.

St. Mary's College in Moraga, California, where Laslie's play was deemed "brilliant" would later become the cornerstone campus to house the Navy's Pre-Flight Program in 1942.

CHAPTER FOURTEEN: THE BLYTHEVILLE HIGH SCHOOL "CHICKASAWS"

At the end of the football season in 1935, his wife due in March of 1936, Bryant needed a paying job. With Coach Thomas's recommendation, he took a job with Union College in Jackson, Tennessee, to coach their offense for $170 a month. In the fall of '36, he accepted Coach Thomas's offer to come back and coach as a bona-fide assistant, and be paid accordingly to the tune of $1,250 a year plus housing and transportation. He was also able to secure his degree in '37, a year later, in physical education, a needed commodity if he was to continue to pursue coaching, which he clearly had a passion and talent for. https://www.uu.edu/unionite/summer03/rememberingthetitans.html

Courier News, Blytheville, AR, October 2, 1934, J. P. Friend, "Gridders Came Through First Tilt of Season in Fine Shape," page 6.

"The Executive Committee shall have full authority for matching the teams and selecting the time and place for all championship games. It shall select the officials and arrange the details. It shall divide the proceeds of the game, 40 percent to each team and 20 percent to the association. . . . The winner of the game shall be declared the state champion and be presented with a trophy." https://www.newspapers.com/image/15221117/ *Camden Times*, Camden, Arkansas, 6 February 1936, page 2.

In 1934, the national football rules committee met in New York in late December, noting that the season of 1934 was especially exciting in the realm of college football. With outside pressure mounting to make the game more spectacular, the committee pointed to the sharp reduction in injuries and concluded the safety of the players would come first. Interesting to note that this was the same year that player Paul Bryant reportedly played a game with a broken leg. The committee did express the most important problem they faced was whether or not further encouragement should be given to the use of the lateral pass. AP. "Grid Rules Group Gives Attention To Lateral Pass", *La Crosse Tribune and Leader-Press*, Friday, December 29, 1934.

For Alabama football fans, a piece of trivia not to be forgotten, is that Hershel (Herky) Mosley, the oldest of the Mosley brothers of Crimson Tide fame, was from Blytheville, Arkansas, and benefited from the careful tutorship of Coach Laslie, who it was said took the "shifty" Mosley and "turned him around." *Blytheville Courier News*, "Chicks To Use Crack Backfield Against Hurricane", J. P. Friend. Wednesday, October 31, 1934, page 6.

Other articles referencing Herky Mosley and Blytheville's first year under Coach Laslie can be found *Courier News*, Blytheville, AR, October 2, 1934, J. P. Friend, "Gridders Came Through First Tilt of Season in Fine Shape," Page 6.

Twenty-five years later, the Mosley brothers were honored at Walker Park in Blytheville where friends of the family gathered to honor their "incomparable athletic history." Included in the event were invited guests, their coaches, who were pictured and identified, one being one of their high school coaches, Coach Carney Laslie, who at the time of the event was assistant coach at the University of Alabama. *Blytheville Courier News*, "A Night for the Moseleys," Saturday May 16, 1959, page 10.

The account of the game profiling the "Ripper" and "Five-Yard" Evans was recounted in the article "Old 'Ripper' Now Is Overseas; Fans

Recall His Gridiron Feats" in the *Blytheville Courier News*, Tuesday March 23 1943, page 8.

The Courier News, "Nazis Are Busy Preparing for Olympic Games," Milton Bonner, Jan 4, 1935, page 6

The reporting about the upcoming Olympic Games in Germany to be held in 1936 was strangely reminiscent of China's Olympic Games in Beijng in 2022.

Coach Laslie hand-picked James Nisbet to succeed him. "Nisbet Is Here To Confer With School Officials," *Blytheville Courier News*, Monday, February 15, 1937.

The undefeated season of '34 for the Blytheville Chicks was also an undefeated season for the Crimson Tide. Every member of Alabama's Crimson Tide that participated in the season of success was designated to make the trip the Rose Bowl, thirty-five players in all, including substitutes whose main duty had been to take the pounding of the varsity throughout the season. When the list was posted, the unexpected inclusion of the substitutes was so thrilling they rushed

to the telegraph office to wire relatives. Laslie teammates now assistant coaches J. B. "Ears" Whitworth and John Cain, were on the list as well, as well as friends/players Jimmy Walker, Paul Bryant, Don Hutson, and Thomas Smith. "Thomas Picks Squad Of 35," Vol. Cxxi—20 Oakland, Calif., Thursday, Dec. 20, 1934 *Oakland Sports Tribune.*

While Laslie was making history in Arkansas, Bryant was making history at the Rose Bowl in 1935 putting on the "greatest exhibition of forward passing seen in the 40 year history of Rose Bowl competition" up to that point, as quarterback Millard (Dixie) Howell completed a record breaking ten of thirteen attempted passes into the hands of the receivers, principally Don Hutson, Paul Bryant and Jim Angelich. *Hope Star*, (AP) "Alabama Smashes Stanford 29–13," Wednesday, January 2, 1935, page 2.

Alice and Mary Lou's summer routine was first established during their years in Blytheville, Arkansas, noted in the society pages of the *Blytheville Courier News* on August 1, 1936: "Mrs. Carney Laslie and daughter returned today from Brunswick, Georgia, where they spent two months at St. Simon's Island with Mrs. Laslie's parents."

The quote referencing the changes in the new playoff plan can be found at https://www.newspapers.com/image/15221117/ *Camden Times*, Camden, Arkansas, 6 February 1936, page 2.

at VMI. Roberts in the meantime proved to be an outstanding boxer as well as football player. He became the first sophomore to ever be named captain of the Alabama boxing team in 1940. He played end on the Alabama varsity football teams from 1940 to '42 and was an alternate captain on the '42 squad. He was accidentally shot on a training range at Camp Campbell, Kentucky.

CHAPTER FIFTEEN: THE FIGHTING SQUADRON

It is interesting to note as well was that Sigma Nu was founded at VMI in 1869. With a military heritage, Sigma Nu retained many military trappings in its chapter ranks and traditions and placed importance on the concept of personal honor.

Kitchen Kapers, Compiled by Lexington Junior Woman's Club, Lexington, Virginia, 1938 Scotch Shortbread Recipe
"Excellent to serve with tea"

| 2 c flour | ¾ c butter |
| 1 egg yolk | ½ c brown sugar |

Sift flour and sugar together and work butter in with fingers. Chill in ice box. Roll as for cookies. Cut with cookie cutter. Brush tops with yolk of egg to which has been added a little water. Bake in moderate oven 20 minutes.

—Mrs. Albert Elmor

Scandinavian Cookies

½ c butter	1 ½ c sifted flour
¼ c brown sugar	½ c chopped nuts
1 egg separated	Jelly

Cream butter and sugar. Add egg yolk and beat. Blend in flour. Roll into small balls. Dip in egg white and then roll in chopped nuts. Make impression in center and put in jelly. Bake 20 minutes in 300 degree oven.

—Mrs. C. G. Laslie

CHAPTER SEVENTEEN: DASHED DREAMS

The Moseley letters are introduced in this chapter and are used as the major building blocks for the subsequent chapters related to the coaches tenure at Kentucky. Frank wrote a letter every day to Edy, starting immediately after they first met in December 1945 until they married in June 1946, and regularly while on the road after that.

Alene Moseley shared how Kentucky found Bryant—a series of events that Frank Moseley had kept between him and Edy for decades.

CHAPTER EIGHTEEN: HIGHWAYS AND BYWAYS

Tony Constantine described Coach Laslie and his recruiting prowess while in Kentucky in his column POSTscripts in *The Morgantown Post* in 1953.

Bryant, Laslie, and Moseley were enthusiastic about supporting rivalries between any group that inspired good competition. As such they were often invited to participate in clinics all over the country, including those conducted at the annual North-South All-Star game in Charleston, South Carolina, where during a two-day clinic, technical discussions, it was reported, were led by head Coach Paul (Bear) Bryant and line Coach Carney Laslie of the University of Kentucky. *Raleigh Register*, Beckley, West Virginia, Thursday Afternoon, August 14, 1947, AP "Sideline Events Take Spotlight As N-S Squads Wind Up Practice," page 14.

CHAPTER TWENTY-THREE: BAND OF BROTHERS

Superstitious routines were related by Dr. E. C. Brock, who traveled with Laslie and Bryant to away games as the team physician.

CHAPTER TWENTY-FOUR: SCANDALS

The subsequent history of Kentucky's basketball star Bill Spivey is well explained in https://www.espn.com/classic/s/basketball_scandals_explosion.html. Rupp famously claimed his team was above reproach, stating he had the utmost confidence his players were not involved in a point shaving scheme. Despite this, the NCAA's investigation resulted in suspending Kentucky basketball for the '52 - '53 season. Kentucky player Bill Spivey would later be indicted for perjury in 1953,, based on accusations against Spivey by teammates. Though the case was eventually dismissed, the NBA refused to admit Spivey to the league.

CHAPTER TWENTY-FIVE: THE DAY THE MUSIC DIED

The title of this chapter came from https://www.kentucky.con/ sports/spt-columns-blogs/mark-story/article-44045568

Following the 1952 football season, Bryant's first season without Laslie or Moseley, Bryant submitted his resignation to go to the University of Arkansas. According to Kentucky's Governor Lawrence Wetherby, Bryant was asked to stay on another year, giving him the option to leave at that time if he was still of the mind to. It is also surmised that Bryant was given the impression that Adolf Rupp would be soon be retiring. Bryant stayed on with the apparent intent to remain for the duration of his ten-year contract. *Sunday Herald Times*, Lexington, Kentucky, Sunday Morning, February 7, 1954. Page 1. "Agreement Was Made For Coach To Leave," Ed Ashford.

CHAPTER TWENTY-SIX: MOVING ON

Coach Bain coached from 1924 to 1938, during which time he had four unbeaten seasons and participated in four Rose Bowls.

Constantine, Tony. *Morgantown Post*, POSTscripts, 1953 was referenced for comments about the coaches.

Linda Draper, daughter of Col. Draper, the athletic director at West Point when the Laslie's arrived, spent much of her time at the Laslie home, long after her father left his position, while dating a cadet,

Robert "Bob" Newton. During that time, she was mothered by Alice, who made it her mission to impart some of her fashion flair to the fashion-challenged Linda. Linda and Bob later attributed Alice's counsel as helping to foster their blossoming romance. They were soon engaged and were married for almost sixty years

"Colonel Reeder had played football and baseball at West Point as a young man, then turned down an offer to play pro with the NY Giants at triple the salary," came from https://www.nytimes.com/1999/01/03/magazine/the-lives-they-lived-russell-p-red-reeder-born-at-reveille.html

CHAPTER TWENTY-SEVEN: THE NATION IS WATCHING

Laslie loved to play golf and often Col. Reeder, Col. Blaik, and Coach Laslie would head to the golf course for some R&R where they bantered good-naturedly. One such exchange was overheard and reported in *The Portsmouth Herald*, in New Hampshire, May 8, 1954, in Murray's syndicated column "Between You 'N Me": "Col. Earl Blaik of Army, after dining recently at the White House, eagerly took his football aides out on the West Point golf course and with a patronizing air, waved, 'You fellows tee off first. I've been consulting with that pro' in Washington and have this thing licked.' . . . So after watching the others slam 223-yarders down the fairway, the colonel teed up, jiggled his hips, waved his driver menacingly—and completely missed the ball. . . . Said line coach Carney Laslie, 'That's what you get for listening to the 'White House pro.'"

The account of player Pete Manus was told to the author in an interview with the former Army football player at the Class of '54's sixty-fifth reunion in 2019. I learned at that time that Mr. Manus and my father, James R. Henry, who had passed away in 2016, were roommates their first year at West Point. The sixty-fifth reunion was the only class reunion held at West Point that Mr. Manus ever attended. In relating his experience of playing football at West Point, he also revealed he had never before spoken of the events which transpired to anyone. Pete passed away in 2021.

By 1956, in a remarkable personal comeback, Col. Blaik was singly recognized by the New York Press Photographer's Award, for his relations with sportswriters, other coaches and people in the world of football, noting he set an example of demeanor and integrity for the sport. Today, however, the scandal is still a source of debate, reflected by ongoing efforts to block erecting a statue in honor of Col. Blaik at West Point.

CHAPTER TWENTY-EIGHT: ARMY VS. DUKE

"With first and goal on Army's seven-yard line, the cadets held Duke on a fourth down quarterback sneak from the two, with forty seconds to play. Throughout the final two minutes of play, especially during Duke's four thrusts at the Army goal, it was almost impossible to hear or think because of the roar from the crowd. Cadets had come down out of the stands, were pressing around the Army bench and close to the sidelines, imploring their defense to hold." ForWhatTheyGaveonSaturday.com

CHAPTER TWENTY-NINE: THE MIRACLE OF '53

Included in the 102,000 fans in the stands that day were also 29 former POWs, officers in the Army, Navy, the Air Force, and the Marines who were prisoners during the Korean War. It was in Prison Camp No. 2, where they were all imprisoned together, that they made a pact, vowing to reunite at an Army-Navy game. November 28, 1953, was to be the glorious day. "We'll be there unless there is fifteen feet of snow and even then we may make it," said the unofficial organizer of the reunion, Navy lieutenant Thornton. "Army Navy Game Is Dream Come True For 29 POWs," by Lee Linder, *Hawaii Tribune-Herald*, Sat 28, 1953, page 7.

CHAPTER THIRTY: COACH HANK

The exact date of Coach Hank's visit in December is not known, but it would have to have occurred after the last game of the '55 season and before January 1, 1956, given Mary Lou's visit with her parents and her moving to Germany

CHAPTER THIRTY-ONE: LIGHTING THE MATCH

Matt Hooper's excellent article about Coach Whitworth's years at Alabama was referenced for much of the information in this chapter. The previous chapter title foreshadows the implosions at Texas A&M and Alabama, but also the explosion that would be coming in the form of Whitworth's successor.

https://web.archive.org/web/20100111184438/http://www.bhamweekly.com/2009/06/10/low-tide-ears-whitworth-and-the-lost-history-of-alabama-football/_

CHAPTER THIRTY-TWO: ONE IN A MILLION

The Auburn-Alabama game was described in *The Birmingham News*, Sunday, December 1, 1957, "War Eagle gives final proof," by

Sid Thomas in addition to interviews with Mary Wooddall, who was a majorette at Auburn in 1957 and who shared her recollections of game-day.

This online article written by Louis Fernandez, published in January 2020, about the 1957 Gator Bowl is an entertaining account. A 4:26 minute video courtesy of Russell Barton Film Production is posted along with the written transcription.

https://www.knoxnews.com/story/shopper-news/bearden/2020/11/05/no-one-wanted-play-us-former-bearden-coach-smelcher-reminisces/6083266002 was also referenced extensively about the Gator Bowl '57.

CHAPTER THIRTY-THREE: THE RETURN

"Carney," he yelled down the hallway, "why don't you call whoever you know up there in Washington and ask them about getting us the rest of that golf course?" as related by Dr. E. C. Brock, team physician.

John Watterson, author of The History of College Football met Amos Alonzo Stagg, Jr. at about the same time Coach Bryant was honored. Stagg, Jr. claimed his father had more wins which were uncredited because father and son had co-coached at Susquehanna College late in his father's life, a number which would have exceeded Bryant's record.

John Watterson, author of The History of College Football met Amos Alonzo Stagg, Jr. at about the same time Coach Bryant was honored. Stagg, Jr. claimed his father had more wins which were uncredited because father and son had co-coached at Susquehanna College late in his father's life, a number which would have exceeded Bryant's record.

CHAPTER THIRTY-FOUR: THE BOYS ARE BACK IN TOWN

The story about Coach Bryant and the injured player came from Tom Stoddard, *The Turnaround*, page 105.

Laslie was beloved by the trainers. After his death, a memorial scholarship fund for future trainers was set up and funded by those in the athletic training department. For more info see epilogue.

CHAPTER THIRTY-SIX: KILL OR BE KILLED

"Tide's '61 team had one of the best defenses in football," by Chase Goodbread, *Sports Writer*, Posted Aug 16, 2011.

https://www.tuscaloosanews.com/article/DA/20110816/News/605309438/TL

1961: "Led by the 'Bear,'" by Jason Morton, tuscaloosanews.com

www.TheSpun.com. "The Tradition Continues." October 22, 2017. Aaron Nanavaty

EPILOGUE

The Danville Register, September 21, 1969. Page 41. "13th Ranked Alabama Defeats Virginia Tech 17–13."

A good article about the troubles Coach Sharp experienced at Virginia Tech can be found at https://www.washingtonpost.com/archive/sports/1977/10/30/idiots-have-fun-as-sharpe-virginia-tech-struggle/abe7a08f-2b0c-4b52-ae74-2697128cf5a3/

Current Head Coach Nick Saban and Bryant have tied for the number of National Championships won at Alabama as of this writing.

During moments of secrecy in practice, hiding its new offense from everyone, Alabama surprised the college football landscape with the Wishbone in 1971, going on to win three more National Championships.

Alene Moseley Danby was the flower girl at Mary Lou's wedding in 1955, and the two remain close. They have beach homes a mile from each other and continue to celebrate July 4th together whenever possible, as well as Thanksgiving, when they traditionally watch the Auburn-Alabama game together—rooting for Alabama, of course.

Seated, L-R: Alene Moseley, Mary Lou Laslie, Ruffy Moseley. Carney Laslie in background, cigarrette in hand. At the Moseley home in Blacksburg, Virginia, July 4, 1954

Picture Credits

Page 9: VMI coaches, 1939. Virginia Military Institute Archives. Used with permission.

Page 17: Air Fleet Command Inspection. Official US Navy Photo. Used with permission.

Page 26: Class Photo, Naval Reserve Induction. Courtesy of Laslie Family.

Page 30: Bryant, Laslie, Walker off to war. Courtesy of Paul Bryant, Jr.

Page 32: Panama Canal.Official US Navy Photo.Used with permission.

Page 33: Williamstown, Massachusetts. Courtesy of Laslie Family..

Page 36: On the golf course. Official US Navy Photo. Used with permission

Page 50: Used with permission from Wilson Library, UNC – Chapel Hill.

Page 52: Carney Laslie, 1910. Courtesy of Laslie Family.

Page 57: Pinehurst Outlook Magazine, January 23, 1911.

Page 60: Laslie family picture. Courtesy of Laslie Family.

Page 62: University of Alabama baseball team, 1899. Courtesy of Laslie Family.

Page 84: Crimson Tide of 1930, UofA National Champions. Courtesy of Laslie Family.

Page 85: Tackle, Carney Laslie. Courtesy of Laslie Family.

Page 99: Coaches Laslie and Patchett. Richmond-Times Dispatch. 1938. Used with permission.

Page 115: Virginia Military Institute Archives. Used with permission.

Page 121: Virginia Military Institute Archives. Used with permission.

Page 123: Alice and Mary Lou Laslie. Courtesy of Laslie Family.

Page 138: Kentucky Coaches, 1938. University of Kentucky. University of Kentucky general photographic prints. Used with permission.

Page 147: Kentucky Coaches, 1946. The University of Kentucky Alumni Magazine. Used with permission.

Page 150: Frank Moseley and Paul Bryant. © The Courier-Journal— USA TODAY NETWORK

Page 158: Coaches and players on the sidelines.© The Courier-Journal– USA TODAY NETWORK

Page 165: Duplex. Courtesy of Moseley Family.

Page 166: Coaches wives. The Bryant Museum. Used with permission. © Catapult Sports.

Page 187: Alice and Mary Lou Laslie. © The Courier-Journal—USA TODAY NETWORK

Page 193: Laslie and Bob Gain. Courtesy of Laslie Family.

Page 198: Lexington train station. Photo by The Lexington-Herald Leader. Used with permission.

Page 223: Coach Carney Laslie. Official photo of the USMA.

Page 230: Cadet James R. Henry. Courtesy of Laslie Family.

Page 241: Framed photo and caption at Thayer Hotel. Used with permission.

Page 249: Ring Dance, West Point. Courtesy of Laslie Family.

Page 250: Photo of Coach Hank with his brothers, Used with permission from the Crisp family.

Page 258: Welcome to A&M. Courtesy of Laslie Family.

Page 259: Bryant and Laslie on sidelines, Alabama vs Auburn, 2958. Alabama Department of Archives and History. Donated by Alabama Media Group. Photo by Tom Self, Birmingham News.

Page 273: Laslies and Moseleys. Courtesy of Moseley Family.

Page 279: Sheraton Hotel, 1982. Courtesy of Moseley Family.

Page 293: I Love Me Wall. Used with permission. The Bryant Museum. © Catapult Sports.

Page 301: Laundry money. Used with permission. The Bryant Museum. © Catapult Sports

Page 304: Kicking Instruction. Used with permission. The Bryant Museum. © Catapult Sports.

Page 311: Wallace Wade Reunion. Used with permission. The Bryant Museum. © Catapult Sports.

Page 312: Sam "The Bam" Cunningham. a Alabama Department of Archives and History. Donated by Alabama Media Group. Photo by Tom Self, Birmingham News.

Page 313: Alice and Carney. Courtesy of Laslie Family.

Page 314: Astro turf. Used with permission. The Bryant Museum. © Catapult Sports.

Page 315: Frank Howard. Courtesy of Laslie Family.

CPSIA information can be obtained
at www.ICGtesting.com
Printed in the USA
LVHW051836140922
728383LV00001B/1